True Competition

A Guide to Pursuing Excellence in Sport and Society

David Light Shields, PhD

Brenda Light Bredemeier, PhD

University of Missouri-St. Louis

Human Kinetics

Library of Congress Cataloging-in-Publication Data

Shields, David Lyle, 1950-
    True competition : a guide to pursuing excellence in sport and society / David Light
Shields, Brenda Light Bredemeier.
        p. cm.
    Includes bibliographical references and index.
    ISBN-13 978-0-7360-7429-2 (soft cover)
    ISBN-10: 0-7360-7429-5 (soft cover)
1. Sports--Sociological aspects. 2. Sports--Psychological aspects. 3. Competition. 4.
Success. I. Bredemeier, Brenda Jo, 1950- II. Title.
    GV706.5.S535 2009
    306.4'83--dc22

                                                    2009001024

    ISBN-10: 0-7360-7429-5
    ISB N-13: 978-0-7360-7429-2

The Web addresses cited in this text were current as of October 1, 2008, unless otherwise noted.

Acquisitions Editor: Myles Schrag; **Developmental Editor:** Judy Park; **Assistant Editors:** Melissa
J. Zavala and Lee Alexander; **Copyeditor:** Patsy Fortney; **Proofreader:** Jim Burns; **Indexer:** Bobbi
Swanson; **Graphic Designer:** Bob Reuther; **Graphic Artist:** Kathleen Boudreau-Fuoss; **Cover
Designer:** Bob Reuther; **Photographer (cover):** © Human Kinetics; **Photo Asset Manager:** Laura
Fitch; **Visual Production Assistant:** Joyce Brumfield; **Photo Production Manager:** Jason Allen; **Art
Manager:** Kelly Hendren; **Associate Art Manager:** Alan L. Wilborn; **Illustrator:** Kelly Hendren;
Printer: Versa Press

Printed in the United States of America   10 9 8 7 6 5 4 3 2 1

Human Kinetics
Web site: www.HumanKinetics.com

United States: Human Kinetics
P.O. Box 5076, Champaign, IL 61825-5076
800-747-4457
e-mail: humank@hkusa.com

Canada: Human Kinetics
475 Devonshire Road Unit 100, Windsor, ON N8Y 2L5
800-465-7301 (in Canada only)
e-mail: info@hkcanada.com

Europe: Human Kinetics
107 Bradford Road, Stanningley, Leeds LS28 6AT, United Kingdom
+44 (0) 113 255 5665
e-mail: hk@hkeurope.com

Australia: Human Kinetics
57A Price Avenue, Lower Mitcham, South Australia 5062
08 8372 0999
e-mail: info@hkaustralia.com

New Zealand: Human Kinetics
Division of Sports Distributors NZ Ltd.
P.O. Box 300 226 Albany, North Shore City, Auckland
0064 9 448 1207
e-mail: info@humankinetics.co.nz

Contents

Foreword

The basketball court and the classroom, the union hall and the corporate boardroom, the Senate floor and the Presidential campaign trail—these are a few of the settings where I have engaged in that sometimes magical and sometimes unsuccessful process that we call *competition*.

My initial appreciation of competition developed along with my love of basketball. Through twenty years of high school, college, and pro ball, I learned the core values that have guided my life. I wrote about these in my 1998 book, *Values of the Game*. While I can no longer play like I once did when the Knicks were winning national championships, I still experience great joy from most of my basketball memories.

After my life in professional sports, I went on to a life in politics and public service. I won a United States Senate seat three times and eventually lost a Presidential campaign. Of course, I much prefer winning to losing, but when I gave my best, I never regretted having competed.

As a Senator, I worked hard for Title IX to make sure girls and women in educational institutions have as many opportunities to benefit from sports competition as guys like me. Sports competition can provide powerful learning opportunities, and knowing how to compete fairly and respectfully, with an eye toward excellence, can enrich our lives. During my 18 years in the Senate and now in my business career, my appreciation for competition broadened as I saw it stir innovations in science, engineering, education, commerce, and communications.

But there is a shadow side to competition as well. In fact, I left the Senate in 1996, deciding not to run for a fourth term, in part because I concluded that American politics had become a form of competition run amuck. Rather than competing over what ideas would serve our country best, we spent far too much of our time contesting over money and producing negative sound bites. The search for truth and the common good was too often sacrificed to political expediency and narrow self-interest.

Competition can bring out our worst, as well as our best. I have seen it on the basketball court and I've seen it in the halls of government. David Shields and Brenda Bredemeier, the authors of this book, are keenly aware of both the potentials and pitfalls of competition in all parts of our society.

I first met the book's authors when I was the guest speaker at a banquet sponsored by the Mendelson Center for Sports, Character, and Community at the University of Notre Dame. They were the founders and co-directors of the center and were widely regarded as leading scholars in the field of sport psychology, particularly as it relates to character development. This book is an extension of that work and it is a pleasure for me to write its forward.

True Competition is a powerful book. The authors clearly separate competition from a destructive look-alike, which they call *decompetition,* as well as its qualities and causes. By separating the concepts of true competition from decompetition, they present a compelling explanation that helps to clarify when and why contests result in bad outcomes, rather than good.

But David and Brenda don't just offer analyses. They also offer solutions. They structure the major portion of the book as a kind of field guide that features "distinguishing marks" of true competition and decompetition, identifies threats to competition, and presents leadership strategies to promote the best that competition has to offer. They root their interpretation in the facts of real life.

I have known the upsides and the downsides of competition, and I appreciate *True Competition* because it has helped me gain deeper insight into my own experiences. More importantly, I feel better equipped to create and sustain the most positive and productive forms of competition in ways that benefit everyone—my family, my work associates, our country, and our world. I want as many as possible to benefit from competitive experiences that fuel excellence and the kind of lasting enjoyment and satisfaction that I have found.

I hope that, like me, you find this thought-provoking book both enjoyable and useful. It is one of the few books that is equally suited for both scholars and practitioners, and for those who work with children and those who work with professionals. Whatever your position or vocation, it can help you turn competition into a positive force. Whether you are a coach or an athlete, an educator or a parent, a businessperson or a politician, or just a curious reader, *True Competition* can help you and those you work with rise to new levels of excellence and enjoyment.

—Senator Bill Bradley

Acknowledgments

Just as competition cannot be done solo, neither can writing a book. Our friends, colleagues, coaches, and teachers have provided ideas and inspiration through various phases of this book's evolution. David wants to extend special thanks to Coach Bill Pendleton of Morningside High School, who first introduced him to the ideals of true sport competition, and to Julia Carol, who embodied a similar marriage of excellence and ethics in a corporate context.

Brenda would like to thank Carole Oglesby, her Ph.D. advisor, who has inspired generations of athletes, especially girls and women, in this nation and internationally to be true competitors, and has helped create opportunities for them to do so. Brenda is also indebted to a group of exceptional former students at the University of California, Berkeley who collaborated to explore the meaning women make of their competitive and cooperative sports experiences: Leslee Fisher, Debby Getty, Nancy Slocum, Gloria Solomon, Dawn Stephens, and Jaimie Warner. Finally, many conversations with former Cal students, especially Themy Jo Adachi, Ellen Carlton, Maria Montes Clemens, Laura Hills, and Steve Miller have been invaluable; our students have been and continue to be our best teachers.

We would like to thank Jeff Beedy for giving us the first opportunity to share some of the ideas that are at the heart of this book in our keynote address at the 2000 Youth Sports Summit. Numerous conversations with our Notre Dame colleagues further enriched the development of our own thinking. Thanks especially to Jay Brandenberger, Matthew Davidson, Sally Derengoski, George Howard, Dan Lapsley, Nicole LaVoi, Blake Miller, Kelli Moran, Darcia Narvaez, Ann Marie Power, and Mary Wooley. We owe a tremendous debt especially to Clark Power, whose deep spirituality and commitment to education and social justice infuse his passion for "the game."

We also offer thanks to those Notre Dame coaches who generously shared their time and their perspectives on competition. Thanks especially to Bob Bayliss (Men's Tennis), Mike Brey (Men's Basketball), Debbie Brown (Women's Volley), Bobby Clark (Men's Soccer), Kevin Corrigan (Men's Lacrosse), Muffet McGraw (Women's Basketball), Tim Welsh (Men's Swimming and Diving), and Tyrone Willingham (Football; now at the University of Washington). We are grateful, too, for the invaluable contributions of the many athletic directors, coaches, and athletes who participated in various Mendelson Center programs, especially the coaches focus group supported by a grant from the National Science Foundation.

A heartfelt thanks also to our colleagues at the Center for Character and Citizenship, University of Missouri-St. Louis, especially Wolfgang Althof, Marvin Berkowitz, Mindy Bier, Sandra Diamond, Liz Gibbons, Matt Keefer, Peggy Cohen, Virginia Navarro, Wendy Saul, Charles Schmitz, and Steve Sherblom. We would also like to acknowledge the important contributions of our close friend and colleague, Vic Battistich, whose tragic and unexpected death in 2008 has left a deep personal and professional void.

We also have had the privilege of working with an extended community of scholars, professionals, and competitors, including Carol Alberts, Bob Bigalow, Susan Birrell, Gus Blasi, Jay Coakley, Joan Duda, Martha Ewing, Kari Fasting, Deb Feltz, Diane Gill, Marta Guivernau, Ed Hastings, Don Hellison, Vickie Krane, Maria Kavussanu, Scott Kretchmar, Richard Lapchick, Frankie Moore Lappé, Holly Metcalf, Steve Miller, Mariah Burton Nelson, Terry Orlick, Pat Polk Simms, Glyn Roberts, Ron Smith, Frank Smoll, Sharon Stoll, Robin Vealey, Maureen Weiss, Peter Yarrow, and Judith Young. We extend our gratitude to each of you, and to Jim Thompson of the Positive Coaching Alliance (PCA) who works tirelessly on behalf of true competition; our collaborative leadership with Jim and the PCA on the *Against the Grain* series of forums was a highlight of our work at the Mendelson Center.

Several people read early drafts of the manuscript and their comments were immensely helpful. We would especially like to thank Marvin Berkowitz and Chris Funk who painstakingly read earlier versions of the entire manuscript and offered detailed responses. We would also like to thank Grace Hogan and Angela Hudek for their valuable comments on parts of the manuscript.

We were privileged to work with an outstanding editorial team at Human Kinetics, and would like to especially thank Myles Schrag and Judy Park for their vision, inspiration, and eye for detail.

Finally, we express our deepest gratitude to our beloved children, Micah Light Shields and Maya Light Bredemeier. Thank you for your patience with us, and for bringing delight, joy, and love to each day.

Prelude

Compass for the Journey

We would like to invite you to take a journey with us into the heart and soul of one of the most misunderstood and taken-for-granted aspects of life: *competition.* Perhaps you're a coach, an educator, a businessperson, an athlete, a student, a lawyer, or an executive. Perhaps you love competition. Possibly, you hate it. Or maybe both. No doubt, you compete in many arenas of your life. You compete on the job, on the playing field, or in the classroom. Sometimes you compete at home, and you may even compete during a night out on the town. What do you think of all this competing? We suspect that sometimes you find it exhilarating, yet at other times you find it draining. Competition can push you toward excellence. It can also push you toward despair. What makes the difference isn't just whether you win or lose.

As you travel through the pages of this book, you will discover how to tap into the positive benefits of competition, while avoiding its dangers. You will learn potent strategies for optimizing your performance, or that of your team, that will also lead to sustained enjoyment. We hope you will come away with a deep appreciation for both the potentials and pitfalls of unleashing the power of competition.

For us, this book reflects a deeply personal journey, because it springs from our own life experiences. Back in the days, we were devoted high school and college athletes. David lettered as a high school freshman and competed in four varsity sports before going on to college, paid for in part by track and field scholarships. Brenda, whose high school didn't offer interscholastic sports for girls, played sports on the streets and in vacant lots. Then she delighted in intercollegiate sports competition during every season she was in college. Brenda also went on to coach volleyball at Smith College and later coached at Temple University.

Like many of you, we have competed in realms other than sports as well; we've competed for grades, scholarships, grants, and jobs, among other things. Our professional activities have also involved working with people in a variety of settings as they struggled with the anxiety, frustration, relief, and exhilaration that spring from engagement in "the contest."

Since we will be traveling together, it may be helpful for you to know a little bit about us. When the two of us met, David was teaching in the Peace and Conflict Studies Program at the University of California at Berkeley and Brenda was a new sport psychology professor there. For almost 20 years we collaborated on a research program examining the psychological and social implications of involvement in sport competition. In the course of our work, we have interviewed dozens of coaches and hundreds of athletes, from youngsters to professionals. We wrote about some of this in our first book, *Character Development and Physical Activity,* which we penned primarily for other scholars in the field.

In 1999, we were invited to become the founding codirectors of a new research and program development center at the University of Notre Dame. The center became known as the Mendelson Center for Sports, Character, and Community. For five years, we conducted research; designed educational programs; engaged in community outreach; built coalitions; sponsored conferences and symposia; and worked with coaches, athletes, school administrators, and league officials. Then, in 2003, we joined the College of Education faculty of the University of Missouri at St. Louis and helped launch their new Center for Character and Citizenship.

We share these brief introductions to make the following point: We have studied competition from an academic perspective, and we have lived it from a human perspective. Through our scholarly and personal experiences, we have come to deeply appreciate the compelling power of competition.

Competition is blood in our veins, fiber in our muscles, wind at our backs. Competition can provide food for the soul, energy for the body, and incentive for the mind. From competition springs desire, from desire springs passion, and from passion can spring a yearning for excellence. When excellence is pursued with vigor, enjoyment comes in the wake.

We believe in the potential for goodness and greatness that is inherent within competition. And we are not alone. Competition, we are often told, is what made Western civilization so prosperous. Our *yes* to competition would seem to harmonize well with those who sing about the glories of competing in our gyms and politics, our markets and newsrooms, our classrooms and courtrooms. Competition, many suggest, is *the* source of our efficiency and productivity. It is said to reduce waste, improve quality, and boost output. Competition may even be peddled as a panacea, essential to curing all ills in our work and our leisure.

So our praise of competition would seem to fit the climate of our culture. Yet, the truth is, we are profoundly concerned with the tenor of our times. We believe that when CEOs, political leaders, school administrators, and sport heroes praise competition, they typically do so for the wrong reasons.

Too often, the meaning and methods of true competition have been mischaracterized. Paradoxically, those who most loudly proclaim the virtues of competition may unintentionally support its vices. They often turn it inside out and subvert its true potential. But we are now getting ahead of our story.

Our reflections in this book generally apply to any situation or domain in which competition is found. Sports, education, work, play—competition is almost everywhere. To make our points, however, we focus primarily on sports. We do so for three simple reasons. First, we have experienced sports firsthand through the roles of athlete, coach, and consultant; and we have studied human development and social relations in sports for many years.

Second, games and sports provide most children in our culture with their first introduction to formal competition. These early experiences provide powerful lessons that may influence how people think and behave in later competitive situations. If young people learn that sports are foremost about glory, power, and privilege, if they learn that competition is primarily about reward seeking and self-aggrandizement, what does this portend for their future competitive experience in other settings?

Finally, sports provide an interesting prism through which to refract the light of the broader culture. The highly public, visible, and condensed nature of sports allows us to observe dynamics that may be more subtle or hidden in other competitive settings. One can witness in an hour of sport what might take weeks or months to observe in other contexts.

Audience and Approach

We have written this book for a wide audience. Because we use sport as our primary point of reference, the book may find its most natural readership among coaches, sport administrators, athletes, parents, sport officials, and sport fans. We hope it will also be of interest to our academic colleagues in sport psychology, sociology, and philosophy, as well as to their students. We also believe the book will be of interest to people in numerous other fields, such as education. As educators ourselves, we hope students, teachers, principals, and others involved in the great educational enterprise will find much of value in these pages.

To help make the connections to fields beyond sports, we have sprinkled the text with illustrations from other domains. Nevertheless, a word of caution is in order. We would be guilty of gross reductionism if we were not to acknowledge important differences between sport and business, or games and politics, or playing fields and classrooms—to name a few of the settings in which contests occur. Indeed, each setting is unique; the insights we develop here will need to be applied with care to other contexts. And yet competition is competition whether in sports or elsewhere. We believe the key ideas will hold regardless of context.

We have sought to make the book accessible to people in quite diverse occupations and circumstances. In writing the text, we did not assume that the reader has advanced knowledge of psychology, sociology, economics, political science, or any other specialty. To the extent possible, we have eliminated academic jargon. What little jargon does appear is limited primarily to the footnotes, which we have kept to a minimum.

How The Book Is Organized

The book contains two parts divided by an interlude. In the first part, the main ideas of the book are introduced. In the opening chapter, we summarize, without getting into detail, the findings of more than a century of research on competition. As you will see, most of that research supports a view of competition that is quite at odds with the positive evaluation that is widespread in our culture. Rather than viewing competition as an engine for efficiency and productivity, researchers have concluded that it often lowers productivity while simultaneously increasing interpersonal tension and hostility. This has led some to even conclude that, as far as possible, we should eliminate competition from our homes, schools, and social institutions.

In the second chapter, we suggest that the negative conclusions about competition reached by many researchers are flawed. Comparing the researchers' case against competition to a legal court battle, we suggest that the prosecutor's charges against competition are based on a case of mistaken identity. True competition involves seeking excellence by trying to meet the challenge posed by the opponent. It is an enjoyable process that pushes us to our boundaries. However, competition can also degenerate into something quite different: an ego-driven struggle for supremacy. When researchers take competition to task, it is this degenerated struggle that is the object of their ire, not true competition. Since the English language currently has no word to designate competition's "twin," we coin the term *decompetition.* We then go on to suggest that if we are to reclaim the power of true competition, we need to clearly distinguish it from its degenerated form, decompetition.

The third chapter offers a field guide to true competition. In many respects, the third chapter contains the heart of the book. In outline form, it offers the key themes and insights that are elaborated in the book's second half. It presents a set of markings that can be used to reliably distinguish between true competition and its imposter, decompetition.

In the interlude between the first and second parts of the book, we offer a reflection on the relation between competition and personal character. Character, we will see, consists of two elements: what we desire and our ability to act consistently with our most cherished ideals. We suggest that for true competition to prevail, we need to choose it deliberately and resist temptations to deviate from its norms.

In the second half of the book, we elaborate on the themes introduced in the field guide. Each of these chapters contains three main elements. First, each chapter elaborates on one or more of the markings that distinguish competition from decompetition. Next, possible threats to true competition are named and examined. Finally, each chapter concludes with suggestions for how leaders such as coaches, teachers, parents, and administrators can support true competition.

Specifically, chapters 4 and 5 deal with two aspects of motivation. Chapter 4 focuses on the reasons people compete, examining that topic through the lens of intrinsic versus extrinsic motivation. Chapter 5 looks at the most basic goals that people pursue during competition.

Chapters 6 and 7 focus on relationships within competition. Chapter 6 focuses on relationships between opponents, whereas chapter 7 reflects on the relationship that competitors have with the rules and those charged with enforcing them.

Chapters 8 and 9 focus on dynamics within competition. Chapter 8 elaborates on the theme of pursuing victory and how a focus on outcome is balanced with a focus on values connected with the process. Finally, in chapter 9, we reflect on the requirements for an ideal contest.

In the concluding postlude, we summarize key ideas of the book and address questions that we are often asked about them. We also point to resources available for those interested in continuing the journey beyond the pages of this book, such as our Web site: www.TrueCompetition.org.

Special Features

Sprinkled throughout the book are a number of special features designed to augment or clarify some of the book's ideas and themes. First, we have included a number of photos to graphically portray relevant themes. Rather than using traditional captions, we offer questions for reflection. In a classroom setting, these questions could provide launching points for group discussions or individual writing assignments.

We have also included letters to the authors throughout the text. In almost all cases, these reflect actual questions people have asked us when we have presented the book's ideas to audiences. Sometimes we use these letters to probe certain issues more deeply. At other times, we use them as an opportunity to spell out practical implications. In similar fashion, we have also included a number of highlight boxes to present ideas that complement what is presented in the main text.

Let's begin the journey. ■

The Case Against Competition
Was Kohn Right?

"I'm open. I'm open," I bellowed as I ran down the right sideline. It was summer and there was no better way to pass an afternoon than in a neighborhood game of flag football. On this particular play, the pass didn't come my way, but Bull did. Bull is the name we used for the snarl-faced boy who lived in the brick house midway down Fourth Street. Even though the ball wasn't thrown in my direction, Bull slammed into me like a 16-wheeler into a Volkswagen Beetle. Slightly bruised, mostly in spirit, I leapt to my feet. "Why'd you do that?" I yelled angrily. "The ball wasn't even coming my way." Smugly, Bull relied, "Yeah, but it might next time."

Getting knocked to the ground had caused me no real physical damage. Though Bull had two years and 20 pounds on me, I was reasonably tough. Still, the joy of competition had been knocked out of me. Not permanently, of course. But for that afternoon, football was no longer about fun and friends, skills and strategies. It was more about surviving attacks, saving face, and even getting back.

> **"Life for us has become
> an endless succession of contests."**
>
> Alfie Kohn

Contests are, indeed, frequent. So, too, are experiences that interfere with our enjoyment of them. Perhaps, like me, you've had your enjoyment of a game bruised by a bully, or a cheat, or simply someone with a bad attitude. Perhaps you've been in the stands and found yourself irritated by an out-of-control, loud-mouthed fan. Perhaps, at a youth sport event, you've overheard a parent cut down her child's spirit with a knife of caustic criticism. Perhaps you've seen a spoiled victor mocking a defeated and deflated opponent. Or maybe you've witnessed the red-faced coach breaking the sound barrier as he roared obscenities into the stoic face of an official. And it was only a T-ball game. Are these inevitable outcomes of competing? Or are they distortions of an otherwise good and noble process?

Recently, I was talking with a fellow who had been a longtime youth sport coach. I asked what must have seemed like a rhetorical and somewhat silly question: "Do you enjoy competition?" Without a moment's hesitation, the words "I love it!" poured out of his mouth like syrup on a pancake. "I love the challenge. I like being able to push myself, give my all, and see if I can come through in the clutch. It makes me work and improve, and I love the excitement, the tension, not knowing how things are going to turn out. I think there's a special bond among those of us who compete, whether we are teammates or opponents."

I then asked him if the kids he coaches experienced competition in the same way. This time his answer was more delayed and reflective. "Not really," he replied. "Sometimes they do, but too often something ugly happens during the game and it just saps the good things out." He then confided that he was actually contemplating quitting as a coach, not because he no longer loved the kids or the sport, but because he thought the competitive element had become too important.

Many of us love competition, yet we frequently find that the experience we hope for isn't what actually takes place. We love competition, but we have an uneasy feeling that something is amiss. Too often, we experience an alarming gap between the reality of competition and our ideal image of it.[1]

It doesn't matter whether we're talking about pickup games among elementary school kids or Division I college sports. The age or competitive level isn't what's important. It also matters little whether we're talking about competition in sports or competition in schools, the marketplace, politics, or even our homes. Whether we are competing in badminton or a spelling bee, for a grade or for a job, similar issues and challenges arise. Competition, by its very nature, seems to come with inherent risks.[2]

© Human Kinetics

Athletes cheat or foul in games; journalist fib about sources; politicians utter false promises; scientists fudge data. Is there something about competition that pushes people to act in these ways?

This book is about competition. More specifically, it is about how to unleash the power of true and worthy competition and avoid distortions of it. You may wonder, *Is there really a need for such a book?* Perhaps you are thinking, *I already know what the problems are. Some people are just too competitive. They get carried away. They try to win at all costs. We just need to keep things in perspective and everything will be fine.*

These reflections certainly contain an element of truth. They are also the kinds of sound bites that one often hears in the media. No doubt, when a fight breaks out in a game or when a scandal hits the business pages, commentators rely on a familiar set of refrains:

- Winning became all-important to them.
- All he cared about was the bottom line.
- Caught up in the emotion of the moment, she had a lapse of judgment.

As we will see, the problems that plague our playing fields and classrooms cannot be reduced to such simple ideas as these. Although there is an element of truth to such folk explanations, they largely miss the mark. Something much deeper and more structural is at work. By focusing on the personal failings of individual competitors, these analyses underplay the very powerful forces that stem from the contest structure itself. Competition, it seems, often leads good people to act in bad ways.

In this book, we probe the benefits and limitations of competition. Most important, we make the case for true competition as a way to pursue both excellence and enjoyment. We also suggest that a fundamental misunderstanding of competition has severely limited our ability to take advantage of its positive potential.

In the next section, we talk about the science of competition. Be forewarned: A century of research on competition has led to some startlingly negative conclusions about its worth and impact. As Alfie Kohn summarized in his highly acclaimed and award-winning book, *No Contest: The Case Against Competition*,[3] a sea of evidence suggests that if competition were a person, it should be jailed. We disagree. Yet there is much to learn from critics such as Kohn and the social scientists who have investigated the workings of competition. Just as we need to learn about history, so do we need to learn about competition so we are not doomed to endlessly repeat its more unsavory elements. So let us listen and learn from the critics—at least for a time.

Competition Research

Competition has been studied from many disciplines: psychology, sociology, anthropology, political science, economics, biology, and ethnology, to name just a few.[4] Although all of these disciplines offer unique contributions, most point to surprisingly consistent conclusions. Economists and biologists sometimes celebrate the positive contributions of competition, but most investigators who have probed the inner dynamics and workings of competition have raised serious concerns. In this chapter, we are particularly interested in the findings of social scientists, especially social psychologists and educational researchers.

Since the late 19th century, social scientists have been interested in competition.[5] In fact, it is one of the most carefully and thoroughly researched topics in all of the social sciences. Obviously, our intent here is not to provide a comprehensive review of this expansive literature. Instead, we will journey to a few scenic highlights from the 100-year exploration.[6] Along the way, we will introduce you to a few of the leading explorers. The trailhead of our journey into this literature is located in Robbers Cave State Park.

The Sherifs and the Robbers Cave Experiments

Robbers Cave State Park is located in the scenic, hilly woodlands of the San Bois Mountains of southeast Oklahoma. It is a terrific place to ride horseback along picturesque bluffs or fish for trout to your heart's content. In the 1950s, it was also the site of one of the most important and influential studies of competition, often referred to simply as the Robbers Cave experiments.[7]

Musafer and Carolyn Sherif, a husband and wife team of researchers from the University of Oklahoma, wanted to investigate the effects of putting people in competitive and cooperative situations. Their findings were stark and startling. Although the Sherifs conducted dozens of studies during their long and fruitful careers, the setting for the most famous investigation was a summer program for adolescent boys. The study began when the unsuspecting 12-year-olds arrived for what they thought was a regular summer camp.

Although none of the boys knew each other prior to camp, they all came from similar middle-class Protestant backgrounds. The boys arrived in two buses and initially were not even aware of the other group. Over the next several days, each of the groups independently engaged in activities designed to build group identity and cohesion and to allow patterns of leadership and hierarchy to emerge. Independently, each group planned outings, cooked together, and solved shared problems. The boys in each group hiked and swam and canoed together. Through these activities, the boys developed a feeling of attachment to their group, and a team structure emerged. One group named itself the Rattlers, and the other group coined the moniker the Eagles. Each group designed a flag, set up a clubhouse, and did other group-building activities.

The second phase of the camp began when the Sherifs introduced a four-day series of competitions, mostly sports, between the two groups. Every day, the contest scores were posted. Although mild tension was evident from the outset, it increased dramatically over the course of the week. Before the week was over, the Eagles had burned the Rattlers' flag, and the Rattlers had ransacked the Eagles' cabin, overturning beds and stealing property. The mild name calling that characterized the beginning of the week had descended into rabid prejudice by the end. The groups, in fact, became so antagonistic that the researchers had to physically separate them.

Immediately following the week of competition, the camp staff sat the boys down and asked them to describe the two groups. Not surprisingly, the boys characterized their own group in highly favorable terms. When asked to characterize the other group, however, the boys used terms that were anything but complimentary.

The Sherifs then shifted the structural situation from formal competition to informal cooperation. They introduced "superordinate goals" that required the two groups to work together to achieve an outcome that everyone desired. The boys were told, for example, that the water supply to the camp had been interrupted. The drinking water came from a reservoir on the mountain to the north of the camp, and the camp staff lead the boys to believe that vandals had clogged it. The two groups worked together to discover that an outlet faucet had a sack stuffed into it, and they jointly brainstormed and implemented solutions. Similarly, a truck bringing food to the camp "accidentally" got stuck in a rut on its way in, and both groups of boys worked to free it. By the end of the camp, the boys wanted a single bus to return them to Oklahoma City, rather than separate buses for the two groups. When told by the camp staff that a single bus would work, the boys cheered. The cooperation phase of the camp had resulted in harmony between the two groups.

So what does the Robbers Cave experiment tell us about competition? There are, of course, numerous limitations to the study. It involved only 22 boys of a particular age. They were all white and all of a similar background. It was relatively short in duration. It entailed competition of a particular kind—games and sports. For these reasons we should not draw too many conclusions from it. On the other hand, since that initial experiment more than a half-century ago, numerous similar studies have been conducted. They have focused on various populations, settings, and forms of competition.[8] What is striking in looking at all these studies is the similarity of their results. Regardless of who is participating, competition (whether in sports or in something else) seems to lead inexorably to hostility and prejudice, sometimes spiraling into open aggression.

It is important to note that the negative outcomes of competition are not dependent on weaknesses within particular people or any particular history of antagonism between the groups. The boys at the Sherifs' camp were all strangers at the outset and were normal, well-adjusted kids. There seems to be an inner force to competition that acts like an invisible hand propelling participants into antagonistic relationships that spill over beyond the bounds of the immediate contest. To learn more about that inner force of competition, we turn to the highly influential work of Morton Deutsch.

Deutsch and Social Interdependence Theory

After his military service in the Second World War, Morton Deutsch began a long and fruitful career studying how competition and cooperation affect individual and group dynamics.[9] Although Deutsch's early career included a number of small group experiments in the labs of the Massachusetts Institute of Technology, he was no ivory-tower, armchair theoretician. Living in the shadow of Hiroshima and Nagasaki, Deutsch was deeply committed to addressing the real-world problems of his day. His experimental work on competition was informed by a rich and textured analysis of dilemmas and conflicts arising from the Cold War, the Civil Rights Movement, campus unrest, poverty, and management–labor tensions. Correspondingly, his research spanned a wide range of competitive settings, from dyads to nations. Simultaneous with his academic career, Deutsch was also a clinical psychologist who helped dozens of individuals and couples navigate the subtle and hidden competitions that creep into and sometimes derail otherwise close and intimate relationships. Toward the end of his career, Deutsch founded the International Center for Cooperation and Conflict Resolution at Columbia University, where he served as the E.L. Thorndike professor of psychology until his retirement in 1990. Deutsch is often considered the pioneer of modern social interdependence theory, an area of social psychology dealing with competition and cooperation.

An understanding of Deutsch's theory begins with a commonplace observation: People are goal directed in much of their behavior. We shop for groceries in order to eat. On the basketball court, we practice free throws so that we can make more of them in the games we play. We attend college to learn and get the jobs we want.

Although people can pursue many goals independently, Deutsch notes that people's goals are often connected; they are interdependent. In these situations, one person's success or failure has an impact on another's goal pursuit, positively or negatively.

Positive interdependence occurs when one person's success makes it more likely that others in the relationship will also be successful. Imagine, for example, an advertising team working on an ad campaign. If one person comes up with a great idea, it helps everyone on the team. Positive interdependence is the defining ingredient of a cooperative situation.

On the other hand, negative interdependence occurs when the success of one party makes it less likely that others in the relationship can be successful. Imagine two advertising teams pitching their ideas to a client. If one team's idea garners her enthusiasm, the other team is unlikely to achieve its

© Human Kinetics

How do Deutsch's theories play out on this tennis court? What would a social interdependence theorist predict might happen during and after the match?

goal of gaining the contract. According to Deutsch's terminology, negative interdependence is the essence of competition.

Most games are designed deliberately to create negative interdependence. In all forms of win–lose games, people's goals are mutually exclusive. If one person wins, the other loses. Winning can be divided into gradients (first place, second place), but the basic structure of a contest requires that some win and others lose. That's negative interdependence. That, according to Deutsch, is competition.[10]

Games, of course, are not the only setting in which negative interdependence occurs. Teachers who grade students on a curve are placing students in such a situation. Candidates running for office are in a similarly structured contest. Virtually all businesses compete for customers, and when people go shopping, they spend money at some businesses (the winners) and not others (the losers).

As the Sherifs' demonstrated, whether a situation is structured competitively or cooperatively makes a big difference. According to Deutsch, each of these two forms of goal interdependence unleashes a predicable set of consequences having to do with human emotion, thought, and behavior. The consequences that flow from cooperation are largely positive; the reverse is true for competition. Specifically, Deutsch suggests that people in competitive settings are likely to do the following:

- Develop a negative view of the other party
- Think of opponents in stereotypic and prejudicial ways
- Act in hostile, demeaning, or aggressive ways toward opponents
- Experience heightened interpersonal anxiety and tension
- Exhibit a disruption of effective communication
- Display a poor use of resources
- Exhibit lower productivity

Whew! That's quite a nasty list of outcomes. And, to be fair, Deutsch would acknowledge that not every competition results in such dramatic negative consequences. Sometimes the negative outcomes that flow from competition may be rather small and innocuous. Still, Deutsch's own extensive experiments, as well as those of many others, have borne out the prediction that competition thrusts people in these directions.[11]

It is worth noting once again that these negative outcomes of competition—distrust, coercion, hostility, deception, intimidation, aggression, and lowered productivity, to name a few—are not based on characteristics of the person. Rather, they seem to spiral out from a logic built into the structure of competition. If you and I both want the same thing but only one of us can obtain it, the resulting clash of interests is likely to set forces in motion. Those forces entail antagonisms that can derail the positive relations between us. This may not happen immediately. It may not be the result of every contest.

But over time consistent participation in competition leads, almost invariably according to Deutsch's extensive research, to such predictable, negative results. This is particularly true, as we discuss later, when the competitive outcome is important.

One final component of Deutsch's theory is worth highlighting. He calls it his "crude law of social relations."[12] Here is how he describes it: The "characteristic processes and effects elicited by a given type of social relationship (cooperative or competitive) tend also to elicit that type of social relationship"[13] What does he mean?

Imagine that you are meeting someone, let's call him Derek, for the first time. Soon you realize that the two of you have a similar idea for a new media delivery product. Perhaps you could cooperate, join in a collaborative effort. But then Derek says something that you know to be false. Although it is not at all related to your business idea, a seed of distrust is planted. Feeling distrustful of Derek, you distance yourself from him. You also decline to share more details about your idea, fearing that he might steal them.

Dear Authors:

Those academics you cite just don't know what they're talking about. Sure, competition gets out of hand sometimes. But come on. It doesn't just automatically generate hostility, anger, resentment, and aggression. I'm a college student, and I've played hundreds of games with my friends, competed with them for grades, and even competed with them for dates. But we're still friends. Most of the time, competition is just fun. Aren't they exaggerating?

— College Competitor

Dear College Competitor:

You're both right! Sometimes people compete just to add a little zest to their lives. Who doesn't enjoy a good game? So you're right – competing won't always lead to all those negative outcomes that show up so frequently in the research. In fact, that's part of the point of this book. On the other hand, the research is strong and compelling. When people's goals conflict, as they typically do in a contest, there is a natural stimulus toward antagonism. Dozens of studies have clearly demonstrated that most people, under most competitive circumstances, will experience some form of negative emotion or outcome. So the question arises: When will contesting be helpful and enjoyable, and when will it be harmful? That's the central question of this book. Read on!

Soon you are in open competition with each other. According to Deutsch, all of the individual outcomes or elements associated with competition can act as triggers to bring out all the other elements. And competition, once unleashed, breeds more intense competition.

The Johnsons Take Competition to School

By the time David and Roger Johnson began their work on cooperative learning at the University of Minnesota in the 1970s, there was already much known about the positive benefits of cooperation and the destructiveness that often comes packaged with competition. For the next 30 years, however, they pioneered efforts to bring such theoretical insights into the classrooms of America and beyond.[14]

Here sits Mitra at a round table in her fourth-grade classroom. She has pieces of an intellectual puzzle and is working to combine them with clues held by other excited children at her table. They work together, sharing insights, building knowledge. The fact that Mitra is not sitting passively at an individual desk lined up in a neat row with other identical desks owes much to the Johnsons.

Although the Johnsons are best known for their work on cooperative learning, they have also carefully investigated the effects of competition in schools. Of course, schools are filled with competition. Students compete for grades, for entrance into select colleges, for spots on sports teams, for

©Andreanna Seymore/Stone/Getty Images

Why do you think children usually learn better in cooperative learning groups than in competitive arrangements?

drama parts, and for first chair in their band section. Is all this competition beneficial? Rarely, according to the Johnsons. They have demonstrated quite conclusively that if learning is the goal, competition is rarely the best process.[15] If you have two groups of children with similar aptitudes and one group is learning cooperatively while the other is engaged in a learning contest, the cooperators will learn more almost every time. The Johnsons found that for most educational tasks, cooperative learning fosters greater academic achievement, while simultaneously promoting self-esteem, intrinsic motivation, psychological health, and enhanced social skills.[16]

Why is competition so counterproductive for learning? The Johnsons suggest several reasons. In addition to the antagonisms and hostilities that competition often generates, it also tends to create self-defeating behaviors. When competition is in place, some people may not work hard so that they can blame a loss on a lack of effort, rather than a lack of ability. Others engage in what's known as self-handicapping behaviors, such as procrastinating, so that they have an excuse ready at hand in case they fail. Still others minimize the importance of the task so that, should they lose, they can simply claim not to care.

There is remarkable uniformity to the findings of the Sherifs, Deutsch, and the Johnsons. Of course, these are only a few of the hundreds of people who have investigated competition in one setting or another. To find a broad summary of this research, we turn finally to the work of Alfie Kohn.

Kohn's Case Against Competition

If you desire a compelling summary of a century of research on competition, there is one place to turn: *No Contest: The Case Against Competition*.[17] Alfie Kohn's powerful treatise won a book award from the American Psychological Association and has stirred a heated debate about the merits of contests. Structured like a legal argument, Kohn's book puts competition on trial and finds it guilty. We close our discussion on the research of competition by summarizing Kohn's key arguments.

For Kohn, all competition is inherently bad. And competition is bad, Kohn argues, for a number of reasons. For the practically minded, competition is bad from a purely *instrumental* standpoint. Contrary to popular belief, competition doesn't lead to improved performance or increased productivity. Whether we are talking about the output of a factory, learning in school, or the acquisition of a skill, Kohn cites numerous studies that all suggest that competition undermines performance. This is true whether performance is measured in quantitative or qualitative terms.

Among the many experts that Kohn metaphorically calls to the witness stand to offer testimony against competition is Robert Helmreich of the University of Texas.[18] Helmreich tells how in one early study he investigated 103 scientists, looking to see how often their work was cited by colleagues. To his surprise, Helmreich found that the more often the scientists' work was cited, the lower they scored on a measure of competitiveness. In other words, productive scientists tend to be less competitive. He wondered whether his results were just a fluke. So he conducted a similar study with academic psychologists. He found the same result. Then he studied male businessmen, measuring achievement by their salaries. He went on to study students, measuring performance by grades. Then he studied airline pilots, then airline reservation agents, then several other groups. In every study, regardless of the measure used, performance was related negatively to competitiveness.

Kohn calls another witness: Theresa Amabile. She tells about her study of a group of 7- to 11-year-old girls who made collages.[19] Some of the girls made their collages while competing for prizes. Other girls made them just for fun. Ambile then had professional artists evaluate the girls' creations. The artists found that those girls who were competing made collages that were less creative, less spontaneous, and less complex and varied than the ones created by the girls who were not competing.

Kohn goes on to call dozens of other expert witnesses. Each offers similar testimony. If the destination you seek is improved performance, then competition, it seems, is the wrong road to travel.

There are probably many reasons why competition interferes with performance, and Kohn cites a number of them. One is certainly the stress that competition often evokes. Although a moderate amount of stress can be beneficial, competition often generates disabling levels of stress for many people. Research has shown, for example, that competition-related stress often has negative effects in educational settings. One illustrative study found that 12 percent of medical students, as a result of their highly competitive environment, experienced stress at a level that led to psychiatric disorders.[20]

Competition also interferes with optimal performance simply because focusing on winning is quite different from focusing on doing well. The contest distracts from the task. If my goal is to outperform others, I may try to perform at my best to reach that goal. Nevertheless, I'm focusing on relative performance rather than on doing the task to the best of my ability.

The next charge that Kohn levels against competition is that it is bad from a *psychological* standpoint. To back up this allegation, Kohn offers several research-supported observations. First, Kohn notes, people engaged in competition tend to look outward instead of inward for their sense of personal worth and validation. Competition provides a highly celebrated and public pathway to the socially valued label "winner," but taking that pathway leads away from anchoring self-worth in an unshakable sense of inner dignity and security. Psychological health is supported best by a rock-solid and unconditional sense of worthiness. Once a person steps onto the treadmill of competition, however, that person is likely to climb endlessly up the Sisyphean hill of external validation based on publicly witnessed performance. Although this may not be inevitable, it is certainly common.

Charge 1: Competition undermines performance.

Supporting Arguments:
- Competition creates stress, which interferes with optimal performance.
- It focuses attention on defeating others rather than on performing well.

Charge 2: Competition has negative psychological consequences.

Supporting Arguments:
- Competition undermines a sense of intrinsic self-worth.
- It fosters insecurity and undermines self-esteem.
- It creates undue anxiety, envy, humiliation, and shame.

Charge 3: Competition is ethically wrong.

Supporting Arguments:
- Competition fosters interpersonal hostility, prejudice, and aggression.
- It encourages a belief that we benefit only at the expense of others.

Kohn's case against competition.

Kohn also notes that for many people, perhaps the majority, competition leads to heightened insecurity and lowered self-esteem. These are not just his personal opinions, of course. They are charges backed by considerable science. Why do these outcomes occur? They might not if people didn't care about winning, but who doesn't want to be a winner? Because being a winner and actually winning, at least most of the time, are typically linked in people's minds, anxiety arises from the realization that even if you prevail in one contest, losing may be just the next contest away. Over time, most people rise to a level of competition at which losing is at least as likely as winning. Tying self-esteem to competitive success, although common, is a recipe for insecurity and lowered self-esteem.

Even those who win consistently are not immune to negative psychological effects. Knowing that their position is envied and comes at the loser's expense, victors often experience stress, anxiety, and insecurity. The psychological costs of winning, in fact, may lead some competitors to sabotage their own performance.

Finally, some experiences of competition, particularly highly public defeats, can lead to devastating feelings of humiliation and shame that stay with a person throughout life. On this point, I am in full accord with Kohn.

Whenever I talk to an adult audience about competition, I invite those attending to share their stories. I am always dismayed by how many people carry with them highly painful memories of youthful defeats. Of course, we all need to learn to deal with failure, but these stifling and painful memories are about as useful in learning to deal with defeat as near drowning experiences are in learning to swim.

Kohn's points about the effects of competition on productivity and psychological health are important. However, like circumstantial evidence at a trial, they may not be enough to convict. To nail his case, Kohn hammers at a final point. Most important, Kohn argues, competition is bad from an *ethical* standpoint.

In short, Kohn's argument is that a process that makes one person's happiness dependent on another's sorrow is fundamentally flawed. As people compete, they learn to take delight in others' defeats. Because winning in competition requires that others lose, competition links your agony of defeat with my thrill of victory. Every win requires a loss, and so the psychological link between my enjoyment and the pain of others becomes as strong as the link between eating and alleviation of hunger. Kohn writes:

> **Strip away all the assumptions about what competition is supposed to do, all the claims in its behalf that we accept and repeat reflexively. What you have left is the essence of the concept: mutually exclusive goal attainment (MEGA). One person succeeds only if another does not. From this uncluttered perspective, it seems clear right away that something is drastically wrong with such an arrangement. . . . Competition by its very nature damages relationship. Its nature, remember, is mutually exclusive goal attainment, which means that competitors' interests are inherently opposed. I succeed if you fail, and vice versa, so . . . the failure of others is devoutly to be wished.[21]**

According to Kohn, competition inherently sets up antagonisms between people. Recall the Robbers Cave experiments. Competition trains us to think that our own interests and well-being can be served only at the expense of others. This is a mind-set that easily persists beyond the bounds of the formal contests in which we participate and infuses our everyday lives. Can this really be healthy and positive? Kohn renders his verdict: *No!*

Competition is guilty of crimes against productivity, psychological health, and ethics.

Competition's Appeal

Is competition as bad as many scientists seem to believe? Is Kohn right? Personally, we are convinced that Kohn's analysis, which of course is far more nuanced and complex than presented here, is essentially correct. It needs to be taken seriously. Though his book is now dated (the revised edition was published in 1992), Kohn summarized a century of research on competition well, and more recent research has added additional nuances but nothing substantially different.[22]

Honest observation leads one to much the same conclusion. If you thoughtfully examine what is happening in our sport arenas, on our playing fields, in our pools, and on our tracks—as well as in our classrooms, boardrooms, and political spheres—you will find just the kind of negative effects that Kohn so aptly describes. From the youth leagues to the pros, we read almost daily of fights, cheating, and scandals, all seemingly spurred on by competition. Of course, many contests occur without these overt distortions, but the problems are too frequent to ignore. The evidence seems overwhelming.

And yet, despite the mountain of evidence that seems to convict competition, we believe it is innocent of all charges. In fact, we believe competition is an incredibly positive mode of human interaction that can build positive relationships, foster personal growth, and promote ethical behavior.

Acting as defense attorneys, how can we rebut the powerful arguments put forward by Kohn and his team? Mistaken identity is the key to our defense. Kohn is right, except he is not really talking about competition at all. The studies of the Sherifs, Deutsch, and others, and the summaries of Kohn, have confused competition with an outwardly similarly but highly different process. In the next chapter, we rebut the charges leveled in Kohn's *No Contest* and make a case for the *noble contest*. ■

---

1   It may be that the rise of action or extreme sports is partly a consequence of disaffection with the emphasis on winning and interpersonal competition within conventional sports. In traditional sports, athletes contest against each other under highly standardized conditions, and the primary goal is to outperform the other. In contrast, adventure sports, as they are also called, place a greater emphasis on overcoming natural resistance—such as wind, snow, gravity, and ice. Although many action sports contain an element of contest, the emphasis on winning is usually not as great as it is in conventional sports.

2   The context within which competition takes place does matter, of course. Competition among Internet providers is not identical to competition in Little League, which is not the same as competition among siblings over parental attention. And yet there are also commonalities. In this book, we focus primarily on the commonalities.

(continued)

(continued from previous page)

3   Kohn (1992).

4   For a more comprehensive literature review that covers numerous disciplines, see Rosenau (2003).

5   There are really two sciences regarding competition. In this book, we focus on the social and psychological dynamics involved in contesting. Research within this tradition seeks to understand how people function in contest settings and what kinds and qualities of processes and outcomes are associated with competing. There is also an emerging science, based in mathematical game theory and experimental methods, that addresses the question of how to manage and optimize the strategic decisions that are made in competitive situations. For an analysis of the latter form of the science of competition, see Case (2007).

6   Our review of the research literature on competition is obviously highly simplified. For an excellent historical review of the relevant theoretical and empirical advances in the study of competition from 1897 through 1980, see the first chapter of Pepitone (1980).

7   For the most complete description, see Sherif, Harvey, White, Hood, and Sherif (1988).

8   Musafer Sherif was the chief architect of realistic group conflict theory (RGCT). The basic premise of RGCT is that intergroup hostility is produced by conflicting goals and reduced by superordinate goals. For validations and extensions of RGCT, see, for example, Blake and Mouton (1961); Bobo (1983); Diab (1970); Langford and Ponting (1992); Rabble and Horwitz (1969); Stendler, Damrin, and Haines (1951); and Zarate, Garcia, Garza, and Hitlan (2004).

9   See Deutsch (1949a, 1949b, 1973, 1985, 2000).

10 This is a simplification. For Deutsch, competition or cooperation only exist as people *perceive* the social interdependence of their goals and take corresponding promotive (helpful) or oppositional (hindering) action.

11 For a review, see Johnson and Johnson (2005).

12 Deutsch (1985), p. 365.

13 Deutsch (1973), p. 365.

14 See especially Johnson and Johnson (2006), as well as Johnson and Johnson (1999, 2003).

15 Unlike Kohn, the Johnsons do not think that all competition should be eliminated from schools and other institutions. Although cooperation is more productive in most situations, they do see a limited role for competition, if it is carefully constrained. Appropriate competition has five characteristics: (1) it is voluntary; (2) the importance of winning is not so high as to cause disabling stress; (3) everyone must have a reasonable chance to win; (4) the rules are clear and fair; and (5) relative progress can be monitored. See Johnson and Johnson (1978, 1989, 2003). It is also important to note that a few studies (e.g., Clark, 1969), in contrast to the majority, found that competition boosts academic performance. One explanation for this inconsistency is that the word *competition* has been used to name two distinct processes, each associated with quite different dynamics. We would hypothesize that when a contest situation more closely approximates true competition, it will be associated with more positive outcomes.

16 Johnson and Johnson (1999).

17 Kohn (1992).

18 For Kohn's discussion of the Helmreich studies, see Kohn (1992), pp. 52-53.

19 Amabile (1982).

20 Liu, Oda, Peng, and Asai (1997).

21 Kohn (1992), pp. 9, 136.

22 For more recent reviews, see Johnson and Johnson (2003) and Rosenau (2003).

Naming the Imposter
Unmasking Decompetition

The year was 1943; the place, Columbia University. A dispute was raging between Lou Little, head football coach, and instructors in the physical education program. The debate focused on the value of competition. More specifically, the question was whether competitive sports were more valuable than recreational physical education programs. Lou Little was fired up:

> I'm convinced that the physical education directors want to get rid of coaches in all sports, build themselves up and have their programs accepted by all. What good is it to have muscles developed if a boy loses the desire for competition? When I take part in a sport, I want to win and kick the brains out of the other fellow. I'm not content to play with someone. I want to play against them. [1]

Coach Little's argument hinged on the added value that competition brings to physical activity. Interestingly, his argument *for* competition sounds much like Alfie Kohn's argument *against* it. Kohn basically shares Little's understanding of competition, but comes to the opposite conclusion about its worth. As we have seen in chapter 1, Kohn argues like a prosecutor and indicts competition on a number of charges.[2] Competition is bad, Kohn alleges, from a *practical* standpoint because it doesn't, contrary to popular belief, improve performance, creativity, or productivity. It is bad from a *psychological* standpoint because it leads to heightened anxiety, lowered self-esteem, dependence on external evaluation, and performance-based standards of personal worth.

Kohn also puts social scientists on the witness stand and they testify that competition is bad from a *moral* standpoint. In short, their testimony is that competition makes one person's happiness dependent on another's sorrow. It trains people to take delight in the pain of others. Competition pits us against each other, and that stance of antagonism easily becomes habitual. If Kohn were to cross-examine Lou Little, he would ask whether the world is a better place when people want to "kick the brains out of the other guy."

> ❝ **The beginning of wisdom**
> **is to call things by their right names.** ❞
>
> Chinese proverb

Contests are everywhere. And, make no mistake about it, contests require winning and losing. In a game, one person wins by outscoring the opponent. In a classroom, if the teacher grades on a curve, students are in a contest for top grades. Two local Italian restaurants are in a contest to obtain the business of those in the area who have a yearning for Italian cuisine. It is a mistake, however, to assume that competition occurs whenever a contest is in place.

The word *contest* literally means "to bear witness together." A contest contains a "test" (such as tossing a ball through a hoop), and contestants seek to "bear witness" to their relative ability to meet the test.[3] The individual or team that provides convincing witness that it can perform the test better or best (e.g., by scoring more points) is declared the winner. For present purposes, what is important to notice is that a contest requires more than just having a structure in place that eventually leads to winners and losers. *How the participants think about the test* is important as well. They must want to excel at it. Similarly, how people think about the contest is important to defining the nature of true competition.

Often, the word *competition* has been used interchangeably with the word *contest.* Likewise, *to compete* has been used to mean the same thing as *to contest.* However, we think this is a big mistake. It has resulted in considerable confusion and mistaken conclusions. When Kohn puts competition on trial and finds it guilty, it is actually a case of mistaken identity. Kohn's prosecution of competition is possible, if unfortunate, because the word *competition* has been used to refer to two quite different things. It has been used to refer to two very different processes, or activities, both of which can take place within a contest. We suggest that *to contest* is a generic verb that can refer to two distinct activities with quite different characteristics.

It is helpful to recall that the word *competition* comes from the Latin *-petere,* meaning "to strive" or "to seek," combined with the prefix, *com-,* meaning "with." So the root meaning of competition is "to strive or seek with."[4] It is

> When I first met my friend Terri, I didn't know that she had a twin sister. Soon, however, I met her twin. At first, I had a hard time telling who was who, so I didn't always know which name to use when I saw one of them approaching. Of course, if both Terri and her twin went by the same name, matters would have been considerably worse. Unfortunately, this is precisely our predicament with competition.

not "to strive *against*," but "to strive *with*." True competition involves striving *together*; it involves seeking excellence together.[5] In true competition, the competitors think about the contest as an opportunity for enjoying a quest after personal (and, perhaps, team) excellence.[6] In true competition, each party pursues excellence by trying to meet the challenge presented by the opponent's best effort.

An alternative and quite different process often occurs in contests. Rather than *striving with* the opponent, one *strives against* the opponent. Although the gulf between *striving with* and *striving against* may be experienced in a myriad of quiet and subtle ways, it is still an immense chasm as wide as it is important. In true competition, the focus is on excellence and the enjoyment that comes from striving for it. In competition's twin, the focus is on conquest. The contest is reduced to a site for self-aggrandizement. Once again, *how people think about the contest matters.*

Part of the problem is that we have a very inadequate language when it comes to competition. We need a richer vocabulary if we are to preserve and promote what is valuable about genuine competition. Imagine the confusion that would be created if we had one name for two twins, one word for both hot and cold. We need a new word, not to replace the word *competition*, but to name what is really its opposite.[7]

Decompetition

The process of competition—of striving with another, of seeking excellence together—is really fairly fragile. As we will see, it balances seriousness with play, intrinsic motivations with extrinsic motivations, and outcome orientation with process orientation. When the balance required for true competition is upset, competition decomposes or degenerates. It becomes something quite other than what the true meaning of *com-petere* suggests. To designate this alternative process that can take place within a contest, we will use the term *decompetition*. The prefix *de-* means "reverse of" or "opposite of." Decompetition is contesting that has devolved or decomposed into *striving against*. Decompetition is the opposite of true competition.

When limestone is buried deep in the earth and exposed to heat and pressure, it transforms into marble. Fortunately, we have two words to distinguish the two rocks. Similarly, when a log decays into mulch, it would make little sense to continue to call it a log. And when *striving with* decays into *striving against*, it ceases to be competition. We need to call it what it is. It is decayed or decomposed or degenerated competition. It is decompetition.

Like competition, decompetition takes place within a contest structure, but it has morphed into the opposite of true competition.

Question: *But, really, why a new word?*

Answer: Because we need words to highlight important distinctions.

Dear Authors:

It seems to me that all you're really saying is that sportsmanship is important. When people are poor sports, it makes for bad competition. Rather than inventing new words, why don't you just talk about good and bad competition or good and bad sportsmanship? Do we really need a new word like **decompetition**? The English dictionary is fat enough already!

— Plain Talker

Dear Plain Talker:

We sympathize with your desire to keep talk simple. No doubt, some people will run from the word **decompetition** like a lizard from a snake. But, hopefully, we're not selling snake oil.

There is such a thing as "bad" competition, but it is not what we mean by decompetition. Bad competition (which is still a form of competition) might occur, for example, when opponents are uneven in ability. It can result when competitors are tired or simply off their game. When officials make egregious mistakes, bad competition may result. Although all of these things may cause competition to be less than it might be, they can all take place within a contest that is still understood as **striving together.** In other words, there is a continuum that runs from ideal competition to bad competition. But when we talk about decompetition, we are no longer on that continuum at all. Decompetition is a fundamentally different process.

Are we simply urging people to be good sports? Not really. Being a good sport is important, but it is insufficient to guarantee true competition. Many decompetitors are polite and civil and obey the rules. Most people would consider them to be good sports. So would we. But they may still think of their opponent as an enemy or enter the sport primarily for the glory. In short, decompetition is a different concept from both bad competition and being a poor sport. Unfortunately, there is no other word available.

Our failure to use separate words for competition and decompetition creates confusion and tends to dull our perception. When Kohn puts social scientists on the witness stand and asks them about competition, they often talk about decompetition without anyone noticing the inadvertent sleight of hand.

It is important to emphasize that decompetition is not just overly zealous competition. It is not competition hyped on caffeine. Nor is it simply competition with an ugly zit on its face. Rather, it is no longer competition at all, just as marble is no longer limestone.

In our legal system, prosecutors and defense attorneys both seek to win. Does this mean there is no room for a shared interest in truth and justice? How would a truly competitive lawyer approach her work differently from a decompetitive one?

As coaches and teachers, we encourage our charges to be competitive, but when they cheat, fight, taunt, or belittle, we admonish them not to get so caught up in competition that they lose their moral compass. In reality, we need to urge them to be *more* competitive, not less. They need to focus more on excellence and enjoying the effort to achieve it. When athletes or students or businesspeople or politicians lie or cheat or steal in an effort to win, *they aren't competing*. They are engaged in a quite different process guided by a fundamentally different way of understanding and valuing contests. Although outwardly they are still contesting, the very purpose and nature of the contest is different. Let us offer one more analogy.

Imagine two people who are each writing a script for a television broadcast. One is writing about the science of global warming. The other is writing a revision of history to cast a favorable light on the Nazis. Outwardly, both are doing similar things, but the purpose and intent of their activity is different. Fortunately, we have different words to distinguish between *communication* and *propaganda*, the latter being a distortion of genuine communication. Lacking such a discriminating vocabulary about contesting, time after time, true competition gives way to decompetition without us recognizing and naming the change.

Twins can look alike, but sometimes they have strikingly different personalities. Lest we kiss the wrong contest twin, we need to learn to distinguish competition from its troublesome look-alike, decompetition. Despite skin-level similarities, the differences are profound.

Genuine competition has great potential to enhance and enrich human life. To unleash its potential, the first step is to clearly distinguish it from decompetition. Decompetition stimulates the kinds of problems outlined in chapter 1. Unfortunately, because we have traditionally used one word, *competition,* for two distinct processes, the problems that infest one have damaged the reputation of the other. Many people have concluded, falsely, that whenever people contest, the problems associated with decompetition will follow.

Meet Jack. He is a fierce competitor. A high-level soccer athlete, Jack is ready to give his all when he enters the field; he's there to win. But winning is still not his ultimate goal. His opponents are not his enemies. Jack plays for the enjoyment of the contest, for the emotional charge of the challenge, and for the desire to push his physical skills to their boundaries. Although he wants to win, that desire is only one part of a deep and abiding respect for the game itself. In our terminology, Jack is a true competitor.

Like a barrel that can hold good apples or bad, a contest is a structure that may contain competition or decompetition. Although Kohn and others assume that the very existence of a contest will lead to *striving against* others, we suggest that this is not the case. Whether competition or decompetition occurs depends on how the participants think about the contest. True competitors think of the contest (and preparation for it) as an opportunity for self-improvement, for feeling camaraderie with others, for enjoying the thrill of a challenge, and related goals. For those involved in decompetition—we will call them *decompetitors*—the contest is viewed as an opportunity to flaunt personal superiority, to reap the shallow pleasures of conquest, and to steal whatever rewards come with victory.

This book focuses primarily on the meanings, values, and purposes that people bring to the contest. These are what divide competition from decom-

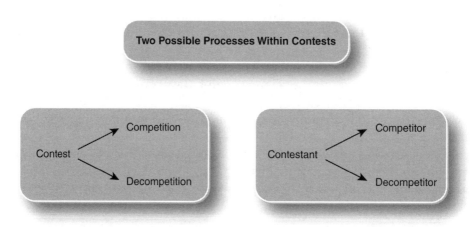

The language of contesting.

petition. And because these are within our collective ability to control, it is up to us whether a given contest will result in competition or decompetition. Of course, in reality, contests invariably involve some mixture of both. No one is completely competitive or decompetitive. The point here is that the ability to recognize and name competition's imposter is a powerful tool in helping us create genuinely competitive contests.

If you are a coach, teacher, or parent, you have a responsibility to ensure that those entrusted to your guidance learn to become true competitors. Why? Because only true competition can support a dedicated pursuit of excellence and lead to lasting enjoyment. Decompetition may look similar, but ultimately it leads to the kinds of problems identified in chapter 1.

Thus far, we have only hinted at the substantive differences between competition and decompetition. In the next section, we probe the root metaphors that guide these two processes. In chapter 3, we provide a field guide to competition and decompetition. The categories of the field guide are then elaborated in subsequent chapters. As you will see, competition and decompetition operate with different guiding metaphors and involve contrasting views of opponents, officials, the rules, the goal, and the process. About the only thing that competition and decompetition share is the external contest structure.[8] Because there is a contest, some win and some do not, but the real meaning and attributes of the contest are quite different for the two.

The Power of Metaphors

Metaphors? you may ask. *Aren't those the fancy devices of poets? What do they have to do with the gritty world of competition?* Excellent question! Many of us are surprised to learn just how important metaphors are to our everyday lives and our way of thinking about things. Humans are *homo sapiens*— thinking beings—and much of our thinking is guided by the metaphors that we employ—often unconsciously—to understand our world. To illustrate the profound differences between competition and decompetition, we begin by identifying the metaphors we use to think about contests.

In their classic book, *Metaphors We Live By,*[9] linguists George Lakoff and Mark Johnson points out how deeply metaphors structure our ways of thinking, feeling, and acting. Far from being the esoteric property of poets and novelists, metaphors guide our everyday lives. They shape our ways of perceiving the world and acting within it.

We say, for example, that time is money. That is a metaphor. One thing (time) is understood with reference to another thing (money). And so we "invest" our time, "spend" our time, "save" our time, "waste" our time, and "donate" our time. The way we perceive of and handle time is influenced by the way we deal with money. This comes so naturally to us that we aren't even aware that we are thinking in a metaphor when we talk about saving time. Yet in some cultures the idea of investing, spending, wasting, saving, or donating time wouldn't make much sense because time is not viewed through the metaphor of money. Metaphors provide a mental model, a cognitive map, of how something is to be thought about.

Metaphors are a natural and indispensable part of our mental apparatus, but they do come with a price tag (to use a metaphor). Although metaphors help to *reveal* important dimensions of something, they also *conceal* other dimensions. Metaphors highlight the common features of the two things, but the features that are not held in common are placed in a cognitive shadow. They become hard to see (to use a cognition-as-vision metaphor). The ways time is not like money become less obvious to the person who thinks of time as money.

Contests provide a rich setting for metaphorical interpretation. In fact, they derive much of their meaning from the metaphors we bring to them. So it is important to recognize and name the root metaphors of competition and decompetition. These root metaphors guide the experience of the contestants and lead them to take certain actions, assume certain attitudes, and adopt certain values. For those who hold it, the underlying metaphor reveals certain things about the contest and conceals other things. Depending on the underlying metaphor through which one perceives the contest, either competition or decompetition will ensue. So what are these metaphors?

Contest as War

The root metaphor for decompetition is a battle or war. The contest-as-war metaphor highlights the ways contestants are pitted against each other in the pursuit of a goal (winning). In games, it is not at all uncommon to speak of "attacking the enemy." Athletes have "weapons," and even the athletes themselves are often described as weapons in the coach's arsenal. Quarterbacks can throw bombs, and so on. Our language about sports is filled with military jargon. In contests, we fight the enemy. Guided by the metaphor of war, decompetitors view their opponents through the lens of rivalry. In a war, the opponent seeks to conquer, to annihilate. When we think about contests through the metaphor of war, we tend to think about opponents as enemy combatants. At best, the opponent is simply depersonalized; at worse, vilified.

It is true that contests share certain features with fights, battles, and wars. Often, contests involve struggle; they involve opposition and tension. It is not that the war metaphor is wrong or inherently bad. Even in true competition, there is a dimension of battle. However, the war metaphor is limiting, and it is problematic when it is the dominant metaphor. What it hides is more important than what it reveals. The war metaphor tends to obscure or hide the fact that worthy opponents are needed to bring out our best. The war metaphor is based on a view of competition as *striving against*. In contrast, true competition is guided by a metaphor that reveals how contests involve *striving with* one's opponent.

Dear Authors:

I've always thought about sports as a battle. Isn't it true that we are fighting our opponents? Sure, it is not an all-out war, but we are on opposite sides. Are you saying that it is wrong to think this way?

— *Fighter*

Dear Fighter:

Not necessarily. As we have said, there is an element of battle in competition. But if the battle image is taken too literally, if war is the dominant metaphor, then there is a problem. Here's a question to ask yourself: If forced to choose, would you rather play poorly and win, or advance to a new height of skill in a losing effort? Under the sway of the war metaphor, decompetitors would rather win ugly than lose beautifully. The competitor also wants to win, of course. But true competitors are accepting of a loss if they have gained through the process. As you continue to read, you will find numerous other questions that will help distinguish true competition from its impersonator, decompetition.

Contest as Partnership

Partnership is the root metaphor for true competition. In this metaphor, each competitor is viewed as an enabler or facilitator for the other. If I am going to improve my game of tennis, I need a partner who can challenge me. In the ideal contest, the skills of the competitors are roughly equal. The play of one is continuously a challenge to the other, and the effort needed for meeting that challenge requires pushing to and beyond previous levels of achievement. The result can be an exhilarating upward spiral that can be hard to achieve apart from the competitive partnership. A synergy results from the mutual challenge that each competitor provides to the other. This synergy enables the competitors to reach new heights of excellence and mastery that could not be achieved in isolation. Embracing the root metaphor of partnership enables competition to be *striving with* the opponent.

Why Metaphors Matter

The metaphor that we use to understand contests will have tremendous implications. For example, the root metaphor that we adopt, consciously or unconsciously, will lead us to desire different things for our opponents. In true competition, I hope that my opponents perform at their best. Why?

©Human Kinetics

Studying a book about chess strategies might improve your game, but can excellence be achieved without playing opponents? In what ways do opponents cooperate even as they compete?

Guided by the metaphor of partnership, I recognize that achieving my own best performance requires a worthy challenge. The better my opponent performs, the higher the bar is set. I cannot achieve my own best performance without the bar set high. Therefore, I hope that my opponents perform at their best. I hope that they do well.

Chris Evert, shortly after retiring, was asked about her favorite match. She named a Wimbledon match against Martina Navratilova as a highlight of her tennis career.[10] She recalled that match because both she and Martina were playing in top form, pushing each other to the max. The fact that she eventually lost was less important than having experienced that upward spiral of heightened focus, emotion, and performance. That's what true competition is all about.

The war metaphor, on the other hand, has different implications. Rather than hope that my opponents perform well, I hope that they trip up. In a war, a "worthy challenge" is a meaningless concept. The weaker the enemy, the better. The easy victory is preferable to the hard-fought fight. When contests are viewed through the metaphor of war, opponents are enemies, and if the opponent doesn't bring his best to the contest, so much the better.

As outlined in chapter 1, social scientists have documented a number of negative consequences that seem to flow from pitting people against each other. To avoid these negative outcomes, Kohn argues that it is far better to place people in cooperative structures than "competitive" ones. These analyses are flawed because they try to predict human behavior by looking only at the external structure—the contest—and do not take into account the metaphors through which the person perceives the contest. Is the contest viewed primarily as a place of battle and war? If so, then participation in the contest will likely promote increased hostility, interpersonal antagonism, outgroup thinking, and heightened anxiety. Is the contest viewed primarily as a partnership enabling each party to excel? If so, then it is unlikely to have the negative consequences Kohn and others describe. Kohn writes about the effects of decompetition, not competition.

Competition and Cooperation

For many, including Kohn, "competition" and cooperation are opposites. Kohn is right with reference to decompetition. In a war, opponents fight; they do not cooperate. Viewed through the metaphor of war, the cooperative nature of the contest is hidden. It goes relatively unnoticed and unheeded. However, genuine competition is really a subset of cooperation. It is a special form of cooperation that enables participants to push each other toward personal excellence.[11] It is a special, oppositional form of cooperation that enables opponents to simultaneously experience the joy of challenge and effort.

Although competition takes place within a contest structure, the psychological goals of the participants are not mutually exclusive, even though winning and losing are. It is possible for both (or all) competitors to simultaneously improve and experience the exhilaration of the contest, regardless of the outcome. Viewed within the metaphor of partnership, the cooperative nature of the contest is highlighted. Even while contesting, opponents cooperate. I cooperate with my opponent by providing my best effort, just as my opponent provides the same for me. The opposite of cooperation is not competition, but decompetition. Under the sway of the war metaphor, decompetitors fail to appreciate the cooperative quality of competition and, therefore, think and act as though the opponent is an enemy.

In chapter 3, we review a number of other important ways competition and decompetition differ. It is important to learn these distinctions because the best way to safeguard genuine competition and to unleash its true power is to learn to spot its troublesome twin, decompetition. Both competition and decompetition share the same parent—contests give them birth—and they may sometimes look quite alike, but in reality they are as different as twins with opposite dispositions. As we will see in chapter 3, competitors and decompetitors differ in terms of their motivations and goals, in how they think about winning and striving to win, and in their view of the rules and officials. Learning to spot and name these differences is one of the best ways to safeguard the genuine values of true competition. ■

Dear Authors:

It sounds to me like you are advocating "competition lite." I don't want to cooperate with my opponents. I want to defeat them. Isn't that what competition is all about?

— Get Serious

Dear Get Serious:

Striving to win is essential. However, striving to win is just one dimension of true competition. There are values to be tapped through competition that are deeper and more enriching than can be captured by a narrow focus on winning. In fact, reducing competition to a mere battle for victory is what creates a "lite" version of the contest.

Would you be upset if your opponents stopped trying hard to win? Our guess is that the answer is yes. You cooperate with your opponents by playing your hardest, even when you think you might lose. No doubt, you expect the same from them. Appreciating the cooperative dimension of competition does not mean that you don't seek to defeat your opponents, but it does require that you respect them and appreciate their contributions to the process.

---

1   See Sperber (1998), p. 97.

2   Kohn (1992).

3   For a more elaborated description of what is involved in both a test and a contest, see Kretchmar (1975).

4   Although considering the etymology of the word is illuminating, we are not suggesting that there was ever a golden age of true competition. We discuss the etymology of the term not to look backward, but to look forward to the potential that is within competition and that is suggested by the word's etymology.

5   For similar perspectives, see Clifford and Feezell (1997); Fraleigh (1984), especially pp. 84-91; Hyland (1978); and Nelson (1998).

6   On the importance of both excellence and enjoyment as *teloi* of athletic competition, see Hyland (1984). Hyland identifies three *teloi* of competitive sport: excellence, fun, and "peak experience." Our concept of enjoyment (see chapter 4) encompasses and extends the latter two.

7   Other writers on competition have sought to make a distinction somewhat similar to our competition–decompetition distinction by using such language as "good" and "bad" competition or "constructive" and "destructive" competition. Similarly, to capture some of what we mean by decompetition, some theorists write about the problems that arise when there is too much competition, intense competition, or hypercompetition. We reject these proposals because they imply that competition (*striving with*) is still taking place even

at the negative pole. These suggestions imply a single continuum that runs from positive to negative competition, whereas we suggest two discontinuous processes. Closer to our view is that of Torres and McLaughlin (2003), who propose a distinction between "outcome seekers" and "resolution seekers." Our view also resonates with that of Nelson (1998), who refers to a conqueror's approach to competition and a champion's approach. Finally, our view overlaps with the distinction between a "zero-sum" approach and a "mutualist" approach to the goals of competition (Simon, 2004).

8   Stated in Deutsch's terminology, both competition and decompetition arise in a social context of negative goal interdependence. However, Deutsch (and Sherif, among others) erred in assuming that people necessarily adopt an antagonistic attitude toward the opponent whenever they perceive conflicting goals. The reality is much more complex. People enter situations with multiple goals. Depending on the relative salience of their goals, different outcomes follow. The true competitor enters a contest with highly salient cooperative goals, most importantly seeking excellence and worthy enjoyment. In contrast, the decompetitor elevates winning or self-aggrandizement above all other values and goals.

9   Lakoff and Johnson (1980). For a similar discussion of how metaphors inform and contour our ethical perceptions and judgments, see Johnson (1993).

10   The story about Chris Evert is from Clifford and Feezell (1997), p. 30.

11   Similarly, Simon (2004) writes: "competition presupposes a cooperative effort by competitors to generate the best possible challenge to each other" (p. 27).

3

True Competition
A Field Guide

In the summer of 1988, we were camping in a thickly wooded area of Yosemite. It was dusk when two men walked up to our campsite and asked if we would like to join them on an owl hunt. "An owl hunt?" I asked, wondering what they were up to. Grinning, one of the men pulled out his camera, obviously expensive, and told us that they were biologists from California State University at Sacramento. There had been an unconfirmed citing of a rare owl in the area a couple of days prior, and they were hoping to document its presence in the region. Joining the hunt, we traveled with them as they snaked their way through the forest thicket. Then we got lucky. We heard the hoots of an owl. To us, the hoots sounded rather plain, like the calls of every other owl we had ever heard. To the biologists, however, they were extraordinary music. Soon the lead owl hunter spotted the bird high in one of the majestic redwoods. Despite his efforts to help us, it took us a while to distinguish the owl from the surrounding foliage. Once we finally spotted it, we were a bit disappointed. The rare owl looked like an ordinary barn owl to our untrained eyes. After numerous clicks of the camera lens, the biologists were off. To this day, I'm not sure what owl species we observed that night.

> " Before you can be externally competitive,
> you must be internally cooperative. "
>
> Mike Fratzky

Like rare and common owls, competition and decompetition may look similar. In both cases, people contest. Still, there are profound differences between the two. We saw in chapter 2 that competition is animated by a root metaphor of contest-as-partnership. In contrast, decompetition springs from a contest-as-war root metaphor. The meanings and values of contests vary immensely depending on which metaphor is predominant. Of course, we all use both metaphors to some extent; and when we contest, we all experience a certain amount of competition and decompetition. This only highlights the need to be crystal clear about the differences.

In this chapter, we provide a field guide to true competition. Just as a field guide to birds enables the budding ornithologist to distinguish closely related fowl species, we hope that this field guide will enable readers to more easily distinguish competition from its foul twin, decompetition. Field guides work by identifying visible markings that distinguish one species from another. In parallel fashion, we identify the markings of true competition, distinguishing them from the markings of decompetition. Later chapters amplify on the distinctions made here and provide a number of practical strategies for promoting true competition.

Competition and decompetition are not birds-of-a-feather, and we can learn to distinguish the rare and prized owl of true competition from the more common owl of decompetition. Why is this so important? Unlike with the observation of birds, when we learn the markings of competition and decompetition, we can start to create what we want to see. Whether a contest results in competition or decompetition is largely within our control. This field guide conveys the knowledge needed for recognizing true competition, and thus motivates and empowers readers to strive toward true competition for themselves and others.

Just as a field guide to birds directs attention to certain body parts and then tells you what to observe there, this guide focuses on selected elements of the contest and then describes the markings of competition and decompetition. The specific elements that we address are motivations and goals, views of opponents, responses to rules and officials, valuing of process and outcome, and views of the ideal contest. Toward the end of the guide, table 3.1 summarizes the distinguishing marks of competition and decompetition and specifies where in the remainder of this book they are elaborated. We begin by looking at people's motives for contesting.

Motivation

Why do we compete? Motivations vary, of course. Some compete for the thrill of it; some, for the glory. Others compete to share camaraderie with teammates; still others, to fortify faltering egos.

Psychologists often distinguish between two types of motivation: *intrinsic* and *extrinsic*. When we are intrinsically motivated to do something, we do it because we find it inherently interesting or enjoyable. In contrast, when we participate in an activity because it may lead to some other benefit, we are extrinsically motivated. For example, if I enjoy my job, then my motivation for doing it is intrinsic. If I do my job purely for the paycheck, then my motivation for going to work is extrinsic. By carefully observing the outer markings of internal motivations, true competition can be distinguished from decompetition.

In true competition, intrinsic motivation is supreme. In sports, for example, true competitors are motivated largely by a love of the game. They are motivated by a desire to experience the intrinsic values that can come from participation. The game provides an opportunity to enjoy camaraderie, thrill in the pursuit, and achieve a personal level of excellence. Competitors recognize that pitting one's skills against a well-matched opponent leads to

FIELD GUIDE

©Josu Altzelai/age fotostock

Some people play primarily because they love the game. Others are motivated foremost by what they can take from the game. What difference does a person's motivation make?

an exhilaration and arousal that can tap deep reservoirs of physical, mental, and spiritual resources that are simply hard to summon in other contexts. A deep and resonant enjoyment sustains their efforts, even in challenging times and experiences of defeat.

In decompetition, extrinsic motivations are primary. In decompetition, the motivation shifts from *love* of the game to *use* of the game. Decompetitors treat the contest like a pirate treats a treasure ship: They seek to pillage the game, extracting such bounty as transient self-esteem, material gain, public praise, or social status. For them, the thrill of *conquest* is greater than the thrill of the *contest*.

MOTIVATION

Markings of the Competitor

1. Listen for expressions of interest in the game itself (including its traditions and lore); interest is not dependent on winning or extrinsic benefits.
2. Look for signs of deep appreciation and enjoyment that does not come at the expense of others.

Markings of the Decompetitor

1. Listen for a heavy emphasis on material rewards or status gains as motives for participation.
2. Look for positive emotions that come only when victory and its attendant rewards are gained.

Goals

In addition to the relative importance of intrinsic and extrinsic motivations, competitors and decompetitors also differ in terms of the goals they pursue. Although motivations and goals are closely related, distinguishing the two gives us another set of markings by which to identify competitors and decompetitors. By focusing on goals, we highlight what each wants to achieve and how they view success.

For true competitors, the goals of competition are multidimensional. Of course, competitors want to win. Yet more important is the opportunity to develop mastery and cultivate excellence. Success is measured according to the effort exerted and the personal goals achieved. When true competitors bring their best selves to the contest, they often experience a host of positive emotions such as joy, exhilaration, excitement, and hope.

Of course, competition can lead to other emotions as well, such as frustration and disappointment. But even these more "negative" emotions are valued by the true competitor as part of the experience. When competitors lose, they recognize, like former U.S. senator and basketball great, Bill Bradley, that "the taste of defeat has a richness of experience all its own." Experiencing a wide range of deep and resonant emotions while striving to achieve one's best is a cherished goal of the true competitor.

Whereas the goals of true competitors are multidimensional and richly textured, those of decompetitors are rather one-dimensional. Decompetitors have but one real ambition: to reap whatever rewards victory can bring. Rather than seeing contests as opportunities to develop and test their skills, decompetitors view contests as opportunities to showcase their superiority over others. For decompetitors, defeating others is the very essence of success. At a minimum, they seek to avoid looking inferior and will sometimes act defensively to avoid appearing incompetent. This may, for example, lead to lowered effort when victory seems in doubt so that a loss can be shrugged off as a result of not trying rather than a lack of talent.

GOALS

Markings of the Competitor
1. Watch for a focus on mastery and growth, both in terms of performance and personal character.
2. Watch for an ethic of excellence that propels high effort in most or all situations.
3. Listen for an equation of success with effort, improvement, and meeting personal goals.

Markings of the Decompetitor
1. Watch for an ego-driven desire to demonstrate superior ability or talent.
2. Look for lowered effort when victory is out of reach and excuse-making following defeat.
3. Listen for an equation of success with outperforming others.

Opponents

True competitors recognize that great contests require great opponents. When well-matched opponents bring their best to the contest, everyone benefits. Recognizing this, competitors view their opponents as partners. Decompetitors, however, view them as enemies. Listen to the language used to talk about opponents. Is the opponent appreciated? Is the opponent respected? Positive language about the opponent can reveal the presence of true competition.

When an opponent is denigrated, through word or action, we have the markings of decompetition. To spot decompetition, watch and listen for disrespectful language and behavior. Failing to appreciate the gift that opponents offer, decompetitors may tarnish the contest by targeting opponents with anger or hate, treating them as if they were enemies or objects. In a tragic mix-up, the decompetitor confuses the contesting of abilities with the combating of persons. Certainly in a contest, one party's abilities are pitted against those of another, but in true competition the *against* dimension is appreciated for how it contributes to the *seeking with* dimension.

OPPONENTS

Markings of the Competitor

1. Listen for positive words about opponents and expressions of appreciation for the challenges they provide.
2. Look for recognition that each person in the contest depends on the other(s).
3. Outside of the immediate contest, watch for positive, helpful behavior toward opponents.

Markings of the Decompetitor

1. Listen for language that depersonalizes the opponent or implies that the opponent is an enemy.
2. Look for a dismissive attitude toward opponents that overlooks their value and contribution.
3. Watch for hostile or demeaning attitudes or behavior toward opponents before, during, or after the contest.

Regulations

Contests must have rules, and those rules must be enforced. To distinguish true competition from decompetition, look at whether the participant takes a floor or ceiling approach to rules. Adopting a moral perspective, true competitors think of rules as a floor below which one cannot descend. Simply

FIELD GUIDE

obeying the rules is not always enough; competitors attend to the spirit of the rules as well. The spirit of the rules may require them to go above and beyond the letter of the rule to uphold the ethical principles of fairness and concern for well-being.

For the decompetitor, on the other hand, rules are a ceiling toward which some approach. Forget the spirit of the rules. For the decompetitor, the most that can be expected is a lack of cheating.

Officials, for true competitors, are personal agents who share an important role in the process of competition by interpreting and enforcing the rules. It is their role to ensure, as far as possible, equality of opportunity, fair treatment, and minimization of risk. Like all humans, officials are fallible, but competitors recognize that game officials have an important role to play that is undermined by constant challenges to their integrity or veracity. Officials will err, but they are due respect. Thus, true competitors cooperate with, assist, and enable officials.

Decompetitors, in contrast, struggle against officials. Although the officials are there to facilitate the game for the players, in an odd sort of way the officials become part of the game for decompetitors; outwitting them is just one more game strategy. In the mind of the decompetitor, officials merge with opponents. They become part of the opposition. For the decompetitor, avoiding detection when violating rules is just another game skill, equivalent to blocking an opponent's shot.

©Human Kinetics

Coaches sometimes try to "work" the officials through intimidation and mind games, just as they try to work the opponent. Do you think this reflects a decompetitive approach?

REGULATIONS

Markings of the Competitor

1. Look for a desire to uphold the spirit of the rules, not just their letter.
2. If you see a contestant giving up a competitive advantage to uphold fairness or reduce the likelihood of injury, you have observed a clear marking of competition.
3. Look also for respectful behavior toward officials, including acceptance of questionable calls.
4. In the face of genuinely bad officiating, look for protests to follow established procedures of review.

Markings of the Decompetitor

1. Deliberate cheating is a clear mark of decompetition, but more subtle markings also exist.
2. In addition to outright cheating, look for signs of seeking loopholes in the rules.
3. Look also for argumentative and hostile interactions with officials.
4. Watch for efforts to play mind games with officials.

Playing and Winning

What is more important—to play well or to win? One of the most important dividing lines between competitors and decompetitors is revealed in their different answers to this question. Whether winning or striving is more important is an old and much-debated issue. The cliché "It's not whether you win or lose, it's how you play the game" is pitted against "winning isn't the most important thing; it's the only thing." Even though the debate is old, framing it in terms of competition and decompetition may shed new light.

Within true competition, contestants value winning and losing because these outcomes enable the contest to take place. Yes, of course, competitors want to win. They may well want to win just as much as decompetitors do. Nevertheless, the true competitor focuses primarily on the benefits flowing from striving to win, more than winning itself. True competitors recognize that the value of the desire to win resides largely in its capacity to drive the competitive partnership. The desire to win is the driving force that brings the competitors together, allowing for the upward spiral of achievement, enjoyment, and performance. That is, wanting to win is seen for what it can contribute to human well-being and flourishing. It is experienced as a spur, as something that can facilitate the seeking of excellence. When true competitors do win, they are quick to recognize that victory is never strictly the accomplishment of the victor.

Decompetitors have quite a different experience of process and outcome. For them, the outcome draws all significance to itself. In decompetition, the outcome, or end, cannibalizes the process, or means. Winning is everything. Getting the W is what counts. The values intrinsic to the process fall by the wayside.

In decompetition, the contest exercises sovereignty over the participant. The structural goal of the contest, to win, is replicated at the psychological level. It becomes the sole or dominant aim, displacing or subordinating all other considerations. When the decompetitor does win, the ego-driven motivation for seeking victory is evident in the way she tends to attribute the triumph to superior personal abilities.

PLAYING AND WINNING

Markings of the Competitor

1. Look for a focus on values intrinsic to the process of participation.
2. Listen for a silver-lining approach to losing and a gracious, credit-sharing approach to winning.

Markings of the Decompetitor

1. Look for a serious focus on winning that overshadows all other values.
2. Listen for a "nothing can be gained in a losing effort" approach to losing and an ego-driven, credit-hogging approach to winning.

The Ideal Contest

As we have seen, competitors and decompetitors prioritize the process and outcome of contesting differently. For the true competitor, the emphasis is on the values that can be gained from contesting. For the decompetitor, winning is what matters most because the key values to be gained from the contest are tied to the outcome. These different views lead to different perspectives on the nature and quality of the ideal contest.

True competitors want to experience that upward spiral of challenge that enables them to summon deep inner resources. As a result, for the true competitor, the ideal contest is an aesthetic event that is saturated with drama and uncertainty, mystery and tension. The tension is not from hostility and antagonism, but rather from an encounter with the unknown. How will things turn out in the end? Playing a game is like watching a play or reading a novel. If the concluding scene or ending chapter becomes apparent too quickly, then the plot is too thin and uninteresting. The ideal contest involves story and plot and turns of event. In the ideal contest, well-matched opponents challenge each other to the fullest. Because they are relatively equal in ability, the outcome remains uncertain. Uncertainty creates drama, which creates tension, which stimulates maximal effort.

In contrast, decompetition is marked by a desire for certainty. Putting the game away early is ideal and running up the score is OK because these guarantee victory and demonstrate superiority. The more quickly and decisively decompetitors can win, the better. In fact, drama and uncertainty undermine their goals. The closer the game is, the less clearly the decompetitor has demonstrated superiority, even if he eventually emerges victorious.

To successfully manage the tension of the ideal contest, true competitors balance seriousness and play. They experience and express positive emotions such as enthusiasm and joy and focus on opportunities that the contest presents, regardless of game circumstance.

THE IDEAL CONTEST

Markings of the Competitor

1. Look for signs of disappointment if the contest is poorly played or one-sided, regardless of whether the competitor is on the winning or losing side.

2. In informal contests that are lopsided, look for the true competitor to seek equalizing modifications.

3. Watch for evidence that seriousness and playfulness are in balance, regardless of who is winning.

4. Look for positive emotions predominating over negative ones.

Markings of the Decompetitor

1. Look for the enjoyment of blowouts if the player is on the winning side.

2. In informal contests, look for players who try to stack the deck in their favor.

3. Watch for an overly serious approach to the contest that curtails all playfulness when behind.

4. Look for negative emotions predominating over positive ones.

In contrast, decompetitors take themselves too seriously, and the play dimension is diminished or lost. Especially when behind in the contest, decompetitors have a tendency to drain the contest of enjoyment, levity, and fun. They may express the tension of the contest through anger and hostility.

This field guide to competition and decompetition is summarized in table 3.1. The chart reviews the major markings of competition and decompetition. Reading down the two columns, you will see that the elements that define each type of contest form a coherent set of ideas, a unified whole. Competition and decompetition are based on closely interrelated elements. Each element of competition arises from viewing the contest as an opportunity for partnership. Each element of decompetition arises from viewing the contest as a symbolic version of war.

TABLE 3.1

Competition and Decompetition: A Summary

	Competition *Striving with*	Decompetition *Striving against*	See chapter
Basic metaphor	Partnership	Battle or war	2
Motivation	Love of the game Shared enjoyment	Use of the game Thrill (at opponents' expense)	4
Goals	Learning and mastery Pursuit of excellence	Domination and conquest Pursuit of superiority	5
View of opponent	Partner or enabler	Obstacle or enemy	6
Regulation	Rules are imperfect guides to fairness and welfare Officials are facilitators	Rules are partially tolerated restraints Officials are opponents	7
Playing and winning	Focus is on process (contesting)	Focus is on outcome (winning)	8
Ideal contest	Balanced opposition Tension, drama, story Play and seriousness in balance Positive emotions predominate	Dominated contest Certainty of outcome Seriousness overshadows play Negative emotions predominate	9

Field Notes

Before concluding this chapter, we would like to make two final points:

1. The elements of competition and decompetition are mutually reinforcing. Each element within a given perspective reinforces each of the other elements within that perspective. For example, if opponents are viewed as enemies, then that view of opponents will support the adoption of domination as the desired goal. The adoption of domination as the desired goal, in turn, will support the focus on outcome over process, and so on. In the social sciences, this is called a relation of *promotive interdependence*. Any element within true competition, once embraced, will encourage the adoption of each of the other elements of true competition. Conversely, the adoption of any single element of decompetition encourages the adoption of the entire decompetitive orientation.

2. Despite the promotive interdependence among the elements of competition and decompetition, it is also important to qualify our discussion with a second, equally true observation: In the real world, neither contest type exists in an entirely pure form. To greater and lesser degrees, we are all competitors and decompetitors. Unlike the rare and common owls discussed in the beginning of this chapter, there are not two completely different birds when it comes to contests. If we switch the metaphor to dogs, all contests are mixed breeds. Our motives are always mixed; our goals, always blended; our focus, always blurred. The competition and decompetition models reflect what sociologists call *ideal types*. They are conceptual models that can help us distinguish two types of social interaction, but they are pure only in thought, not in reality. Nevertheless, people have strong tendencies to live within one model far more than the other. Moreover, by carefully noting the markings of true competition, we can go a long way toward minimizing the grip that decompetition so often has on our contests.

In this chapter, we expanded on the meanings of competition and decompetition. In reality, much of what transpires today under the banner of competition is really more akin to decompetition. Decompetition is what occurs when the primary metaphor is contest-as-war. Opponents are viewed as enemies, and the goal is to conquer the opponent and display dominance. The contest is pillaged for extrinsic rewards tethered to winning, which is the main locus of value. Because winning is supreme, putting the game away early and avoiding the drama of tight, teeter-tottering games is ideal. Rules may be followed, although cheating is likely if rule breaking is not being detected.

It is no surprise, then, that social scientists who study competition often find that people who contest with one another experience negative outcomes. Decompetition has come to dominate our contests, and critiques like those offered by Alfie Kohn carry considerable sting because they capture the truth of decompetition.

An alternative to decompetition does exist. We need not give up our delight with contests. We can revel in the exhilaration of a closely contested race, game, match, or meet. To do so, however, we need to recover the transformatory potential of striving with, rather than striving against. By seeing the contest as an opportunity for a unique form of cooperative partnership, we can reclaim its rightful place in our lives.

In the following chapters, we amplify on each of the categories introduced in this field guide. We also offer advice for leaders in how to promote true competition and diminish the negative influences of decompetition. Importantly, the following chapters also identify forces that tend to knock competition off its tightrope and into the gutter of decompetition.

What triggers decompetition varies somewhat from person to person. For some, it has simply become habitual. Many people have come to believe that decompetition is the only way to contest. Others may enter a game or contest with a competitive orientation only to lose it. It is important to identify the triggers that may push people to become decompetitive. If people learn to recognize such triggers, they can more easily push back and resist the lure of decompetition. Such is the hope that inspired this book.

True competition will not occur spontaneously. The natural push of the contest structure is toward decompetition. To sustain true competition, those who engage in contests need to be committed to its values and principles. Stated differently, true competition requires character. So before we elaborate on the elements of true competition, let's briefly look at the relationship between competition and character. ■

Interlude

Character and Competition

> **❝ Let yourself be silently drawn
> by the stronger pull of what you really love. ❞**
>
> Rumi

Oil and water. Lions and lambs. Olives and ice cream. Do *character* and *competition* go together like these incompatibles? Kohn certainly thinks so. And when he denounces competition for its negative effects on character, he is easily heard above the din because he speaks through the megaphone of a century of research. Far from suggesting that competition promotes positive character, a tall stack of scientific literature suggests that competition too often encourages self-centeredness, fosters prejudice, creates hostility, promotes aggression, and triggers cheating.

But wait! No doubt, you've heard other voices. Praises for competition and its character-building capacities echo through congratulatory speeches at sports banquets, business luncheons, and political rallies. These voices sing a familiar refrain: Competition builds competitiveness; competitiveness fires ambition; ambition drives industriousness; industriousness powers accomplishment. And character, it is said, fuels each step along the way.

In this interlude between the first and second parts of the book, we explore the character–competition link. To preview, we suggest that true competition can only be sustained by a resolute commitment to core ethical norms. When character is weak, decompetition is likely to ensue.

Can participation in sports and other competitive endeavors contribute to positive character development? *Most certainly.* Not only can competition develop many positive values and qualities, learning to handle the stresses and temptations of contesting is also an integral part of character growth.

On the other hand, can involvement in sports and other contests undermine character? *Most definitely.* When guided by wrongheaded values or distorted emphases, "competition" (really, decompetition) can nurture character like poison nurtures health.

But what is character?

On the surface, we all know what character is. When we think about positive character, words like honesty, compassion, integrity, respect, fairness, and service come to mind. While commonsense gives us a pretty good idea of what character is, to understand how it relates to competition, we need to elaborate on its psychological structure.

Etymologically, *character* means "distinctive mark." Indeed, each person's character is unique. Everyday observation confirms what is now widely accepted in the social sciences: People have distinctive marks of character.[1] Each person is marked by a particular configuration of virtues and vices, moral strengths and limitations. And the qualities of a person's character make a big difference in the real world. For the most part, a person's character guides their moral behavior. True, environmental factors or personal stresses may trump the influence of character in particular circumstances. Nonetheless, people have strong predispositions to act in certain ways in situations requiring ethical choice. That's character.

The word *character* refers to the moral, or ethical, components of personality. In this interlude, we suggest that character has two main components, or dimensions.[2] Both are relevant to how people participate in contests. First, character reflects a person's cherished ideals or deepest desires. Obviously, people are unlikely to act in a manner consistent with true competition if all they really want is to get rich. Second, character reflects our ability to act in a manner that is consistent with our values. Sometimes, people may become decompetitive, despite valuing competition, because they simply are unable to marshal the inner resources to resist temptations or stay focused on their real priorities. After we explore these two dimensions of character more closely, we end with a consideration of why character is so important to true competition.

Character and Desire

At the root of character is desire. Our character is a reflection of what we really want. Character is contoured by our responses, usually unarticulated, to such questions as these: What do we most deeply desire in our relationships? From our activities? Out of life? What kind of person do we most want to be? What kind of society do we want to live in? Such questions extend into contest settings: What is our ideal for competition? What do we most want to gain from our participation? Which do we desire more: to partner with our opponent for excellence, or to use our opponent for personal gain? These are questions that go straight to the issue of character.

The first component of character, then, is desire. Desire focuses our attention, guides our choices, and energizes our values. The stronger our desire, the more attuned our attention, the more consistent our choices, and the more primed we are to act on related values.

If I am a selfish person, I am constantly noticing opportunities to advance myself at the expense of others. My desire leads me to notice and leap at possibilities for self-aggrandizement. My values center on myself. In contrast, if I desire a world in which people help one another, I will notice opportunities to offer assistance. In some situations, helping others may be easy. At other times, the choice to help may come at considerable personal cost. If my desire is strong, I will still help. The consistency of my action depends in part on the strength of my desire. If my desire to help is quite strong, I may develop the virtue of compassion.

We have suggested that the deeper or stronger our desire, the more potent it is in directing attention, guiding choices, and activating values. But our desires are not all alike. Some are mere superficial attractions to what provides immediate pleasure or gratification. Others are deeper and more resonant.

First- and Second-Order Desires

The philosopher Harry Frankfurt likes to talk about two types of desire.[3] Immediate desires are somewhat akin to impulses. We see a pumpkin pie, and we want to take a bite. We hear a funny joke, and we want to retell it. We step onto the wrestling mat, and we want to win. These types of desire arise in a nearly automatic fashion. Frankfurt calls these first-order desires.

There is another type of desire. Frankfurt calls them "second-order" desires. These are desires that we consider and deliberately embrace. We consciously choose to act on them rather than just spontaneously respond to them. Second-order desires begin like all desires: They are felt as a tug drawing us in a particular direction. In other words, all second-order desires begin as first-order desires; but then something uniquely human happens. Rather than just being driven by the tug of immediate desires, we intervene. We make choices about which of our many desires to ignore or stifle and which to follow and strengthen. In Frankfurt's words, we have "desires about our desires." The point is that we are not simply slaves to whatever impulses we feel. We can choose to nurture some of our more immediate desires, while starving and stunting others.

If we are health minded, we may experience a first-order desire for a box of dark chocolates, yet reflect on that desire and decide to stifle it. We do so because we have a more considered desire to nurture a well-functioning body. Similarly, when we see the new gadget in the technology store, we may desire it, but then decide not to buy it because we want to save for our son's college education. In the sport contest, we may desire victory, but when an opportunity to cheat arises, we may desire fairness more.

Because of our capacity to reason and plan, we prioritize some desires over others. We subject our desires to scrutiny and decide that some, despite their immediate appeal, are not worthy of our time and effort. We decide that some values are more important than others. When desires do not reflect our considered values, we may seek to diminish them, to rob them of their motivational pull.

Moral Desires

Desires cover a large landscape. We have desires that are mere preferences, such as desires about foods. We have desires about things we want to accomplish, such as obtaining a degree or making a team. We also have ambitions, which are desires guiding sustained efforts toward long-range goals.

Of particular importance to character are moral desires. We have moral values and ideals that are important to us. We may believe in certain moral principles or guides. We may be committed to certain relationships and ways of interacting with others. Like other second-order desires, our moral desires reflect our best thinking about what is genuinely worthy of our commitment.

The specific content of our moral desires gives shape to our character. One person's character may be highly focused around a deep valuing of compassion, whereas another may focus on justice. Yet another may be deeply committed to honesty. Each of these people may have strong character, but each has a somewhat different configuration of values. Although there are only a relatively small number of core moral values, there is an infinite variety of ways to combine and nuance them. This is one reason no two people have identical character.

Most of us behave appropriately most of the time not because we have to, but because we want to. The person with no desire to act ethically is rare indeed, a true sociopath.[4] Why do we want to act ethically? There are many reasons. We want to live in relationships of trust and goodwill. We want to experience the benefits and blessings of cooperation. We recognize that a world in which people treat each other with respect and dignity is a better world than one in which people don't. We choose to act ethically because we like ourselves better when we do. Even when there is a personal cost to doing the right thing, we may prefer to do it for one simple reason: We believe it is right.

Morality is often a weak first-order desire. But moral desires can be quite powerful second-order desires.[5] My impulse (first-order desire) is to keep the extra change, seek revenge for a minor infraction against me, or cuss out the player who makes a strategic blunder. However, if I've reflected on what is truly valuable to me, on what kind of person I want to be, and if I've committed myself to a set of beliefs about what is genuinely right and good and beneficial, then most likely I will restrain myself. I will act out of my second-order desire. To summarize: Ethical decision making isn't about suppressing desire. Not primarily. It is about choosing considered desires over more impulse-like desires.

Moral Imagination

We have said that our moral desires reflect our best thinking about what ethical norms (e.g., the golden rule, honesty, integrity) are worthy of our commitment. That may be true. Nonetheless, the content of our moral desire is often unclear, even to ourselves. We believe that honesty is important, for example, yet at times we feel perfectly justified in being less than fully honest. Moral life is complex. We may have strong moral convictions, and yet not be able to put them into clear and precise words. One reason is that our moral insights rarely lend themselves to pure cognitive or logical expression. Our moral decisions are often guided as much by inchoate images lodged in our imagination as by well-defined principles reflecting our rational thought.[6]

Meet Marlos. He is coaching a youth basketball game. Unfortunately, Marlos has not read this book, and he thinks of the game as a battle. Still, Marlos is a decent fellow and would never condone cheating. But the game is tight. The lead has been swinging back and forth, and emotions have risen to a fever pitch. Then, late in the game, one of his players goes up for a rebound and on the way down his elbow smashes into the jaw of an opponent, who falls to the wooden floor in agony. It is unclear whether the act was intentional. The ref calls an injury time-out.

What does Marlos say to his gathered team? There is no moral principle that can provide a specific script. Rather than being guided by moral logic, Marlos will be guided by an image of what a good and responsible coach should do, an image formed over years of experience and reflection. Our point here isn't to suggest what Marlos should say. There are probably several good responses, as well as a number of bad ones. Our point is simply that what Marlos does is likely to be based as much on moral imagination as on moral principle. Like the rest of us, Marlos' character embodies the values, ideals, and principles that he can articulate and defend, as well as more subtle images, intuitions, and story plots that live in his imagination.

When it comes to morality, we are dual processors. In addition to logic, we are guided by subtle and only partially conscious images about what a good parent, friend, neighbor, coach, boss, and employee acts like. We may be attracted to particular ethical principles, but our character simultaneously lives within stories and narratives.

Perhaps we have moral tag words—such as *trust, honesty, caring, fairness, respect*, and *responsibility*—that guide us. Perhaps certain moral maxims, such as "treat others like you would want to be treated," express our inner sense of moral logic. However, to flesh out the full meaning of these words or maxims, we process them through internal images that resonate with us. Our brains work simultaneously with both reason and imagination.

Responding consistently with moral wisdom takes sound moral logic plus a rich moral imagination. Reasoning plus intuition. Principle plus metaphor. We need to think clearly about the requirements of ethics, and yet have our reasoning enriched through cherished stories and narratives. One resource that faith communities provide is a rich reservoir of treasured stories that exemplify key moral insights. Alert leaders in every context often use the power of stories to energize the moral imaginations of those with whom they work.

The Possible and the Ideal

One final point. Our moral desires are shaped by both our deepest convictions about what *ought* to be and what we believe is *possible*. Character limitations can come from either source. Some people may have narrow and immature views of the requirements of fairness, justice, and compassion. Jaela may retaliate against an opponent's aggression, returning it twofold, simply because she does not perceive any obligation to dampen the spiral of violence. Jaela exhibits a shortcoming in moral reasoning capacity.

Other people may acknowledge that they *should* do something ideally, but dismiss their sense of obligation because they consider it impractical. Janet may believe that she should, *in an ideal world*, refuse to go along with her company's clear yet unstated policy of overcharging customers. However, given the rough-and-tumble real world, Janet believes ethics are beside the point. She exhibits a failure of moral imagination. Janet has an overly constrained view of the possible.

Group norms sometimes support less-than-optimal behavior. Bullying may be expected in some peer groups. Retaliation may be expected in some settings; drug use, in others. On some teams, members may expect that when the game starts, ethics stop. Responding appropriately in such contexts requires both sound moral reasoning and an ability to imagine a better alternative. It also takes moral courage. This point is a good transition into the second major component of character—moral will.

Character and Will

To desire something is one thing; to have sufficient focus and skill to obtain it is another. Just because I may want to be honest doesn't mean that I will tell the truth. Moral desire provides the navigation system to our character, but *willpower* keeps it fueled. Our priorities give substance to our character, but the strength of our character comes from our *will*.[7]

Earlier, we observed that morality is often a weak first-order desire but a potentially strong second-order desire. Stated differently, our immediate impulse may not always be to do as we ought, and yet we may consistently act with integrity because we commit ourselves to core values. The *will* component of character reflects our ability to act consistent with our second-order desires rather than be driven by our first-order desires. This demonstrates self-control in the fullest sense of the word and an ability to regulate our emotions and thoughts.

Contrary to popular ways of thinking about it, willpower is not primarily a matter of inner strength, exertion, or force. If I'm tempted to eat the chocolate mousse, refraining from doing so is less about some mysterious inner strength than about having a set of relevant mental competencies.

Unpack the bag called *willpower,* and what you find is *skill power.*[8] Willpower is really a set of related and interlocking mental skills. It involves, for example, the ability to focus attention, keep distant goals in mind, and break down our intentions into a sequence of specific tasks. The will involves a set of skills that operate in the brain's prefrontal cortex. In psychological jargon, these mental operations are called *executive skills* because they enable people to organize, plan, and execute their intentions.

There is an important implication to viewing willpower as a set of skills. Skills can be learned. Although there are no doubt genetic differences in people's abilities to control impulses, delay gratification, focus attention, and engage in sequential thinking, executive skills can be developed. What's more, contest settings—what we typically call competitive settings—can be ideal places to practice the executive skills associated with willpower. We will have more to say about this in the closing paragraphs of this interlude.

Character and Virtue

A person with a strong, well-developed character is, to use an old-fashioned but still useful term, a virtuous person. And just as character has two important dimensions, virtues come in two broad categories: moral virtues and performance virtues.

Moral virtues arise from moral desires. Such virtues are dispositions to act in a positive, prosocial manner. Although we can give names to specific moral virtues—honesty, integrity, compassion, fair-mindedness, altruism, humility, and so forth—they all tap into a deep, underlying desire for *goodness.*[9] Virtuous people desire to be good. Not "good" in a shallow, conformist, or moralistic sense, but in a strong, principled, and compassionate sense. Moral virtues are really at the heart of a well-developed, positive character. A second type of virtue, however, is also important.

When people have developed considerable willpower, when their executive skills are well honed, they may possess *performance virtues*. These are virtues such as persistence, resilience, courage, perseverance, optimism, and loyalty. None of these qualities are good in themselves. An addict can be highly persistent. A jewel thief may be highly courageous. Performance virtues must be tethered to moral desire before they have any real moral

For More on Character

For those interested in pursuing the topics of character and character education in more depth, the following organizations can provide a wealth of information:

Association for Moral Education: www.amenetwork.org
Character Education Partnership: www.character.org
Center for Character & Citizenship: www.characterandcitizenship.org

significance. Moral desires, on the other hand, need the performance virtues to give them strength.

Virtues develop most naturally for those relatively few people who integrate moral desire into the very core of their sense of identity.[10] Mother Teresa was so committed to compassion that her moral desire defined who she was. Dr. Martin Luther King, Jr., became almost synonymous with a search for justice. These, of course, are just a couple of famous examples. Many people in everyday life fit a similar pattern. However, only a relatively few people are so committed to their moral beliefs that they define themselves by them. Yet virtue is relevant to all of us.

If moral desires are felt only weakly, they are unlikely to win out in a head-to-head contest with more self-serving goals. They are unlikely to be married to willpower. Character is strong only when moral desire is strong. When moral desire is strong, willpower will naturally bond to it, and the marriage will give birth to the virtues. However, the relationship between desire and will is circular. Strong moral desires don't just come naturally; they must be chosen, nurtured, and sustained. They must be *willed* into strong second-order desires. Nowhere is this truer than in competitive situations.

Character and Competition

Character consists of moral desire and will. What people most sincerely desire—what they care most deeply about—provides the guiding light to their character. The strength of their character, on the other hand, corresponds to their ability to sustain a focus on their real priorities, avoiding distractions and temptations. How does this view of character help us think about the challenges of competition?

As we have seen, true competition springs from an underlying metaphor of partnership. It originates in a desire to partner with another (the opponent) to seek excellence through the mutual challenge of the contest. Did you catch the word *desire* in that last sentence? True competition is all about desire, but not just any desire, of course. In true competition, excellence and enjoyment are larger than the self. As with any partnership, such as a marriage or a friendship, a narrow focus on self-interest is an acid that dissolves mutuality.

It is common in sports to talk about competitive ethics. In reality, competition *is* an ethic. Competition springs from a desire for excellence and the enjoyment that comes from striving for it. Competition involves mutual respect and respect for the process. Without that respect, there is no competition, only decompetition.

Decompetition is rooted in desire as well—the desire to feel superior, to gain the goods that come from winning, or to feel powerful. Decompetition is consistent with an indulgence of first-order desires. Hey, who doesn't want to look good? And when the ultimate goal is the gold, there's a natural tug to do whatever it takes. True competition, by contrast, can only be sustained by a commitment to a second-order desire. True competition can only come from a deep consideration of the meaning of the contest and the values it has to offer.

People must desire true competition for it to exist. An image of what true competition looks and feels like must be lodged in the moral imagination, and the ethic of respect must be understood in its depths. In the process of competing, there will be many opportunities to deviate. There will be distractions, temptations, and pressures. Beyond desire, it takes willpower to sustain true competition. When competition occurs, though, its benefits unfurl.

Like a good teacher, competition can help us learn about the world and ourselves. Like a puzzle, it can exercise the mind. Like a good counselor, it can help us manage emotion and stress in a positive manner. Like a good leader, it can teach us that self-sacrifice for a worthy group can be noble. Like a loving parent, it can give us both support and challenge to nurture growth in body, mind, and spirit. In short, competition can be an ideal process within which to build character. Contests, however, like fires, can either serve or destroy.

In the coming chapters, we amplify on the main dimensions of competition introduced in the field guide while discussing the obstacles to true competition connected with each. Some forces, left unchecked, will push competition off balance and into decompetition. Distractions, temptations, pressures—competitors must meet these with the executive skills that constitute willpower. When the challenges are successfully overcome, character is strengthened, much as muscles are strengthened from working against resistance. Competition is a gym for the exercise of character.

The following chapters also provide guidance to people such as parents, teachers, and coaches who are responsible for guiding youth in the arts of competition. These folk—and you are probably among them—can help young people learn that competition, through adversity and challenge, can bring them to new levels of performance. They can learn, but will not without guidance, that hard work fueled by passion really does yield results. They can learn that there can be true joy in loss and sadness in victory, and that the quality of their lives is not measured by outcomes alone.

Sports, which is where many young people first learn about organized competition, need to be seen as an ethical challenge—in fact, an ethical feat—just as much as a physical challenge. Asking whether sports build character is like asking whether sports build physical excellence. It depends on whether one prepares for the challenges and successfully meets them. And whether people will successfully meet them depends, in part, on their motivations and goals. These are the topic of the next two chapters. ■

1   See, for example, Alzola (2008).

2   For our discussion of the nature of character, we borrow heavily from the work of Augusto Blasi, most especially Blasi (2005). However, our description departs from his in that we isolate only two components of character (which correspond roughly to his description of *will-as-desire* and *will-as-self-control*), whereas Blasi elaborates a tripartite model of character.

3   Frankfurt (1988).

4   For more on the universality of moral desire, see Haan, Aerts, and Cooper (1985).

5   Blasi (2005).

6   For more on the importance of moral imagination and the role of metaphor in structuring moral perception, see Johnson (1993).

7   Blasi (2005).

8   Ibid.

9   See, for example, Ramsey (1997).

10   Blasi (2005).

Motivation
Pathways to Enjoyment

Imo is a competitive swimmer. He gets up early each morning to devote an hour to swim practice before school, then practices for two hours more after school. I asked Imo why he does it. After pondering the question, he said there were at least three reasons. He loves the feel of his body gliding through the cool, fresh water; he finds the rhythm and feel of swimming deeply pleasurable and aesthetic. Imo also said, despite what a novice might think, that he is constantly learning new things, and he loves learning. He finds real satisfaction in discovering, for example, that cupping his hand in a slightly different way or changing the focus of his attention during a flip turn makes a difference. Finally, he said, he revels in the challenge to outperform himself. If he achieves a new personal best, he fills from head to toe with delight. The challenge, however, not the accomplishment, is what matters most. Simply attempting to surpass himself, Imo said, is pleasurable, exciting, and satisfying, regardless of whether he actually succeeds.

Emma is a talented high school basketball player—actually, an emerging basketball star. She's a sophomore now, but already starting on the varsity team. She has risen to this level of achievement in part through plenty of support from her parents, especially her dad. When she turned 10, he put a hoop up over the garage door so she could practice more frequently. He still rewards Emma with extra spending money whenever she puts in an extra hour of practice at home. He is always out there giving her tips. I asked Emma what she likes about basketball, and she rattled off a list. Some of her favorite things are the roar of the crowd when she sinks her jumper in a tight game, the accolades from visiting college scouts who already have their eye on her, and the newspaper articles and pictures that her mom has cut out and saved.

> ❝ Find something you really love that gets you going, so that every day you want to make yourself better. Once you find that, it's easy to stay motivated. ❞
>
> Kerri Strug

Many things in life are limited—time, energy, and resources, to name a few. Usually, when something is in short supply, it holds great value. So why do people invest their valuable time, energy, and resources to contest with others? Why do athletes devote countless hours, days, weeks, months, even years to the perfection of skills that, in the end, have very limited use beyond the games? Why do students invest time studying when it might be more fun to spend it elsewhere? Why does an entrepreneur stay up late creating a well-crafted marketing plan? Some motives are obvious. Others are not.

Often, when we think about motivation, we think about it in quantitative terms. "Just how motivated is she?" we might ask. When psychologists study motivation, however, they examine a broader array of issues connected to why people start, continue, or quit particular activities or behaviors. Motivations, they have found, vary both in terms of quantity (how much) and quality (what kind).

In this chapter, we probe two kinds of motivation: intrinsic and extrinsic. We suggest that intrinsic motivation can dance gracefully with true competition. Extrinsic motivation can come to the dance as well, but watch your toes! Extrinsic motivation does not lead invariably to decompetition, but where decompetition flourishes, extrinsic motivation has become the dance partner.

The chapter has four major sections. It opens with an exploration of intrinsic and extrinsic motivation and relates those concepts to our themes of competition and decompetition. Then, in the second section, the discussion of motivation transitions into the closely related topic of enjoyment. As much as speed is part of racing, enjoyment is part of true competition. In fact, along with the pursuit of excellence, experiencing enjoyment is one of the hallmark characteristics of true competition. In the third section, we take up threats to competition. Like a hidden virus that undermines one's health, external "bugs" can enter a contest and quietly destabilize healthy motivation; soon, the disease of decompetition sets in. Finally, we discuss leadership strategies that can encourage and support those motives that sustain the true competitor.

Two Types of Motivation

Imo and Emma, the two athletes discussed earlier, are fictional, of course. Imo is intrinsic motivation personified. In short, his motivation arises from internal sources such as enjoyment, curiosity, and a desire for mastery and

© Marlin Levinson/Icon SMI

Our characters Imo and Emma are quite different from Amber, who is only on the hockey team because her overbearing dad insists. She is apathetic and reflects what psychologists call **amotivation.** If each child (Imo, Emma, and Amber) were of the same gender and ability, what would your expectations be for their respective contributions to team success? Why?

growth. Imo is intrinsically motivated when he spends hours practicing in the pool; he doesn't need external pressure or rewards to get him to practice. Emma's motives, however, arise from external sources, and so we call her extrinsically motivated. Her basketball practice and performance are means to get to other ends; she is motivated to play and perform well to please her parents; earn extra spending money; win a scholarship; and gain positive attention from her family, peers, and community.

Although Imo and Emma are quite different in many respects, they share some qualities. For example, they are both highly motivated athletes. They have achieved a good deal of success through talent and hard work. Since both Imo and Emma are highly motivated, does it really matter what type of motivation they experience?

Let's try an exercise. Answer the following questions about Imo and Emma:

■ Which athlete do you think will be better able to sustain enthusiasm during a losing season?

■ If they were both to sustain injuries that permanently prevented them from competing at an elite level, which one do you think would be more likely to stay involved in the sport?

■ Do you think one athlete is more likely to bend the rules if doing so would facilitate a win?

■ Years later, which athlete will look back on his or her experience with a greater sense of satisfaction?

■ Which athlete is more likely to seek excellence and enjoyment through contesting *with* an opponent?

Based only on what we know about their motivation, the scientific literature is clear: Imo is the correct answer to all of the preceding questions, except the one about bending the rules. Emma would be more likely to cheat. Imo derives pleasure and satisfaction from swimming itself, so in a losing season he is more likely to sustain his motivation, just as he is if an injury prevents him from returning to elite form. And because the rewards of winning are not central to his reasons for participating, Imo is also less likely to cheat to win. Imo is more likely to derive greater long-term satisfaction from his athletic career because it is saturated with a deep and resonant enjoyment that he can experience continuously. Finally, Imo's orientation builds on the intrinsic values of excellence and enjoyment, and these provide little incentive to think of the opponent as an enemy.[1]

The many advantages to intrinsic motivation can be found far beyond swimming pools and basketball courts. People with higher levels of intrinsic motivation across a range of life contexts usually report more enjoyment, more positive emotions, and greater life satisfaction than those with lower levels. Here's one more finding from the desk of researchers: intrinsically motivated people also tend to perform better. On average, they perform better in sports, in school, on the job, and in relationships. In the classroom, for example, students who are intrinsically motivated learn faster and process information more deeply than those who are not. They are able to concentrate better and stay with a challenging task longer. They also exhibit more creativity and problem-solving ability.[2]

Does this mean that we should seek to eliminate all extrinsic motivation from our lives? The answer is an emphatic no. Extrinsic motivation is not inherently wrong or bad, and it is certainly common in everyday life. If we brush our teeth to avoid cavities, we are extrinsically motivated; still, few of us brush for the sheer joy of feeling the bristles rubbing against our pearly whites. A student who burns the midnight oil to get an A on an exam is extrinsically motivated, but is not doing something blameworthy. Also, we often do things for multiple reasons.

We can experience both intrinsic and extrinsic motivations simultaneously. We can go to work both because we enjoy our job *and* we need the paycheck. The problems with extrinsic motivation tend to arise when we engage in important life activities primarily, or exclusively, for extrinsic reasons. Over time, reliance on extrinsic motivation is likely to undermine our intrinsic motivation. If my primary focus is on getting good grades, the joy I get from learning may gradually subside. If my main motive for playing sports is to gain popularity, bolster weak self-esteem, or populate my shelves with trophies, my zeal for playing the game is likely to gradually lessen.[3]

Let's pick up on Emma's career:

> As a senior, Emma found it increasingly difficult to get up for practice. Over the past couple of years, she experienced a great deal of pressure to live up to everyone's expectations. She continued to excel on the court, but inwardly she was losing the drive. She often felt as though she wasn't playing for herself; she was playing to please her coach, her teammates, her fans, and, especially her parents. Things that had motivated her earlier, such as seeing her picture in the paper or gaining a bit of extra spending money, no longer held the same appeal. Though she knew she had an excellent chance of landing a college scholarship, she began to doubt whether she wanted to play in college.

Emma is not alone. One major source of athletic burnout is an overreliance on extrinsic motivators. Of course, not all athletes will follow Emma's

Dear Authors:

I run a midsize youth indoor soccer program for kids ages 6 to 12. To motivate the participants, we present high-quality trophies to the members of the team with the best record each year. Are you suggesting that this is not a good idea?

— Trophy Trumpeter

Dear Trophy Trumpeter:

Truthfully, we suggest that you trash the trophies, especially at the younger ages. Though we know this suggestion will meet with considerable resistance among a number of sport enthusiasts, we believe that trophies, as external rewards, do have a tendency to undermine children's intrinsic reasons for participation.

Also, as children are learning about sport, it is vital that they come to appreciate the benefits to participation that are independent of winning and losing; trophies tend to mask that lesson. Although it is OK to recognize that an important dimension of sport is trying to win, trophies exacerbate an overemphasis on game outcome relative to other values. If adults seem to care only about winning, then children are misled about the benefits of contesting. So we suggest that rather than present trophies, you look for other creative ways to celebrate the children's effort.

path or follow it as quickly. However, the more a person's motivation comes from extrinsic rewards, the more difficult it becomes to sustain genuine interest in the activity. Also, as intrinsic motivation declines, the dangers of decompetition increase. Just how problematic extrinsic motivation may be depends in part on which subset of extrinsic motivation it belongs to. When we dig deeper into the theme of motivation, it turn out that not all forms of extrinsic motivation are alike.

According to Edward Deci and Richard Ryan, two of the most influential writers on motivation, an important way that extrinsic motivations vary is in terms of the relative freedom they embody. In psychological jargon, different types of motivation can reflect different degrees of self-determination.[4] A person who acts in fear of negative consequences or who chases after promised rewards is controlled largely by others. True, she is still exercising some level of choice, but others are setting up the conditions for that choice. Even though Emma wanted the extra money offered by her dad, she had an uneasy sense of being manipulated. At the other extreme, people may engage in an activity that they don't really enjoy to achieve an outcome that is self-chosen and freely embraced. Even though I may not like exercising, for example, I may choose to do it because I value fitness, not because somebody has dangled a reward, such as cheaper health insurance, in my face.

Four Types of Extrinsic Motivation

To illustrate the four types of extrinsic motivation, imagine that Emma has four sisters who are all basketball players. Their coach has added an additional practice to their regular routine. Each sister plans to attend the practice, and each is extrinsically motivated. However, they attend for different reasons.

A-B-C-D (Alberta, Betty, Connie, Dana) are on a continuum. Dana's form of extrinsic motivation is focused purely on externals. She believes that she has no choice in the matter and feels compelled to go to practice. Because she is being manipulated by rewards and punishments, Dana exhibits the most extreme form of extrinsic motivation. Alberta's motivation, on the other hand, is the most self-chosen. Although not intrinsically motivated, Alberta freely chooses to practice for reasons that are congruent with her values and sense of self. She gets an A in extrinsic motivation because she exhibits the most positive form of it.

Here's the key point: Intrinsic motivation is preferable to all forms of extrinsic motivation. However, Alberta's form of extrinsic motivation (let's call it *chosen*) is preferable to Betsy's (we'll call it *embraced*), which is preferable to Connie's (*accepted*), which is still better than Dana's (*imposed*). Clearly, Dana gets a D in motivation because she has the least beneficial form, only one step above an F—failing to have any motivation at all.[5]

Those who benefit most from an activity tend to be those who do it because they love doing it. Those who benefit least, and who are at highest

Emma's Sisters

Dana

She will go to the practice for one reason: The coach has imposed a strict rule that failure to attend will result in failure to play. The motivation for Dana's behavior is totally external; it comes from the outside. She feels forced to go.

Connie

Like Dana, Connie will go to practice, but not because she wants to. If it were a voluntary practice, she would not be there. But unlike Dana, a thin slice of Connie's motivation is coming from within. She attends the practice out of a sense of obligation. Connie would feel guilty if she were a no-show. She accepts the coach's authority to regulate what she does.

Betsy

Like Dana and Connie, Betsy doesn't much like practice. But even if the coach didn't require it, Betsy would be there. She knows she needs the work, and she wants to get better. Although the practice itself holds no appeal, Betsy readily follows her coach's instructions because she has embraced the same goal.

Alberta

Though Alberta, like her other sisters, finds no intrinsic pleasure in conditioning or drills, she is enthused about going to the extra practice. *Bring it on! Why?* Because basketball is central to her identity, and she yearns to be the best player she can be. She freely and enthusiastically chooses to do whatever the coach says will help her improve.

risk for undesirable consequences, are on the opposite end of the spectrum. They do it only because they are forced. Figure 4.1 shows the motivational continuum.

Thus far, we have talked only about the *form*, or *type*, of motivation. It is also important to consider its *intensity*. It is possible, of course, for a person to experience a high level of intrinsic motivation, a moderate level, a low level, or none at all. Dwain might really love to swim, whereas Craig might enjoy it only moderately. A similar range of intensity exists for each form of extrinsic motivation. Because people often have multiple reasons for doing something, and they experience each motivation to varying degrees, a person's motivational profile can be quite complex. Beneath that complexity, however, is a rather simple idea: The more a person's motivation draws from the left side of the continuum in figure 4.1, the better.

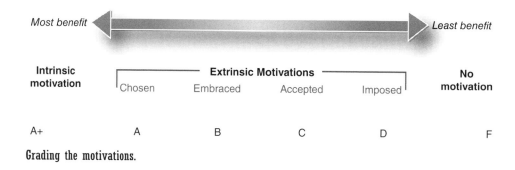

Grading the motivations.

Motivation and Competition

So what is the connection between motivation and competition? In short, the more a person is intrinsically motivated during a contest, the more likely that person will be to engage in true competition. Conversely, the more a person slides down the A-B-C-D continuum of extrinsic motivation, the more likely that person will be to slip into decompetition. Although high levels of intrinsic motivation act as an inoculation against the decompetition virus, extrinsic motivations are all carriers. Whether a person breaks out with an active case of decompetition depends both on the specific motivational virus (The D variant is the most virulent) and other characteristics of the person and situation.[6]

Extrinsic motivations pull toward decompetition primarily because they rely on external values. The ability to obtain such values can be threatened by opponents. If opponents defeat you, fans can drift away, scholarships can be lost, and coaches can become angry. Relying on externals for motivation can pit you in a battle with the opponent. Such is not the case when the primary motivation is intrinsic.

The very existence of a contest makes pure intrinsic motivation nearly impossible. Consider a child at play. That child is motivated by the sheer pleasure of the activity. Now turn that activity into a contest. Sheer pleasure gives way to goal-directed behavior aimed at winning. The desire to win focuses attention away from the intrinsic enjoyment of the activity itself. Winning, after all, is an outcome. It is external to the actual playing of the game.

To the extent that I am motivated by the desire to win, I am extrinsically motivated. Depending on *why* winning is important to me, I will be somewhere on the A-B-C-D continuum. If I'm playing sports and I want to win solely because I'm afraid of getting chewed out by the coach if I lose, then I get a D in motivation and I am at considerable risk for becoming decompetitive. On the other hand, if I want to win because I have chosen to make my

Given the risks attending extrinsic motivations, should the goal be to replace them all with intrinsic motivation?

athletic ability core to how I see myself, then I have a more advantageous form of motivation. However, it is still extrinsic, and all forms of extrinsic motivation push in varying degrees toward decompetition.

Although extrinsic motivation is a carrier of the decompetition virus, a limited amount of extrinsic motivation is fine. Contests, in fact, depend on it. However, if the whole focus is on winning, if winning and its rewards becomes the *raison d'etre* for contesting, then competition will give way to decompetition. To sustain true competition, the primary motivation should be intrinsic.

The 3 Cs of Intrinsic Motivation

Finding fun, excitement, interest, pleasure, and satisfaction—all forms of intrinsic motivation—in the process of contesting will help guard against decompetition. But what evokes and sustains intrinsic motivation? There are several possibilities. Sometimes it stems from the simple bodily pleasure that the activity brings—such as the feel of the water for Imo. Sometimes the suspense built into the contest can elicit delight. Sometimes the learning available is what sustains interest.

The real key to understanding intrinsic motivation, however, is to appreciate the three Cs.[7] Like iron filings attracted to a magnet, people are drawn to activities that increase their sense of *competence, connection,* and *control.* Meeting people's need to feel competent, connected, and in control is the primary path toward increased intrinsic motivation. Let's look at each of these more closely.

We experience *competence* when our skills match the challenge present in a situation. Stated differently, feeling competent comes midway between feeling bored because a task is too easy and feeling overwhelmed because it is too difficult. When we skate right up to that edge between "can do" and "can't quite do yet," the feeling of competence arises and intrinsic motivation is stimulated. Think of a child with a set of puzzles of varying difficulty. Some puzzles are too easy. She may play with them for a time, but will likely become bored rather quickly. Puzzles that are too difficult will not hold the child's interest either; she will probably become frustrated and quit trying to solve them. The child's interest is piqued most by puzzles that are optimally challenging. We are intrinsically motivated to engage in challenging tasks that allow us to demonstrate or expand our competence.

Everyone wants to experience competence. We also want to experience *connection* with others. No man—and no woman—is an island. We all have a deep-seated need to connect with others, to build relationships of love and friendhsip. Again, think of a child. He spontaneously seeks to play not only with objects, but also with other children. Ask him why he wants to join a team and you are likely to hear about the fun of being with friends. We are intrinsically motivated to involve ourselves in situations in which we can experience positive connections with others.

© Human Kinetics

How might playing baseball help a child feel more competent, more connected to others, and more in control? How might the sport experience interfere with these basic needs?

Finally, people want to feel in *control* of their own lives. We want to pilot our own plane. Although we desire connections to other people and to share a certain level of intimacy, we don't want to be controlled by them. When a child is told she must play with puzzles, she has two options: She can obey, or she can rebel; she can comply or defy. Neither option supports her intrinsic motivation. If she were invited to play, she could reflect on her interests and accept the invitation if she chose to do so. We are intrinsically motivated to participate in valued activities in which we can feel a sense of autonomy, of personal choice and control.

Competence, connection, and control—these are the three Cs that directly support intrinsic motivation. There are many reasons to support people's intrinsic motivation. Importantly, it tends to improve their performance. Perhaps even more importantly, it adds to their enjoyment. And one of the key reasons we have contests in the first place is to provide an opportunity for enjoyment. We turn now to a discussion of this hallmark feature of true competition. As we will see, intrinsic motivation may be the primary diet of enjoyment, but it is not its only nutrient.

Enjoyment

" You have to love a sport to play it well and love grows out of enjoyment. "

Jack Nicklaus

True competition is rooted in intrinsic motivation. It is most easily sustained when the activity is fun or pleasurable and quenches our thirst for feeling competent, connected with others, and in control. In chapter 3, we suggested that true competitors are motivated by a love of the game, whereas decompetitors seek foremost to use or exploit the game.

We are, as always, employing the term *game* both literally and metaphorically. The term can apply to any form of contest, whether in the realm of play, games, and sports or in education, politics, or work. When extrinsic motivations predominate in any of these situations, the contest, whether formal or informal, may rapidly devolve into decompetition.

Enjoyment is a natural partner to true competition. In fact, when participants are not enjoying the contest, it is highly unlikely that true competition is taking place. Conversely, decompetitors may experience thrills and excitement, but they rarely experience real and sustained enjoyment. So where does enjoyment come from? Of course, we have already been reflecting on one major source of enjoyment—intrinsic motivation. Whenever we are intrinsically motivated, we are likely to enjoy what we are doing. But, as we will see, the motivational well that enjoyment taps draws from more than the pure waters of intrinsic motivation.

Enjoyment can be hard to write about because there is a great deal of confusion surrounding it.[8] In fact, before we focus directly on the kind of enjoyment true competitors experience, it may be helpful to clear away some of the gnarly underbrush that has grown up around the term. In the following sections, we briefly distinguish between enjoyment and such related ideas as fun, pleasure, and positive emotion. We then discuss the tension that many of us experience between two clashing cultural forces, both of which can interfere with our experience of enjoyment. On the one hand, we live within a culture that celebrates instant gratification. On the other hand, we are constantly lectured to sacrifice in the present so that we can enjoy the future. Despite the fact that both ideas contain kernels of truth, they need to be challenged.

Beyond Fun

Fun is that bubbling, lighthearted pleasure we get when we engage in activities that are exciting or entertaining. Fun typically springs from pure intrinsic motivation. It is often prescribed as a medicine to cure the ills of contests, especially at the youth level. Jim Thompson, founder of the Positive Coaching

Alliance at Stanford University, is an expert on coaching youth sports. Here's one piece of advice that he offers coaches: "Remember the F-word." He is referring, of course, to fun. The advice is contained in his book *The Double Goal Coach,*[9] which is a treasure chest brimming with gold coins of wisdom. Remembering the F-word is good advice, but it can be carried too far because *fun* is not a synonym for *enjoyment.*

Ironically, we sometimes emphasize fun too much in youth sports and other child-centered activities. Kids can get the mistaken idea that enjoyment flows from swimming in an endless river of fun. The goal of continuous fun, however, is not only impossible, but also unhealthy.

Don't get me wrong. Having fun is a good thing. Coaches and teachers *should* try to make learning and practice fun. But fun should take its natural place in the broader scheme of enjoyment. Sticking with our youth sport example, the more important goal of the coach should be to encourage a love of the game, not just having fun.

Sometimes sports will not be fun, and that is OK. One of the great life lessons of sport is that enjoyment does not rule out hard work, sacrifice, and discipline. Loving the game, like loving a person, involves struggling through hard times. The same is true of school, work, or any other context in which achievement or performance matters.

Fun springs from pure intrinsic motivation. Enjoyment, too, taps deep into intrinsic motivation. Yet enjoyment, unlike fun, can also draw from extrinsic motivation. Imagine two climbers on the face of Half Dome in Yosemite. Climbing up Half Dome may require belaying in rotation, even though one climber experiences no elation when he belays. Enjoyment taps into intrinsic motivation to the extent possible, but also draws from the higher forms of extrinsic motivation where necessary to accomplish the aim. For the climbers, the whole experience is enjoyable, even though fun may be experienced only intermittently.

Beyond Positive Emotion

Another misconception about enjoyment is that it is a positive emotion. Emotions, however, tend to be a flash in the pan. Although they may sometimes endure for a time, they are often quite transitory. This is part of what distinguishes positive emotion from enjoyment. The emotion of joy may rise and fall quickly, but the experience of enjoyment endures. In fact, enjoyment is as much a retrospective experience as a present one. Imagine that you are one of those climbers on Half Dome. It is a cold day, and the crisp wind is chilling you to the bone. It has been a hard climb, and your muscles are aching. Yet somehow you make it to the top. No doubt, your immediate emotional experience is exhilaration and euphoria. Days later, as you look back on the climb, you talk about how much you enjoyed it—all of it, not just the final ascent. Enjoyment often includes an extended afterglow that arises when a person puts out great effort to accomplish a meaningful goal. Enjoyment is supported by positive emotions, but it may include a broader range of affects as well as periods when little emotion is directly experienced.

Beyond Pleasure

Finally, enjoyment is not equivalent to pleasure. This may be a particularly important point to emphasize because the mistaken assumption that we can become happier by experiencing more pleasure is widespread in our culture. Enjoyment contributes to happiness, whereas pleasure often does not.

In his book *Authentic Happiness*, Martin Seligman points out that there is now considerable scientific evidence regarding what does and does not lead to life satisfaction, well-being, contentment, and sustained happiness.[10] One of the great myths of our time is that pleasure, in itself, leads to happiness. Pleasure may be good, but happiness cannot be bought with the currency of pleasure. The belief that the good life can be reduced to the pleasurable life has been an illusion feeding disappointment, depression, and despair.

The assumption that pleasure is the pathway to happiness has led many to seek shortcuts to feeling good. As a result, we may seek sensation without sacrifice, delight without dedication, entertainment without exertion. Pleasure, in this view, is good in itself without concern for the path that led to it. So we may indulge in such things as mind-altering drugs, habitual TV, mindless amusement, loveless sex, needless shopping, and food binging. None of these bring real enjoyment, nor do they contribute to an overall sense of contentment and well-being.

The belief that enjoyment can be bought with pleasure, that it can be had on the cheap, pervades contests as well; it is a major contributor to decompetition. The boost to the ego that may come from touting superiority over another doesn't really bring lasting satisfaction, only a cheap thrill. Because the pleasures of decompetition tend to be hollow and short-lived, the decompetitor often gets ensnared in a fruitless effort to renew them, seeking an endless stream of new victims from whom to extract the pleasure of conquest. And every loss also acts as a stimulus to renew the cycle.

There's a profound difference between the superficial pleasures of consumption and conquest and the more resonant pleasures that result in enjoyment. In reference to the former, Seligman notes, "Positive emotion alienated from the exercise of character leads to emptiness, to inauthenticity, to depression, and as we age, to the gnawing realization that we are fidgeting until we die."[11] The more resonant pleasures arise from our considered desires and are consonant with our character. Enjoyment draws from the resonant pleasures and is the pathway to a meaningful and authentically happy life.

> Enjoyment flows from using your skills to their fullest in the pursuit of worthy goals consonant with your values.

The key point is this: *Enjoyment arises from using our talents to pursue an objective that is personally meaningful.* It comes from using our skills and resources to pursue goals that express our values. Pursuing the goal may be fun at times, but not always. It will probably require considerable and sustained effort, but the journey will be alive with richness and possibility. And enjoyment is possible at every step along the way. This brings us to the final misconception about enjoyment that we need to address.

Beyond Sacrifice

Ironically, our culture is simultaneously infatuated with pleasure shortcuts and committed to the idea that we must postpone enjoyment. We are often told that we must sacrifice now to find enjoyment in the future. That leaves a void in the present that is often filled by tantalizing but shallow pleasure shortcuts.

The irony is created by the tension of living simultaneously within two contrasting cultural traditions. On the one hand, we have a tradition of *instant gratification*. Culturally, we tend to be very impatient. We are immersed in the present, hampered by an emaciated view of history and a truncated view of the future. We want satisfaction *now*. We want results. If we have a problem, there must be an immediate fix to it. We are better at short-term thinking than long-range planning. The future is lunchtime.

On the other hand, we are influenced by the old Protestant work ethic. That tradition suggests that we must sacrifice now, putting our collective noses to the grindstone, so that we can benefit later. Much later. Often in the afterlife. This is an austere belief that instructs us to work hard, delay gratification, and put enjoyment on the layaway plan.

When it comes to enjoyment, neither tradition works well. The desire for instant gratification promotes a pernicious pursuit of pleasure shortcuts. Delaying gratification leaves a void in the present and often leads to disappointment in the future.

Consider Tal Ben-Shahar. When he was 11, he set a goal for himself: to win the Israeli national squash championship. For the next five years, he trained exceptionally hard, despite the fact that he really wasn't enjoying the work. Why did he do it? He thought that if he achieved his goal—winning the championship—the gold medal would become his golden key to happiness. Then he won. He was elated and celebrated with friends for hours. Here's how he tells the story of what happened next:

> ❝ **After the night of celebration, I retired to my room. I sat on my bed and wanted to savor, for the last time before going to sleep, that feeling of supreme happiness. Suddenly, without warning, the bliss that came from having attained in real life what**

had for so long been my most cherished and exalted fantasy disappeared, and my feeling of emptiness returned. I was befuddled and afraid. The tears of joy shed only hours earlier turned to tears of pain and helplessness. For if I was not happy now, when everything seemed to have worked out perfectly, what prospects did I have of attaining lasting happiness?[12] **"**

Tal's story is a common one. Coaches the world over tell athletes to sacrifice and work hard so that they can later enjoy the fruits of victory. Students are told to study hard so that they can get good grades, get into a good college, and land a good job. Is that when they are supposed to start enjoying life? Once there, of course, the new employee is told to work hard to save for a house, to fund her children's education, to get a promotion, or to save for retirement. The train of reasons for delaying enjoyment is endless.

True, it is often important to work hard for future goals, and hard work is not always fun. However, delaying enjoyment rarely works. That is what Tal discovered. During his years of training, the bulk of his motivation was extrinsic. He hoped to win the championship to reap the benefits that victory would bring.

In reality, enjoyment will not come when you win the next game, get the good grade, or achieve the next promotion. Expecting enjoyment in the future because of sacrifice in the present puts us on an endless treadmill powered by extrinsic motivation. We can run toward the goal, but we are really running in place. The gratification that we may experience when one of our goals is achieved tends to be short-lived.

Enjoyment deferred creates an emotional vacuum in the present. That void too often gets filled with hollow pleasures. If I no longer love to play, I take delight in the victor's spoils. If I can't find enjoyment in learning, I'll seek satisfaction from a good grade. If my job fails to bring enjoyment, hopefully I'll earn enough money to buy my way to happiness. But these strategies do not work.

The upshot of this discussion is this: *If you want to enjoy the future, enjoy the present.* If you want to enjoy the game, enjoy the practice. If you want to enjoy the victory, enjoy the play. If you want to enjoy the career, enjoy college. Build on intrinsic motivation whenever possible. This does not mean that we don't need to work hard for future goals. Far from it. It doesn't mean that we can be intrinsically motivated constantly. That's not going to happen. To find enjoyment in the present, we still need to delay gratification. But it is important to keep in mind that lasting enjoyment comes when strenuous effort is combined with meaningful purpose.

Enjoyment blends intrinsic motivation with the higher forms of extrinsic motivation. To find enjoyment, you need to work toward personally

What factors will influence how much enjoyment an athlete will experience from an athletic accomplishment?

meaningful goals that reflect your considered values and deepest desires. In one sense, those goals stand outside the immediate present, and yet they don't entirely. Worthy goals infuse the present with meaning and amplify the intrinsic reasons for performing the task. Progress toward future goals is enjoyed in the moment. True enjoyment is both a present reality and a future hope. That's the kind enjoyment that the true competitor experiences.

Tal Ben-Shahar, distraught that his athletic success did not lead to enjoyment, went on to study philosophy and psychology. He was eventually hired by Harvard University, and he became the teacher of its most popular course. Ironically, the theme of that course is happiness. In his book *Happier,* Dr. Ben-Shahar notes:

> **❝ Research in this area indicates that there is a qualitative difference between the meaning we derive from extrinsic goods, such as social status and the state of our bank account, and the meaning we derive from intrinsic goods, such as personal growth and a sense of connection to others.[13] ❞**

When we focus on intrinsic goods, we can experience enjoyment now. It is not at the expense of preparing for the future. That is important too. The best preparation for the future, however, is done when one is also deriving meaningful enjoyment from the present.

Running solely on the treadmill of extrinsic motivation will never get you to enjoyment, but it will get you somewhere when it comes to contests. The person who sacrifices present enjoyment for future benefit runs straight to decompetition. Why? When the outcome becomes valued over the process, it tends to become all important. Hoping to find enjoyment in victory, decompetitors envision opponents as obstacles in the way to achieving personal fulfillment; the opponent becomes the enemy. If you're a decompetitor, the opponent appears to stand between you and your happiness.

We noted earlier that when people postpone enjoyment, when intrinsic motivation is sucked out of their daily lives, they often use shortcuts to pleasure to fill the void. Similarly, when people no longer participate in contests because they love the game, the pleasure of winning becomes an emotional shortcut. It is not a resonant pleasure that stems from a deep sense of satisfaction in a job well done. It is not the pleasure of the competitor, and it does not flow into lasting enjoyment.

Decompetitors' pleasure often comes at the expense of their opponents. It comes from the kick of conquest; from the sense of superiority. It provides an ego boost, paid for by a character drain. Their thrill in the yearned-for victory substitutes for deep enjoyment. So what is the alternative? Where does the competitor find enjoyment?

Finding Enjoyment in True Competition

Competitors enjoy winning. When they celebrate victory at the conclusion of a challenging contest, their joy springs from a sense of accomplishment, from the release of tension, from delight in the plot of the story now ended. True competitors experience victory as an affirmation of the hard work that led to it. Although the opponent lost, they do not celebrate their defeat. Rather, they celebrate their own accomplishment, which the opponent facilitated. Even more than victory, however, true competitors find enjoyment in the contest well-contested. The game is the thing. Even preparation for the game is infused with enjoyment.

What makes the contest enjoyable? Sometimes it is the intrinsic pleasure associated with skillful or powerful movement, thought, or action. As we have noted, contests can be playgrounds for meeting one's needs for competence, connection, and control. Certainly the camaraderie that develops on a team can be enjoyable. Even in the midst of a serious practice or game, there's room for playfulness, amusement, curiosity, spontaneity, humor, and levity. These, too, are important sources of enjoyment in true competition and help to sustain intrinsic motivation.

Olympic Flow

You may recall the 2002 Winter Olympics, in which 16-year-old Sarah Hughes, in a stunning upset, won the gold in women's figure skating. Afterward, she described how, believing she wasn't really a medal contender, she just skated for the sheer pleasure of skating. She entered a state of flow in which her technical expertise combined effortlessly with an inner joy that overflowed in an inspiring and graceful performance.

A related source of enjoyment for the true competitor is the experience of *flow*. This concept may be unfamiliar to many readers, but it can be an important tributary to the river of enjoyment. It is a term used by the highly regarded psychologist Mihaly Csikszentmihalyi.[14] To begin to understand flow, try the following exercise. Think of a time when you were engaged in an activity and became so fully absorbed in what you were doing that you barely noticed the passage of time; you were so immersed in the activity that your concentration narrowed and you performed almost effortlessly. Such are the characteristics of flow.

Elite athletes often describe peak experiences in which they performed at the very top of their skills, but did so with little deliberate effort. These are seamless experiences with a high level of challenge and yet a nearly effortless response. Joe Montana, the great 49ers quarterback, described a critical, late-game drive in which he said everything just happened in slow motion and he didn't really consciously think about what he was doing. He had an experience of flow.

You don't have to be an expert or elite performer to experience flow. The experience can happen for anyone and almost anywhere: on the job, during a hobby, at play. Regardless of where it occurs, flow experiences stand out like sparks against a night sky. They are flashes of intense living. When experiencing flow, people are fully absorbed in the activity to the extent that that they often lose consciousness of self and time. Regardless of skill level, the result of flow is an optimal performance for the person experiencing it.

Like fun, experiences of flow signal the presence of intrinsic motivation. Unlike fun, however, the experience of flow is not dependent on positive emotion. In fact, in the midst of flow, people often report an absence of emotion. Only in retrospect do people describe the experience in positive terms. Flow experiences are enjoyable, although that enjoyment is often not felt in the moment. Sometimes the beauty of the day is recognized only at sunset.

Even though experiences of flow signal the presence of intrinsic motivation, even extrinsically motivated people can experience it.[15] Experiences of flow become increasingly common the more a person's motivation comes from the intrinsic motivation end of the continuum described earlier. The more a person is motivated by the poorly graded forms of motivation, the less likely he is to experience flow. Why does this matter? Because flow contributes to both optimal performance and enjoyment.

Fun and flow are positive, in-the-moment experiences that can result in enjoyment. The enjoyment of the true competitor, however, extends beyond both fun and flow. As we've noted, the deepest motivation of the true competitor springs from a love of the game. Loving the game requires finding meaning in it, even a noble purpose. Former Knicks star and U.S. senator, Bill Bradley, author of *Values of the Game*,[16] did not see the basketball court as simply a place to showcase his ability to toss a ball through a hoop. He saw it as an opportunity to develop and express the values that guide his life.

The businessperson who is interested only in profit is missing a great opportunity. She would experience more life satisfaction and enjoyment if she focused on the values and service that she or her company provides. The lawyer who takes no interest in justice, the teacher who takes no interest in fostering a love of learning, the doctor who cares more about salary than improving health care, and the coach who cares more about the scoreboard than his athletes are all missing the boat. In each case, there is nothing wrong with taking home the paycheck or the win. However, such attitudes raise the question of desire. What is the primary motivation? In what is the sense of accomplishment rooted? In any competitive context, the immediate desire may be to win, but the deeper motivation of the true competitor stems from the intrinsic values of the activity.

Love of the Game

True competitors ultimately contest because they love the game. Love of the game is imbued with an element of transcendence, as is the love of another person. Those who love are no longer the center of their own universe. There are meanings, goods, and values beyond the self. The game can be fun, but more than that, it can be meaningful. It can give expression to deeply held values. When it does, it is enjoyable in the full sense of the word.

True competitors often take a keen interest in the history, lore, and traditions of the game. If you are in love with another, don't you want to know about that person's childhood and earlier experiences? The game's history provides a framework for understanding and appreciating the feats accomplished. If you are a golfer, you are likely interested not only in the physical techniques of golf, but also in the contributions to the game by such notables as Arnold Palmer and Babe Didrikson. A devoted basketball player would want to know of Nancy Lieberman and Earl "the Pearl" Monroe. Becoming involved in a sport means becoming involved in a living tradition.

Just as people in love want to help each other grow, true competitors want to make a positive contribution to the game. They want to help make the game achieve its potential. They are devoted to the ideals and values of their sport, profession, or endeavor. Although this is true of all who compete, it holds special relevance for the unusually gifted. The exceptional athlete who is a true competitor has a desire to leave a legacy, to contribute to the game's positive character and qualities. The game becomes a living tradition that is always ready for new contributions.

In summary, the enjoyment of the true competitor arises from dedication to meaningful activity. It comes from placing one's talents at the service of goals that express one's character. Such activity also provides a blueprint for experiencing competence, connection, and control. It expands our capacities, connects us with others, and affirms our chosen values. Such activity is energizing, expansive, and growth producing. During such activity, the competitor may have moments of fun and flow; such experiences add to their enjoyment, but they are not its defining characteristics.

The enjoyment of the competitor requires balancing both intrinsic and extrinsic motivation, and a future orientation with a present orientation. We turn now to one of the most significant threats to the balance necessary for true competition.

The Threat of Rewards

❝ **What rewards do, and what they do with devastating effectiveness, is smother people's enthusiasm for activities they might otherwise enjoy.** ❞

Alfie Kohn in *Punished by Rewards*

The motivation of the true competitor is largely intrinsic, though it is often complemented by the better extrinsic motivations. There's nothing wrong with wanting to win, with enjoying the praise that comes with achievement, with taking pleasure in standing on the victory platform. But remember this: *The greater the rewards for victory, the more difficult it is to keep motivation in balance.*[17] The more winning actually matters, the more pressure there is to fall into decompetition.

Meet Caesar, a fifth-grade science prodigy.[18] He loves everything science. When he has free time, he reads science magazines or watches science videos. In school, he enthusiastically looks forward to every science lesson. His teacher, eager to keep Caesar highly motivated, decides to institute a weekly "science quiz bowl" with prizes for winning. At the beginning of each week, the teacher announces a science topic that will be the focus of the contest. Because no class time is allowed for preparation, all study must be done independently at home. The teacher announces that the first quiz bowl will focus on weather and that the winner will receive an iPod.

Caesar is delighted. He studies hard and easily wins the contest. The teacher then announces that the second contest will be on geology, and the winner will get a $25 gift certificate to a local electronic games store. Caesar loves electronic games so he studies hard and wins again. The next week a free pizza is offered. This time Caesar studies enough to win, but his enthusiasm has begun to wane. He hopes the teacher offers a better prize next time. However, the following week, the teacher, now low on cash, announces that the winner will just receive a certificate. Caesar doesn't really want the certificate, so he doesn't bother to study at all. In fact, he says, he's really not all that interested in science anymore.

What has the teacher done? She has added rewards to an activity—studying science—that Caesar originally did for enjoyment. Not surprisingly, Caesar began to focus on the rewards. When the teacher removed the external rewards, she found that Caesar no longer felt intrinsically motivated to study science.

The teacher unintentionally stumbled onto an important psychological principle: *Extrinsic rewards tend to erode intrinsic motivation.*[19] This is particularly true if the rewards are viewed as diminishing one's personal choice and control. Caesar may well have perceived the prizes as little more than friendly bribes. In reality, that's what they were. Anytime the message is given, "Do this and I'll give you that," there is an effort to externally control behavior.[20] Such rewards, rather than supporting a sense of personal control, undermine it. And a sense of personal autonomy is one of the key contributors to intrinsic motivation. The science prizes were effective while they lasted, but over time such extrinsic rewards undermine intrinsic motivation. The same thing, you may recall, happened to Emma.

When winning the contest results in rewards, there is a natural tendency to focus on the value of winning rather than the values intrinsic to the process. Rewards, whether in the form of tangible items, recognition, status, or even affection, communicate that what really matters is whether you win or lose. Such an emphasis, again, is likely to diminish intrinsic motivation.

Is it any wonder that students, athletes, businesspeople, politicians, journalists, teachers, scientists, and multitudes of others often lose much of their intrinsic motivation? Students compete for rewards attached to grades. Athletes contest not just to win, but for the scholarships, trophies, or adulations that follow. Businesspeople seek contracts and clients who will reward them for outdoing their opponents. Journalists know there are benefits that come from scooping the rival paper. Teachers may get merit increases if their students outperform others. Scientists recognize that federal grants are more likely if they publish more than their colleagues do. Virtually everywhere people contest, rewards are offered for victory. To some extent, this is inevitable. Such rewards, however, act like the prizes of Caesar's teacher. They have a strong tendency to erode intrinsic motivation. They tend to make it more likely that the person will fall into decompetition. *The more valuable the external rewards, the greater the temptation to adopt a decompetitive orientation.*

Extrinsic rewards, indeed, tend to erode intrinsic motivation. But let's not forget the most important two words of that sentence: *tend to.* We are not talking about the laws of physics. External rewards, even when substantial, do not lead inevitably to a loss of intrinsic motivation. They do not result in decompetition invariably. In our discussion of character, we noted that it is strengthened when it overcomes challenges. Extrinsic rewards present a challenge to the character of the competitor. As the rewards for success become greater, the challenge to stay rooted in intrinsic motivation increases. This is a threat, but it is also an opportunity—an opportunity to strengthen character.

Ideally, sports can provide a progressive learning environment in which people develop the capacity to stay focused on their intrinsic motives for participation, despite the presence of external rewards. This capacity is rooted in the willpower component of character which can be developed through guided practice.

Often, when children are young, the rewards for winning are relatively insignificant. The minimal attraction posed by such external rewards is a fitting match to the level of maturity that children bring to the contest. The lure of such rewards is unlikely to overwhelm the child's capacity to stay connected to their intrinsic motivation, particularly if parents and coaches focus on the intrinsic benefits of participation. Then, as children successfully meet the challenges posed by such minimal rewards, they become better equipped to handle the temptations of increasingly valuable rewards that arise later. Generally speaking, the older one becomes (or the higher the competitive level), the more winning matters. The progressive increase in the value of external rewards can provide a ladder for the increasing development of character. However, all this presupposes that coaches and parents maintain a truly competitive orientation. Unfortunately, this happens too rarely.

Extrinsic motivation can be like sugar. When there are rewards for winning, tasting those rewards can be mighty sweet. And, of course, taking pleasure in dessert is fine. But a sweet tooth can lead to the neglect of the basic food groups, which, in the case of contests, are the joy, learning, and growth that come from intrinsic motivation.

The challenge, stated simply, is to maintain focus. It is to stay grounded in a love for the game. How do we do that? It is important to remember that focus is guided by desire. If we desire the intrinsic values that come from participating in the game even more than we desire the sweet rewards that may come from winning the game, we are likely to remain true competitors.

So what do we do if we become distracted by our sweet tooth? We remember that we have two types of desire. Some desires arise almost instinctively within us; extrinsic rewards tend to stimulate such desires. But if we are mature, we recognize that true competition requires that we focus our attention elsewhere. So we exercise choice. We deliberately nurture those desires within us that arise from our valuing of the contest itself. Our intrinsic reasons for participating in the contest guide us toward true competition as surely as the stars guided the early sailors. If we desire true competition, we will stay focused on our intrinsic motives for participation.

Dear Authors:

I've read your argument that rewards tend to undermine intrinsic motivation. Fine. But what if you really need the reward? I'm a professional runner. If I want to train adequately, I can't take a regular job in which I work on my feet eight hours a day. Most of my current income comes from product endorsements. If I don't win often enough, those contracts will dry up. I need the benefits of winning if I'm going to keep running professionally. Is true competition just for amateurs and others who don't really need the rewards that come with victory?

— *Running for the Money*

Dear Running for the Money:

You're right. Maintaining true competition becomes more difficult when the benefits of winning become more important. Nevertheless, it is far from impossible. And true competition is worth the effort!

Keep in mind that true competitors often outperform decompetitors who have the same level of talent. So focusing on excellence, enjoyment, and the internal values of the contest, rather than the outcome, doesn't diminish your likelihood of obtaining future goals, including victory and whatever rewards come with it. When the rewards for success are important, focusing on them as your primary motivation is often dysfunctional. It can create considerable stress and anxiety, for example, and divert attention from the demands of the moment. We believe it is best, therefore, even when the rewards are important, to stay true to true competition.

The temptations that are most likely to snag us are those that we fail to recognize. That is one of the problems with glitter and gold. Most people do not realize the effects that rewards tend to have on intrinsic motivation. Teachers who place gold stars on papers do not do so out of malice. Ironically, their intention is to motivate learning. But what is the effect? With enough gold stars, the child begins to focus more on pleasing the teacher and getting the reward than on the joy of expanding competence. Unfortunately, the role of gold stars in greasing children's slide into extrinsic motivation is usually unrecognized by teachers, parents, and children. The same is true of rewards in sports and other domains. To build and sustain true competition, leaders must know its characteristics and the dangers that threaten it.

Building, sustaining, and nurturing true competition is nearly impossible without guidance and support. Whether you are a sport administrator, an official, a coach, or a sport psychologist, your help is needed. If you are a principal, a teacher, a counselor, or a parent, your assistance is required. If you are the CEO of an organization or just lead by example, you have a vital role to play.

Good leaders are both visionary and effective. They know where they want to go, they have the people skills to make their vision contagious, and they possess the organizational skills necessary for mobilizing a group to accomplish shared goals. In the present context, leadership means having a clear vision of what true and noble competition looks like, the ability to share that vision effectively, and the skills to galvanize collective efforts to achieve it.

Make no mistake about it. Wherever there are contests, the structural win–lose setup will exert a downward pull toward decompetition. Unless people learn to recognize and value the cooperative underpinnings of true competition, decompetition is the most likely outcome of contests. That is why research into the effects of competition, reviewed in chapter 1, points to hostility, aggression, prejudice, insecurity, lower productivity, and group dysfunction.

Because the dynamics of sports, education, work, and play differ, the following recommendations for leaders, as well as those in subsequent chapters, are necessarily broad. As you read, we hope you will consider how best to elaborate on them to fit your situation.

Importance of Democratic Leadership

> " I know that you can have success being an autocrat and not relating to your players. But you know what, that isn't the kind of success that I want to have. The satisfaction of success cannot be measured by wins and losses. It is about making a difference and helping people achieve their goals within a team situation. "
>
> Marty Schottenheimer

What can a coach, teacher, parent, or other leader do to nurture intrinsic motivation and enjoyment in competition? The place to begin is with the three Cs. When leaders provide experiences that expand competence, build connection to others, and allow people to take control over important decision making, they boost intrinsic motivation. Competence, connection, and control—these are the names of three major tributaries to the river of intrinsic motivation, which provides the main water supply for the city of enjoyment.

All three of the Cs are important, but in any particular situation or context, one or another may come to the fore. Why do kids participate in clubs or sports? For many, friendship is the answer. Their motivation springs from the opportunity to build their sense of connection to others. A coach who overemphasizes winning or performance may unintentionally undercut the intrinsic motivation of these young people. For them, a recreational approach that meets their social needs is probably more appropriate.

For other kids, joining a sport team may be more about enhancing their sense of competence. These kids may thrive on the challenge of building their skills. Rather than losing their intrinsic motivation, they may blossom under a more rigorous training approach. However, it is vitally important not to overemphasize performance or underplay the other two Cs. All people, young and old, have continuing needs to feel competent, connected, and in control.

For a few kids, the motive for participation may be about exercising control and leadership. Of course, all kids have these needs. But sports (and many other adult-organized youth activities) too rarely support them. Frankly, far too many coaches think of the team as their team, not the kids' team.

Decades ago, the informal games kids played in streets and vacant lots offered many opportunities to experience self-determination. The kids themselves decided what to play, how long to play, who was on what team, how to deal with unequal teams, how to adapt the game to circumstances, how to resolve disputes, and so on. Children's informal games were incredibly rich settings that supported their developmental needs for autonomy and control.[21] Such games, however, are largely gone. Even the unsupervised playground games of youth are now primarily miniaturized versions of the big league games of adults.

Adult-organized programs have advantages over children's unsupervised games. They may be safer, adults can lead a more systematic learning process, and vulnerable kids can be shielded from rude or abusive peers. However, the loss of a rich informal games culture is still a real loss. Perhaps some of

Building a Work Ethic

Coaches, parents, and teachers sometimes attempt to enhance young peoples' perceived competence by building their work ethic. This is certainly a worthy goal. These efforts are most successful, however, when the young people enjoy the work. Otherwise, they are likely to get turned off to the activity, rather than develop a lasting work ethic. Although not every practice or drill need be fun, a pervading sense of overall enjoyment is important. The goal is for the children to learn, over time, that working hard and stretching themselves can be enjoyable. As odd as it may sound, learning to enjoy and learning to work go hand in hand.

what made yesterday's informal games so beneficial, though, can be built into today's sports. To do so, we need to turn the games back over to the youth who play them, to the extent feasible in specific situations.[22] This recommendation, in fact, is consistent with a substantial body of literature on effective leadership.

When it comes to coaching and teaching, we are advocates of democratic leadership. This form of leadership maximizes the third C—people's need for an internal sense of control and responsibility. Including team members in decision making builds their sense of ownership, fosters a sense of responsibility, enhances communication, and promotes mutual respect. These are the social, ethical, and psychological gains. Because democratic leadership boosts intrinsic motivation, it can also optimize performance. People tend to perform better when they are intrinsically motivated.

"But what about [fill in the name of your favorite successful, authoritarian coach]?" No doubt, there are many controlling, drill-sergeant coaches who have achieved a high level of success. Democratic leadership is not the only pathway to the victory stand, but it can get you there just as surely. More important, it carries fewer risks and more benefits. Most important of all, because it builds intrinsic motivation, it is more likely to foster true competition.

The media loves to celebrate strong personalities, and strong personalities, mistakenly, are often equated with authoritarian styles. The movies *Remember the Titans*, *Coach Carter*, and *Miracle* all feature authoritarian coaches. There's a similar adulation of authoritarian educators in such movies as *Stand and Deliver* and *Lean on Me*. The coaches and educators celebrated in such movies achieved remarkable success. For that, we can applaud them. But that does not mean that their methods should be imitated. Back in 1974, Marin Ralbovsky was one of the first to write about the dark underside of such authoritarian practices in his book *Lords of the Locker Room: The American Way of Coaching and Its Effects on Youth*.[23]

The media, unfortunately, rarely shows the frequent costs of authoritarian leadership: the broken spirits, the deep resentments, the loss of interest, the failure to thrive, the overconforming disposition. Enamored with the image of the strong, authoritarian personality, the media is even less likely to profile coaches or educators who achieved their success through more democratic processes. And there are plenty of examples.

Have you heard of Coach George Davis? Probably not. This maverick coach spent much of his career coaching high school football in the poor northern California lumber town of Willits.[24] He was also one of the true pioneers of democratic coaching. Back in the late 1960s and early 1970s, he instituted "the vote"—a form of player democracy. Team members took responsibility for such crucial matters as discipline, team life, and strategy. Although

> Coaches can and should inspire. They can and should channel desire. But they must be careful about what they require.

Coach Davis was an excellent teacher who instructed his players on skills and the technical aspects of the game, virtually all key decisions, including the starting lineup, were made by vote of the players. A sure recipe for failure, right? His teams won consistently, attracting national attention.

In a similar vein, Coach Bob Ladouceur of De La Salle High School in Concord, California, violates conventional wisdom by consulting his players on strategy and other important decisions. During a game, he may call a time-out only to have the players decide what adjustments need to be made. From 1991 to 2003, De La Salle went undefeated, racking up a 151-game winning streak, the longest in the nation.[25]

There are plenty of other examples. Coach Lute Olson, the men's basketball coach at Arizona, has the members of his team spend time with potential recruits. The players then vote whether to offer each player a scholarship.[26] When Pat Summitt was the head coach of the U.S. Olympic basketball team in 1984, she had to reduce the number of players on the squad from 18 to 12. How did she do it? She passed out confidential ballots.[27] Tom Osborne, former head football coach of the Nebraska Cornhusker, used a "Unity Council" to democratize decision making.[28] John Kessel of USA Volleyball recommends that coaches routinely call time-outs and let the kids tell themselves what to do.[29]

The list could easily be extended tenfold. From youth sports through professional sports, many highly successful coaches use democratic strategies. Not all do so perfectly, but the effort pays dividends. As performance-enhancement expert Jeff Janssen puts it, "Involving your players in determining their destiny is the key catalyst in changing mindsets from 'have to' to 'want to.'"[30]

Not only is democratic leadership useful in amplifying intrinsic motivation, but it also helps to promote a commitment to shared values.[31] We noted earlier that true competition brings enjoyment in its wake and that enjoyment flows from using one's talents to pursue goals consonant with one's ideals. This especially happens when those ideals are shared and the pursuit of them is corporate rather than individual. Through engaging everyone in discussion and decision making, democratic leadership builds a shared commitment to common values. We will have more to say about this in chapter 8.

Practically speaking, the team meeting is at the heart of the democratic approach to coaching. In team meetings, members discuss and decide on team rules, discipline, norms, goals, and values. Everyone should have input and feel heard. The team meeting provides the coach with an opportunity to advocate for the values and norms of true competition, yet the goal is to achieve consensus, not to impose a viewpoint.

Of course, democratic leadership is not the invention of sport coaches. Involving people in decision-making processes has been a key recommendation in the business world for some time. Just as we recommend that coaches use team meetings to share decision making, company-level "town hall meetings" in which employees share suggestions and offer reflections on company priorities and strategies can increase both job satisfaction and corporate profitability. In fact, restructuring management to increase industrial democracy has been reported to increase productivity between 10 and 40 percent.[33] In education, as far back as John Dewey, increased democracy has been advocated.[33] The famous "just community" schools associated with Lawrence Kohlberg, Clark Power, and Ann Higgins-D'Alessandro helped to demonstrate the effectiveness of democratic schooling.[34] Marvin Berkowitz, Professor of Character Education at the University of Missouri at St. Louis, writes in his book *Parenting for Good* about how important it is to include children in family meetings in which problems are resolved collaboratively.[35]

Objections to democratic leadership often stem from misconceptions. We close this chapter with four myths about democratic leadership. Future chapters will amplify on specific strategies democratic leaders can employ to support true competition.

Myth 1: Democratic leaders give up all control.

Leading in a democratic way does involve recognizing the fundamental equality of all. However, democracy doesn't mean that members are all free to do as they please, that all decisions are turned over to the team, or that a leader's authority is diminished. Democracy is not chaos or mob rule. The coach who exercises democratic leadership still exercises leadership, but it is leadership earned by expertise, character, and inspiration. The authority of the democratic leader relies less on institutional power and more on the power of personal strength and wisdom. It is a power that comes from being a servant to the whole.

Most settings, sport included, have built-in constraints on time that do not allow all decisions to be made through a democratic process. Sometimes the coach will need to make decisions on behalf of, and in the interest of, the whole team. Moreover, coaches do not live on islands. They live within broader structures and systems of accountability that may not allow for the implementation of a fully democratic approach. What is most important is a *democratic spirit,* which is a guiding belief in inclusion, empowerment, and a sense of equality. Such an attitude conveys respect for every participant.

Myth 2: Democratic leadership takes too long.

Sometimes people think that voting is the heart of the democratic process. This is not true. The heart of democracy is an effort to find common ground, shared interests, and mutual agreement. Democratic leaders facilitate discussion. The skilled democratic leader helps a group to uncover, through dialogue, what is in the interest of all. Conversation, of course, does take time. Precious time. But it is time well spent. Rather than being inefficient or a waste of time, effectively guided group discussion builds a sense of camaraderie and shared values. It becomes the platform for shared commitment and vision. Out of that commitment springs dedication and loyalty. Could time be better spent?

Myth 3: Democratic leaders do not discipline.

Here's a true story. Coach George Davis did not require players to participate in drills, conditioning exercises, or even practices. He told them what he expected, but he also told them that it wasn't his job to enforce participation. It was their responsibility. Not surprisingly, one day a player, Tom Blanchfield, decided to test him. "Coach, I think I'll pass on the wind sprints today," he said. "OK, fine," Coach Davis responded. "That's what I'll tell the team if anyone asks—that you didn't feel like running them." Blanchfield ran them.[36]

In most endeavors, discipline is required for success. Coach Davis understood, however, that coach-enforced discipline doesn't lead to self-discipline. Real discipline needs to come from a sense of responsibility to yourself and others, not a fear of reprisal from authority. Feeling responsible to peers is a better pathway to discipline than obedience to a domineering coach.

Myth 4: Promoting hard work requires an authoritarian approach.

Throughout this chapter, we have emphasized the importance of intrinsic motivation. But doesn't the enjoyment associated with intrinsic motivation undermine hard work? Quite the contrary. The enemy of enjoyment is not work. For that matter, it is not even extrinsic motivation. The real enemies of enjoyment are boredom and compulsion.

The football coach at St. John's University in St. Cloud, Minnesota, John Gagliardi, brings this truth to life.[37] If you attend a team practice, you will not see the players doing monotonous calisthenics or mundane conditioning. You won't even see contact drills. Coach Gagliardi removed the forced and routine drills that interfere with enjoyment. *OK, you say, but doesn't eliminating those dreaded parts of practice lead to a softening of players?* If so, it doesn't show up in the stats. St. John's has the second-highest number of wins in college football history. Gagliardi's players develop a strong work ethic using an enjoyable approach.

If enjoyment is an important outcome of true competition, the seeking of excellence is probably its most clearly defining property. In chapter 5, we delve into that theme more deeply. ■

---

1   For a summary of the correlates and outcomes of intrinsic and extrinsic motivation in sport, see Vallerand (2001).

2   For a user-friendly discussion of how intrinsic and extrinsic motivations influence a wide range of activities and outcomes, see Deci (1995). For a more scholarly treatment, see Deci and Ryan (2002).

(continued)

(continued from previous page)

3   Ryan and Deci (2000).

4   For a good overview of Deci and Ryan's self-determination theory, see Ryan and Deci (2002).

5   In the language of self-determination theory, these four forms of extrinsic motivation are labeled (from least to most desirable) external regulation, introjected regulation, identified regulation, and integrated regulation. See Vallerand (1997).

6   As yet, no valid and reliable measure of decompetition or decompetitive orientation exists. Consequently, assertions throughout the book about what leads to decompetition, although drawing from related empirical evidence, are necessarily hypothetical.

7   Once again, we are drawing from self-determination theory (SDT). Our use of the terms *competence, connection,* and *control* parallel the concepts of competence, relatedness, and autonomy, which are viewed as basic human psychological needs within SDT (Ryan & Deci, 2000a).

8   Our analysis of enjoyment borrows from Seligman (2002).

9   Thompson (2003).

10   Seligman (2002).

11   Ibid, p. 8.

12   Ben-Shahar (2007), p. 4.

13   Ibid, p. 72.

14   Csikszentmihalyi (1990).

15   See Vallerand (2001).

16   Bradley (1998).

17   See Kohn (1993).

18   This story is a remake of an old joke that Alfie Kohn (1993) tells as follows: "An old man . . . endured the insults of a crowd of ten-year-olds each days as they passed his house on their way home from school. One afternoon, after listening to another round of jeers and how stupid and ugly and bald he was, the man came up with a plan. He met the children on his lawn the following Monday and announced that anyone who came back the next day and yelled rude comments about him would receive a dollar. Amazed and excited, they showed up even earlier on Tuesday, hollering epithets for all they were worth. True to his word, the old man ambled out and paid everyone. 'Do the same tomorrow,' he told them, 'and you'll get twenty-five cents for your trouble.' The kids thought that was still pretty good and turned out again on Wednesday to taunt him. At the first catcall, he walked over with a roll of quarters and again paid off his hecklers. 'From now on,' he announced, 'I can give you only a penny for doing this.' The kids looked at each other in disbelief. 'A penny?' they repeated scornfully. 'Forget it!' And they never came back again" (pp. 71-72).

19   Ryan and Deci (2000).

20   See Kohn (1993).

21   For more on the developmental benefits of children's informal games, see Devereux (1976).

22   The point about returning youth sports to the kids is forcefully made by Bigelow, Moroney, and Hall (2001).

23   Ralbovsky (1974).

24   For more on the innovative techniques of Coach George Davis, see Amdur (1971).

25   See Hayes (2003).

26   The reference to Coach Lute Olson is taken from Janssen (1999), pp. 158-159.

27   The reference to Coach Pat Summitt is taken from Janssen and Dale (2002), p. 177

28   A thorough description of Osborne's "Unity Council" is provided in Osborne (1999).

29   Cited in Thompson (2003), p. 224.

30   Janssen (1999), p. 56.

31   Building shared values through democratic leadership was a cornerstone of the "just community" approach. See Power, Higgins, and Kohlberg (1989).

32   Rosenau (2003), p. 71.

33   Dewey (1916/1966).

34   For a thorough description of the "just community" approach to education, see Power, Higgins, and Kohlberg, (1989).

35   Berkowitz (2006). The importance of democracy to parenting was also heavily emphasized by the highly influential writings of Rudolf Dreikurs. See, for example, Dreikurs (1964).

36   The story of Tom Blanchfield and Coach Davis is contained in Amdur (1971).

37   For a description of a number of Coach John Gagliardi's practices, see Murphy (2001).

5

Goals
Pathways to Excellence

Dear Reader: Please welcome to these pages the top-seeded tennis players, Task and Ego.

Task, by all accounts, is a fierce competitor. Task isn't his real name, of course. It's a nickname given to him by friends because of his tendency to become fully absorbed in the task at hand. Whenever he's playing, Task seeks to do his best and learn from the experience. Task believes that by trying hard, he will continue to improve. As a result, whether in a practice or a championship match, Task always gives his all. He finds enjoyment in learning and is constantly focused on mastering new skills or refining existing ones. For Task, success is growth.

Ego, as you might imagine, is a nickname as well. It was given to him because of his unwavering concern with looking good. Ego believes that effort may help, but ultimately, success comes to the most talented, and Ego wants to prove that he belongs in that elite category. For Ego, success depends on demonstrating that he is better than his rivals. Ego's goal is to be the star that outshines all others.

> " I never played to get into the Hall of Fame.
> I only tried to be the best that I could be. "
>
> Walter Payton

Do you desire success? Do you want to achieve? Then competition is for you! Contests are all about achievement and success. They provide an opportunity to develop and demonstrate talents and skills. Competition is a gateway to growth, a pathway to pride, and an expressway toward excellence. True competition is, however, a road less traveled. Taking it makes all the difference.

In chapter 4, we suggested that the true competitor experiences high levels of intrinsic motivation. Such a person discovers a resonant enjoyment that is deep and sustainable. True competitors take a compassionate, egalitarian approach to contests and are motivated by a deep respect for the game, officials, themselves, and their opponents. In contrast, decompetitors approach contests like pirates, seeking to capture jewels in the form of money, goods, power, praise, or status. Decompetitors' enjoyment is a buccaneer's pleasure.

In this chapter, we examine a different aspect of motivation: the reasons people seek to achieve. What are the ultimate goals that competitors and decompetitors pursue? How do they know whether they are achieving their goals? How do they define success?[1]

The conceptual table for this chapter was set by a number of prominent educational and sport psychologists, such as Carol Ames, Joan Duda, Carol Dweck, Diane Gill, Rainer Martens, John Nicholls, Glyn Roberts, and Robin Vealey.[2] Despite differences among them, they all suggest that a person's "competitiveness" springs largely from an internal desire to achieve success and feel competent. Although this may seem obvious, it is a somewhat different perspective from that held by the scientists we discussed in chapter 1. For Musafer and Carolyn Sherif and Morton Deutsch, for example, the external situation—the contest structure—stimulates the internal competitive orientation. Of course, these are not incompatible perspectives, but they do have different emphases.

Both competitors and decompetitors are interested in achievement and success, but they think about them differently. To preview: competitors feel successful whenever they develop new skills or achieve new levels of mastery. Personal excellence is their ultimate goal. The goal of decompetitors is to demonstrate their superior abilities, and they experience success only when they outperform others.

In this chapter, after introducing the goal orientations of the competitor and decompetitor, we take a closer look at the concept of excellence. We will see that it springs from desire, is connected to personal achievement, and is distinct from perfection. We will also see that it requires balance and character and is connected with the concept of virtue. In the next section, we identify and address additional forces that tend to push contestants into decompetition. We conclude the chapter with practical advice for leaders.

Two Views of Success

Our opening scenario describes two highly motivated athletes. However, that is where the resemblance ends. Interestingly, when Task and Ego face each other on the tennis court, they pursue quite different goals, even while they both seek to win.

For both Task and Ego, the external goal, dictated by the contest structure, is to win. But what they are really trying to achieve is different. Task sees the contest as an opportunity to learn and grow, to push past previous levels of achievement and to measure his progress toward mastery. Although Task would much rather win than lose, he feels like a winner, regardless of the outcome, if he believes he has stretched himself. Consequently, Task is always hustling, always trying hard.

Ego's goal is to demonstrate his superiority over Task. He defines success as outperforming others. Consequently, Ego often gets engulfed in what we might call the *reveal–conceal syndrome*. He wants to reveal his ability when it is superior, but conceal it when it isn't.

Ego is very careful about how much effort he puts out. He recognizes that trying hard is a double-edged sword. In a match, if he hustles and wins, terrific. He achieves his goal of looking like the more talented player. However, if he tries really hard and still falls short of the victory stand, then everyone will see that he is the less talented player. Better to slack off a bit. Then if he loses, he can shrug it off. He can imply (to himself and others) that he didn't lose because he was less talented, but only because his opponent cared more and tried harder. Ego's concern, after all, isn't with demonstrating superior effort; it is with demonstrating superior ability. At the very least, he doesn't want to look incompetent. So whenever Ego's confidence starts to slip, he looks for ways to buffer the implications of loss.

Task is a true competitor. Ego leans toward decompetition.[3] Ego turns others into objects for his own purposes. Opponents are simply the canvas on which to paint the picture of his own superior ability. The more opponents resist by trying hard, the more they become a threat. They are the enemy of Ego's ego.

These two caricatures represent two types of goal orientation. In the psychological literature, they are often called *task orientation* and *ego orientation*. John Nicholls, one of the key architects of achievement motivation theory, suggested that people differ in their tendencies to become motivated in these two ways.[4] Place two people in a setting in which achievement

TWO GOAL ORIENTATIONS

Task Orientation

1. The primary goal is to develop competence.
2. Success is defined as growth (learning, improvement, mastery).
3. Success is self-referenced (measured by personal improvement).

Related beliefs

4. Effort is what really matters for success.
5. Talent and ability are not fixed and can be expanded through hard work.

Ego Orientation

1. The primary goal is to display competence.
2. Success is defined as performing better than others (winning).
3. Success is other-referenced (measured by the frequency and extent of outperforming rivals).

Related beliefs

4. Talent is more important to success than effort.
5. Talent and ability are largely fixed; effort will make relatively little difference.

matters, such as a classroom, and they may spontaneously pursue different goals. One may be motivated by the challenge to improve, learn, and grow, whereas the other may be motivated by the challenge to outperform others.

Young children are naturally task oriented.[5] They are easily absorbed in the process of learning and don't think much about how well others are doing. By later childhood, however, most people demonstrate some of both goal orientations. Over time, relatively stable tendencies develop. Just as some people tend to be shyer than others, some people find task goals more motivating, whereas others find ego goals to be more engaging. Even the shy person, though, can become a chatterbox in the right situation. In parallel fashion, a person with one goal orientation can become motivated by the other type of goal in particular contexts.[6]

In chapter 4, we saw that a person's motivational orientation (primarily intrinsic or extrinsic) has consequences. Most of the positive consequences follow from intrinsic motivation. Similarly, it matters whether a person is task or ego motivated. And the scientific literature is strikingly uniform: Most of the positive benefits flow from adopting task goals. For example, those with high task motivation[7]

- exert more effort and do so more consistently,
- persist at challenging tasks longer,
- employ more effective learning strategies,
- recover more quickly from emotional set-backs,
- develop higher perceived competence,
- experience less dysfunctional stress,
- enjoy both practices and contests more, and
- cheat less.

The last point is particularly important. The evidence here is conclusive. Those who are charged up with ego-rich motivation are more likely to cheat than those who are task motivated.[8] This is not surprising because ego-involved people are not really all that interested in the contest itself. Their primary motive is to use the contest as a stage on which to perform. Opponents are props in their one-act play titled, *See My Talent*. For some, if they need to cheat behind the scenes, so be it. This is one of the key reasons ego motivation tends to promote decompetition.

Social Comparison

A point of clarification is important here. We noted earlier that young children are naturally task oriented. One reason is that they don't yet have the cognitive abilities necessary for the pursuit of ego goals.[9] To be ego motivated, people need to be focused on how their performance stacks up relative to others. An ability to engage in *social comparison* is a prerequisite, and young children don't have that ability.

As a youngster, Stephanie thought she was a budding Rembrandt because her parents bubbled with enthusiasm whenever she showed them her scribblings. When Stephanie began to compare her artwork to that of her classmates, however, it slowly dawned on her that the lavish praise of her parents was overblown. Although such a realization may be personally unsettling, it represents an important cognitive advance. To understand what a "good" performance looks like, it is necessary to see how well other people do at it. Gradually, as children move through the upper elementary school years, they learn how to judge the quality of their own abilities by comparing their performances with those of relevant others.[10]

By the middle to late elementary years, children have developed the mental capacity for social comparison. This cognitive advance provides a launching pad for rocketing into ego motivation. However, just because people can use social comparison does not put them on an inevitable trajectory to pursue ego goals. Nor does it necessarily place them into decompetition's orbit.

Even after a child has developed the ability to use social comparison, she may still not pursue goals that require it. She may be able to assess how she stacks up relative to others, yet still choose to focus on personal growth and learning, measuring success by self-referenced progress. Whenever a person is absorbed in a task, exerting effort to improve, that person is task involved. Sure, she may notice how her performance compares with others, but that's not where her motivation is coming from. For the ego-involved individual, however, social comparison is central to her motivational system because her primary goal is to outperform others.

How does social comparison relate to competition? The difference between competitors and decompetitors is not that the latter make use of social comparison whereas the former do not. Both competitors and decompetitors may want to know how their performance compares to that of their peers. The question is *why* they want to know. What use do they make of the comparison?

Competitors engage in social comparison to gain information. They want a reasonable guide for assessing their current ability. Those who want to know their strengths and vulnerabilities must engage in social comparison. It is a process of self-discovery. Decompetitors, on the other hand, are less interested in information than in finding opportunities to flaunt superior ability. There is a subtle yet important difference between comparing performances to assess relative ability and comparing them to boost a sense of superiority. One is focused on gaining knowledge; the other is ego driven. Decompetitors turn opponents, whenever possible, into stepping-stones on a path of personal showmanship.

In short, the goal of most decompetitors is to bask in the glow of victory. An alternative form of decompetition, however, focuses on a different goal. We turn to it next.

Decompetition in D Minor

In chapter 2 we talked about how decompetition is based on a war metaphor. The decompetitor is focused on winning. His goal is conquest, to demonstrate superiority over others. The dance for this form of decompetition is inspired by the triumphal beat of a military march. It is up-beat, confident, and in-your-face. It is a fight song, shouted. It is played in D major.

A more somber form of decompetition also exists. It is played in a solemn D-minor key. Rather than focusing on winning, this alternate form of decompetition is driven by a different goal: to avoid defeat.[11] Instead of trying to demonstrate superiority, a person with this form of decompetition is focused on hiding inferiority, real or imagined. Seeking victory and avoiding defeat are two quite different goals, but both focus on outcome over process, and both are concerned with self-presentation. Both are pathways to decompetition.

Fear is the melody of decompetition when played in D minor. It is the fear of being revealed as an imposter, embarrassed by incompetence. It is the fear, finally, of feeling unworthy. Although this may seem like the opposite of the boastful confidence of the typical decompetitor, it is really just its shadow. It is the flip side of the same record. When confident, the decompetitor will dance to a D-major tune. When confidence is shaken, the goal switches, the tune changes, and the decompetitor's orientation becomes colored by fear.

Fear leads to a fight or flight response: Fight the opponent (perhaps with dishonest or deceitful means), or flee the game. Conquer or surrender. Both responses are premised on thinking of the contest through the metaphor of a battle. Both turn the opponent into the enemy. Although some decompetitors are more interested in avoiding loss or saving face than they are in pursuing victory, the underlying metaphor for the contest is the same. It is a battle.

What does the surrender response look like? It often takes the form of diminished effort, of giving up early. Decompetitors who surrender don't do so openly, but often disguise their surrender under a cloak of indifference. "I lost because I didn't really care enough to try my hardest" is the message. Understandably, those involved in a battle are self-protective. To avoid wounds to the ego, decompetitors who lack confidence in their abilities may wear a shield of apathy or a cloak of cool. If they continue to experience loss or if their confidence deteriorates, they may well drop out of the activity entirely.

Neither the fight nor flight response to fear is productive. Nor is dropping out. These negative responses are minimized with true competition. "Seeking with" another does not lead to the same vulnerabilities. In true competition, opponents are not enemies; they are partners who enable one to seek excellence.

The Ultimate Goal of True Competition

In contrast to the decompetitive goals of flashing superiority or covering inferiority, those who are involved in true competition see the contest as an opportunity to push for excellence. In the school scramble for grades, the true competitor focuses on excellence of understanding, not the grades themselves. In sports, the focus is on excellence of athletic skill; in politics, excellence in public service; in business, excellence in rendering customer satisfaction. Contests, when neither overused nor distorted by decompetition, strengthen human community and well-being by encouraging and facilitating enjoyable pursuits of excellence.

Those who experience high levels of task motivation have a boost toward true competition. As we have seen, those who are task involved pursue such goals as learning, growth, improvement, and mastery. Excellence is an

Dear Authors:

I'm a high school history teacher in a disadvantaged region of Denver. Most of the kids who populate my classroom seem totally indifferent. They are not interested in putting time into test preparation or doing extra credit to earn better grades. They certainly are not excited about learning for its own sake. Does your analysis of "decompetition in D minor" fit these kids? If so, how does it help me?

— Desperate in Denver

Dear Desperate in Denver:

Whether teachers intend it or not, most students consider school a place where they must vie for attention, recognition, and grades. Those who believe that they may not fare well in the school-as-contest may emotionally withdraw and outwardly display apathy. It may well be that many of your students fit in this category; they are ego bruised and cover their sense of academic inferiority with a cloak of indifference. What to do? Clearly, there's no simple formula. Before you can encourage these students toward true competition, you may well need to take a step back and try to develop a strong, cooperative, trusting community. Focus on building a climate of mutual encouragement. Let them know through your actions that you care about them, trust them, and believe that they can achieve. Don't give false praise, but provide opportunities for genuine accomplishment. Remember that high expectations are important, but high expectations without personal support will fall on deaf ears.

extension of those goals, the fulfillment of their trajectory. That's the reason we provide strategies for promoting task motivation in the concluding section of this chapter.

But what about ego goals? Do they signal decompetition as surely as the rising sun signals morning? It is true that where there is decompetition, people are likely embracing ego-oriented goals. Yet the reverse is not always the case. We believe that some people, at least some of the time, may pursue ego goals without slipping into decompetition. It is certainly normal for people to want to excel, and the desire to excel may be expressed as a desire to come out on top. If you're a sprinter, you want to run the fastest race. When you're up for a job, you want to be the best candidate. Wanting to be the best at something, at least at a particular moment, does not exclude you from the realm of true competition. So when does ego motivation descend into decompetition?

Let's return to basics. Decompetition comes from viewing the contest as a war, and one of the first casualties of war is truth. A sure sign of decompetition is when the person is less interested in *being* the best than in *appearing to be* the best. Seeking to win through deception or deceit, sabotage, or subterfuge is decompetition, pure and simple.

True competition, in contrast, reflects a view of the contest as a partnership. Can ego goals support such a view? Yes, if outperforming the other is not equated with being superior to the other. When contests are used to divide people into the worthy and unworthy, the better and the lesser, the gifted and the rest, then the partnership has been destroyed and true competition has been rendered impossible. Competitors appreciate the mutuality inherent in their partnership with an opponent. They recognize that all talent is fundamentally shared talent. If my performance is better than yours one day, it is because you have helped me become better. Perhaps on another day, the challenge that I provide will enable you to surpass me. Moreover, the results of the contest have very limited meaning. If we were to compete at something else, I may well be the

Ego Goals and Hedonic Adaptation

Of course, we all want to believe that we are good at something, to both develop and demonstrate our abilities. "Look at me" is not just the plea of the immature child.

If an athlete works hard only because she hopes to become a star, however, she is destined for disappointment. Few ever become stars, and the rare person who does may still not be happy. The psychological principle known as hedonic adaptation refers to people's tendency to rapidly become accustomed to present advantages.[12] The person who becomes a star may quickly adjust to her status and soon want more: to be a superstar. When the focus is on gaining status or wealth, enough is never enough.

The decompetitor is rarely satisfied with present achievements. He will always want to defeat somebody better than those he has already defeated. Decompetition puts people in a vain struggle for supremacy. Decompetitors want to demonstrate superiority over an expanding range of opponents. In such a struggle, skill development takes a backseat. It is simply a means to an end. This is out of balance.

Although true competitors may experience ego motivation intermittently, their primary goals are defined in task-oriented ways. For the true competitor, the primary focus is on *developing* competence, gaining mastery, pursuing excellence. Yes, there can be joy in *demonstrating* competence and receiving praise, but learning and growth are primary. The enjoyment of pursuing excellence is its own reward.

loser. True competitors keep the contest and the victory in perspective. Truth requires humility.

Why do we have contests? At least implicitly, the true competitor's answer is *to enable people to experience an enjoyable quest for excellence.* Such a quest enriches life, builds enthusiasm, promotes partnerships, and inspires community. Whether a person in any particular moment or situation is primarily fired up by ego or task goals is not the critical question. True, task motivation is a much more natural ally to competition than ego motivation, but ego motivation, in limited doses, is not inherently excluded. The real question is whether the participants are seeking excellence or simply using the contest for personal glorification or benefit. This brings up the questions, What is excellence, and where does it come from?

Excellence

❝ The heart of human excellence often begins to beat when you discover a pursuit that absorbs you, frees you, challenges you, or gives you a sense of meaning, joy, or passion. ❞

Terry Orlick in *The Pursuit of Excellence*

Tim Gallwey, author of the classic *The Inner Game of Tennis*, wrote, "to achieve an ambitious goal requires great effort that must come from great desire."[13] Excellence is born in desire. It is desire extended into work. It is work sustained with determination and courage through difficulty and challenge. Talent without heart, and brains without dedication, will not result in excellence.

Excellence is born in desire, but not all strong desires give birth to excellence. Excellence itself must be the goal of the desire. Desire for fame or fortune will not lead to excellence because neither fame nor fortune have much to do with it. If my goal is limited to standing atop the victory stand, I may achieve victory, but I am unlikely to achieve excellence. If, on the other hand, I yearn for excellence, I am likely to be as successful as my talents and circumstances allow.

But is this realistic? Can all true competitors really pursue excellence? Isn't excellence necessarily rare and exclusive? On the one hand, excellence can be viewed externally and objectively. In this case, excellence refers to the best that humanity can be in a particular task or domain. If asked to consider excellence in basketball, you might think of Michael Jordan and Nancy Lieberman. Who doesn't think of Albert Einstein or Madam Curie when the topic of excellence in science is raised? Excellence in morality is often associated with people such as Mother Teresa. Such people provide useful models. They are exemplars. However, no matter how long I practice basketball, I'm not going to join the NBA. Does this rule out my pursuit of excellence in this area?

Competitors seek self-referenced excellence. My excellence is different from yours. What I can pursue is an excellent version of me. That doesn't mean that excellence is limited by a person's self-imposed restrictions, however. Most people have greater capabilities and capacities than they realize. Competition teaches us that we have deep reservoirs of energy, creativity, and capacity beyond those that we have previously tapped.

Seeking excellence often involves breaking out from the prison of our own limited expectations. To reach personal excellence requires pushing beyond comfort, doubt, fear, and a myriad of self-imposed boundaries. *Beyond* is defined as an expanding horizon that one can never quite reach. Excellence is a journey that is never fully completed. It is a journey of self-discovery, and the journey is what matters. Excellence is more about process than outcome.

Progress toward excellence requires sustained focus and attention to detail. The goal of excellence is the big picture, but like a digital photograph, it is comprised of tiny pixels of mini-goals. If life were a room, excellence would not just be in the neatly arranged furniture. It would be in the cracks, under the chairs, hiding in the corners. In sports, excellence is not just exhibited in the game; it is revealed first in the practice. In the classroom, it is not just

What does *excellence* mean to you? Can a backup player be excellent? To what extent is excellence an individual accomplishment?

exhibited on the test, but in the daily mastery of knowledge. Excellence is pursued through a thousand little steps more than a few giant leaps.

Excellence also requires a healthy dose of pride. It requires believing in our own value and worth. There is no point in working so hard for excellence if I believe that a primary benefactor—myself—is unworthy of the effort. That sense of worthiness, however, must be the ground, the starting point, for the quest for excellence. We don't earn worthiness by becoming excellent. We must begin with a sense of *intrinsic* worthiness that is not based on performance or productivity. I am worthy because I am a human being with dignity. Without that rock-solid sense of intrinsic worthiness as the starting point, the quest for excellence will become warped into an effort, doomed from the outset, to prove self-worth. When that becomes the goal, decompetition infests the process.

Beyond the Individual

Excellence is also a journey into community. It takes a village not only to raise a child, but also to approach excellence. The star athlete who explains to the media that she could not have scored the winning point if not for her teammates is not just being modest. She is sharing a truth. Excellence relies on community. As Isaac Newton said, "If I have seen further than others, it is by standing upon the shoulders of giants."

The goal of the true competitor is to seek excellence, but not just solo excellence. The competitor asks two questions: "How can I bring out my best?" and, "How can I bring out the best in others?" Excellence finds nourishment in service.[14] It builds on community and gives back to community. Consider a sport program. Almost any team can have a good year, but an excellent program requires consistently good years. That happens through the process of crafting a vision, planning carefully, and working hard. We're not talking

Excellence in the Classroom

In his inspiring book, *An Ethic of Excellence*, elementary school teacher Ron Berger writes that individual excellence is best nurtured through a culture of excellence. He laments the fact that so much of our current educational policy, focused as it is on artificial and external forms of accountability, directly interferes with developing such school communities. To build a culture of excellence in the classroom, we need models of excellence. We also need to focus on work that matters, building a commitment to progressive revision and supportive peer critique, and public presentation. Although Berger doesn't directly address competition, ironically the title of his book defines the very core of competition. The book is a terrific read. If you're an educator, you might want to pick it up.

about joyless work, but determined effort sustained by the abundant energy that flows from having a purpose. When the community, the team, embraces the vision, then each individual is able to commit to a transcendent value. When that happens, excellence takes hold in the collective.

Beyond Winning

Excellence does not depend on outward success, and it is critical to distinguish the two. The goal of the true competitor is excellence, not victory. Of course, true competitors want to win (more on this in chapter 8), but winning is not essential to feeling successful. When Michelle Kwan failed to win the gold in the 1996 Winter Olympics, she was asked by a reporter to describe her disappointment. Undeterred by the question, she responded that her goal was to do her best, that she felt she had, and that she felt very good about it.[15] Sports writers and sportscasters often ask questions that reflect our culture's obsession with winning. They asked the same question of Lance Armstrong when he won the bronze. Armstrong acknowledged that on that day, other riders were faster. Was he disappointed? No. He had done his best and was pleased with his medal.[16]

Bonnie Blair is one of the most celebrated speed skaters of all time. In the 1988 Calgary Olympics, her rival, Christa Rothenburger of East Germany, set a world record. It was a record that didn't last long. Blair skated next and captured the gold, setting a new world record time of 39.1 seconds. Five years later, at the age of 30, Blair met her ultimate goal of shattering the 39-second mark with a time of 38.99. After Blair retired from speed skating, she was asked about her best race. She didn't name the Calgary Olympics, or her second world-record race. She pointed to, of all things, a 1,500-meter race in the 1994 Olympics in which she didn't even medal. Why? "It was my first personal best since the 1988 Olympics. I had won gold in the five hundred and one thousand [in 1994], but that was the best I could be in the fifteen hundred."[17] Excellence is about finding one's personal boundaries.

The life of legendary runner Steve Prefontaine (Pre), who died at age 24 in a tragic car accident, is memorialized in the movie *Without Limits*. In the film, his coach (played by Donald Sutherland) speaks at Pre's funeral. In a slightly edited version, here is what he said:[18]

> **❝ All of my life, I've operated under the assumption that the main idea in running was to win the damn race. I tried to teach Pre how to do that. Tried like hell to teach Pre to do that. And Pre taught me. Taught me I was wrong. Pre, you see, was troubled by knowing that a mediocre effort can win a race and a magnificent effort can lose one. Winning a race wouldn't necessarily demand that he give it everything**

> **he had from start to finish. He finally got it through my head that the real purpose of running isn't to win a race. It's to test the limits of the human heart.** "

Accepting Limits

Excellence is about testing limits and seeking to surpass them. The film title *Without Limits*, however, is misleading. There are limits. Excellence is not perfection. Prefontaine's best race was not a perfect race, and Pre was not a perfect person. Nor are we. Excellence is not about denying our vulnerability, our shortcomings, and our weaknesses. We are all limited beings. To put on a mask of invincibility distracts us from the pursuit of excellence. To dream the impossible dream is not helpful.

Seeking excellence, far from requiring us to turn a blind eye to our inevitable failings, requires us to be fully honest with ourselves. That entails admitting our weaknesses. Perfection is not the goal; perfectionism is not a virtue.[19] Becoming the best that we can be—given our limitations—is the goal. And even that is a goal that we will never fully achieve. It is the striving that is important. To progress well on our journey, we need to strive with focus, determination, and energy, but also with a sense of humility and humor. We need to be charitable with ourselves and others.

In her book *Embracing Victory*, former Stanford and professional basketball star Mariah Burton Nelson relays the story of Anne Audain. Anne ran in her first Olympics in 1976 and her last in 1988.[20] In 1981 Audain competed in her first 5,000 meters. The result? She broke the world record. Altogether, she had a 22-year career as a top-flight competitive runner. This is a remarkable career for any athlete, but perhaps especially for someone who had been born with deformed feet and underwent extensive surgeries as a young teenager. In an interview, Nelson asked the retired star how she had managed to stay injury free for more than two decades of competitive running. "Maybe because of what I went through with my feet—all that rehabilitation and physical therapy—I learned to listen to my body, and never pushed past stress and into injury," she replied. Accepting limits is important.

The epidemic use of performance-enhancing drugs and hormones in sports is a symptom of a reckless disregard for limits. Excellence is not just about performance. It is even more about the quality of the path that leads to performance. Drug use sacrifices the future for the present, excellence for expedience. From the standpoint of true competition, whether there is an immediate boost in performance is irrelevant. Invariably, the use of such performance enhancers is decompetitive because it is not about pursuing excellence and enjoyment through the challenge posed by the opponent within the structure of game rules. It is only about seeking to exploit the situation for self-benefit. Ultimately, it also sacrifices the self.

Dear Authors:

I find your discussion of performance-enhancing drugs superficial. I am a collegiate shot-putter, and I don't want to sacrifice excellence for expedience, as you say. I would prefer that none of us use steroids or HGH. But I'm simply trying to "keep up with the Joneses." I have a good shot at going to the Olympic trials next year. How can you expect me to put myself at a disadvantage by not doing what I know many of my opponents are doing? Is that fair?

— Reluctant User

Dear Reluctant User:

You raise a very important issue and one that many of us wrestle with. But the claim to have the moral norm of "fairness" on your side is questionable. Let us try to answer your question with a few of our own: If you have a daughter and she says that others are cheating in school, would you recommend that she cheat as well? If the CEO of a pharmaceutical company thinks competitors might be fudging the results of a drug trial to gain an advantage, should the CEO fudge his own data? If you're an airline mechanic and you think that competitive carriers are reducing costs through shoddy maintenance checks, should you do so as well? Of course, all these things happen. But should they? Where does the downward spiral end? Decompetition, unfortunately, tends to beget more decompetition. The only way out is for each person to accept moral responsibility, and that, frankly, sometimes entails putting yourself at competitive risk. If you are unwilling to be a true competitor, it may be time to exit the contest.

Character

We noted earlier that excellence is born in desire. Desire reflects our inner priorities, what we most deeply cherish. Because this is true, it is also true that our pursuit of excellence is inseparable from our character. Our character mirrors what is important to us. It reflects our ability to exercise self-control and determination in the pursuit of what we care about. Excellence is unimaginable apart from solid character.

Some talented athletes manifest questionable morality. Some successful entrepreneurs build profitable companies through less-than-honorable means. Public officials win elections through subterfuge. Some straight A students cheat. Don't these observations contradict what we're saying? Don't they suggest that good character is not necessary for success? Yes, if by *success* we mean victory on the scoreboard. No, if by *success* we mean maximizing our potential.

When we were codirectors of the Mendelson Center at the University of Notre Dame, we designed a coaching education program built around the theme, "Play Like a Champion." At first, some people objected: "Why are you focusing on champions? Is winning really all that's important?" We would answer their question with one of our own, "Does a champion always win?" Invariably, the answer was no. Champions do not always win. A better view of a champion is a person who *champions* the ideals of his or her sport. A champion is interested in excellence, not just performance. True champions engage in true competition.

Good character involves looking beyond the self. It involves commitment to ideals, values, and moral principles that are bigger and broader than the individual. Similarly, pursuing excellence is a much larger endeavor than simply trying to perform at one's best. It involves being the best person one can be. Excellence walks hand in hand with justice and compassion. It breathes integrity. In contest situations, staying focused on true competition builds both performance skills and character.

Virtue

Millennia ago, Aristotle had it right. He believed that the good life is found in striving for excellence and in dedicating one's talents to the pursuit of worthy goals. He used the contexts of both sports and crafts to illustrate how striving for excellence is the very essence of virtue. According to Aristotle, exercising one's capacities, developing them fully, and placing them in the service of a communal good were worthy goals. Interestingly, the words *virtue* and *excellence* have both been used to translate the classical Greek word *arête,* which is the central concept in Plato and Aristotle's ethical thought.[21] Excellence, according to this line of thinking, is not just about performance. It's about becoming the best human beings we can become. It is about developing the virtues that define excellent character.

Aristotle also emphasized the importance of balance in a person's life. Should a person sacrifice all else to achieve excellence in a specific skill or endeavor? Let's explore this for a moment.

Balance

Imagine that we could take a baby and begin a training program that would optimize her capacity to play tennis. Even in the crib, we would intervene to develop rudimentary skills needed for the sport. As she got older, we would structure all of her time and activities to build her tennis skills. In reality, of course, such a program would be an utter failure. But imagine it could work. Would the result be excellence? From a narrow performance perspective, perhaps. From a broader perspective, however, the answer is clearly no. Regardless of the level of skill she ultimately obtained, she would live a narrow and distorted life, not an excellent one.

To achieve any meaningful goal, devotion is important. There is nothing wrong (and often something admirable) about dedicating a major portion of one's time and energy to a singular purpose. But there still needs to be balance. Einstein had interests beyond physics. Michael Jordan did not spend all his time playing basketball.

There's no easy formula for determining what makes for an appropriate balance in a person's life. Perhaps the best gauge of adequate balance is a person's sense of identity. Does a person wrap all of his or her sense of self into a single domain? If so, it is problematic. Athletes who do not have identities beyond the playing field or court are at greater risk of decompetition than those who have multiple interests and commitments. To become so dedicated to one endeavor that all else falls by the wayside invariably leads to decompetition. If baseball is all one lives for, then a failure in baseball is catastrophic. Such an attitude, once again, turns the opponent into an enemy.

In our culture, we are action focused and tend to equate excellence with astonishing, mouth-dropping performances. Excellence, though, needs to also drink from the quiet wells of reflection and contemplation. Similarly, there is a time to be an athlete and a time to be a lover, an artist, an intellectual, a mystic. Most important, there is a time to compete and a time to set aside all competition. Although contesting with others can be a noble path toward excellence, it is not the only one. Competitors must also acknowledge, embrace, and celebrate other paths to excellence. There is a time to contest, and a time to come together in other ways. Everyone needs to find a sense of balance that includes values other than those based on performance and contest.

True competition occurs when contestants give their all in the pursuit of excellence. They do so respecting both opponents and their own limits. Their quest for excellence springs from their inner character and serves the larger community. It is a quest that balances narrow focus with broader values. Sustaining true competition is never easy, but it becomes even more challenging when participants bring to the contest their own insecurities and problems. We turn now to a consideration of psychological dynamics that tend to draw participants into decompetition.

The Threat of Insecurity

> " Big egos are big shields for lots of empty space. "
>
> Diana Black

In chapter 4, we suggested that the balance needed for true competition can be threatened by external rewards. The greater the prize for victory, the stronger the pull toward decompetition. Why? Because external benefits lure us away from intrinsic motivation. Rewards stimulate desire, and the roar coming from our desire for victory's loot can drown out the whisper coming from our desire for the intrinsic benefits of participation. Our own long-term interest, however, is better served by listening to the whisper. How do we tune our ears to the whisper? It's simple (in concept): We *choose* to do so. Like a good pair of noise-canceling earphones, consciously choosing true competition can amplify the whisper and minimize the static.

When rewards for winning are high, it is also difficult to sustain task motivation and to stay focused on learning, improvement, enjoyment, and self-referenced goals. True enough. But we've already discussed the issue of rewards in chapter 4. In this chapter, in our search for forces that push us toward decompetition, we shift our focus from external factors to internal ones. Specifically, certain psychological qualities or conditions, much like rewards, grease the slide into decompetition. Learning to recognize these qualities within ourselves and others can help to reduce their potency.

Let's be clear. None of us are models of pure psychological health. We all have wounded egos and buttons that can be pushed. We state this obvious truth because it is important to recognize that virtually all deviations from optimal psychological health, large and small, can become points of entry for decompetition. And we all have such points of vulnerability.

In his book *No Contest: The Case Against Competition*, Alfie Kohn argues that the psychological root of people's desire to compete is insecurity. The ultimate reason people contest, Kohn suggests, is to compensate for small or wounded egos. We compete to compensate for low self-esteem, hoping that in victory we can win feelings of self-worth. Kohn goes on to argue that the effort to gain self-esteem through competition is doomed to failure from the outset. Every victory generates the fear that defeat looms just around the corner. When self-worth is tied to defeating others, it is inherently unstable, leading to an ever-increasing need for further affirmations.

We do not agree that competition stems from feelings of inadequacy, low self-esteem, or other forms of psychological insecurity. Nonetheless, we do believe that such feelings and needs can easily trigger decompetition. When a person experiences a need to be better than others, whatever the psychological source of those feelings, then the pathway into decompetition has been cleared. Decompetition is highly likely whenever people feel an inner compulsion to win, rather than just a desire to win. Insecurities are often the source of that need.

We're not, of course, going to ask you to hop on the couch and spill your guts. Nor are we going to play therapist or pop psychologist. Our point is simply this: Winning is a salve that many use to dress a variety of psychological wounds. Regardless of the specific origins of our insecurities, the heightened stresses and pressures of the contest are likely to bring them to the fore and, unless we are careful, stimulate decompetition.

Although virtually any psychological deficiency or weakness can provide an entryway for decompetition, one in particular deserves attention because of its pervasiveness. We speak of insecurities stemming from distorted concepts of gender.

The Role of Gender

One source of decompetition is the insecurities created by gender stereotypes.[22, 23] For some men, decompetition is simply *manly* and is used to buttress a sense of masculinity. For such a person, an aggressive, dominance-seeking, in-your-face style of contesting is an outward expression of an inward definition of what it means to be male. In this view, men should have a killer instinct; they are supposed to go for the jugular; they ought to engage in testosterone-driven reckless behavior. Hostility, combativeness, king-of-the-mountain belligerence—these prove manliness. It is good to be bad. Conquering is masculine; defeat is emasculating. For boys and men with such a warrior view of masculinity, one of the extrinsic rewards for winning is an enhanced sense of male potency.

Where do young boys get their ideas of masculinity? Parents, siblings, friends, teachers and the media certainly play a role. For a great many boys, sports also play the role of gender educator. Sports are important places for learning about what it means to be masculine. Too often, boys learn that

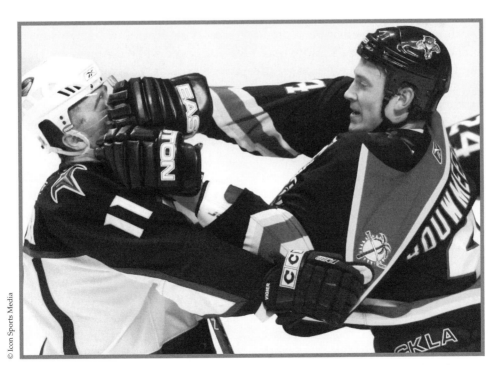

Does a warrior view of masculinity lead to decompetition in sports, or do boys learn from decompetitive sports a warrior view of masculinity?

to "take it like a man" means to deny pain. Openly or subtly, they may be taught that violence is manly, that physical strength equals psychological power, that exercising power *over* another is more manly than exercising power *with* another. Even if most boys in sports don't totally embrace these views, the pervasiveness of such views in many athletic settings is likely to rub off to some extent.

A prominent feature of this view of masculinity is that it is defined in opposition to a rigid and denigrated view of the feminine.[24] Boys are chided to not be pussies. They are told not to throw or play "like a girl." Coaches have been known to put tampons in the lockers of underperforming boys. In this view, males and females are opposites. Girls are weak; boys are strong. Gals are soft; guys are rugged. Women care about others; men watch out for number one. When boys think of males and females as opposites, they may similarly think of competition and cooperation as opposites and opposed to each other. They are likely to view the partnership metaphor that underlies true competition as somehow feminine.

Thinking in terms of opposites and dualities, however, is simply distorted thinking.[25] It exaggerates difference and values extremes. Because no one really fits these rigid stereotypes, embracing them leads to insecurities and an exaggerated emphasis on aggressiveness and dominance (in males). Once again, this can quickly lead to decompetition and all of its attendant problems.

Decompetition, however, is not just a male problem. It also lurks in the shadows of the insecurities created by stereotypic femininity. According to one cultural script, girls and women are supposed to be diminutive. They are not supposed to compete for power, position, or recognition. The only domain in which they are allowed to contest is for male attention. Girls who embrace this view may enter beauty pageants. They may seek to be the best dressed, the youngest looking, or the most sexy. They may seek first to become stereotypic cheerleaders and then trophy wives. By their very nature, such "contests" are invariably decompetitive. All that really matters is winning.

To unleash the power of true competition and benefit from its dynamics, we must embrace open and flexible views of gender. We are not interested in rehashing the old fruitless debate about whether some traits are inherently more masculine or feminine. We are simply emphasizing the obvious: Men can be tender, kind, compassionate, weak, and nurturing. They can be soft and caring. They can be dependent. They can lose and cry. There is nothing unmasculine about these qualities, which are universal to the human experience. Strength comes from flexibility, not rigidity. Girls and women, on the other hand, can be, and often are, powerful, strong, combative, and assertive. And there is nothing unfeminine about these qualities. "Throwing like a girl" can be a compliment because many girls throw much better than many boys. With more flexible views of gender, some will not feel as drawn into the self-defeating dynamics of decompetition.

Although the rigidity of the old-school views of gender have eased considerably over the past decades, they are still alive. They hang around like house guests who have overstayed their welcome. They continue to flourish in the media. Challenging them is essential to supporting and sustaining true competition. Similar problems, of course, lie in other forms of stereotype, prejudice, and discrimination. These can create insecurities that lead, in contest settings, to a need to achieve victory in an effort to prove personal worth or the value of one's group. All such efforts push toward decompetition. Consequently, leaders who are interested in promoting true competition need also be concerned about reducing every form of prejudice and discrimination within their team or organization. This is a challenging task, no doubt, but a critical one.

This brings us to the final topic of the chapter. In the next few pages, we discuss how leaders can promote true competition. In this section, we are especially focused on how they can encourage a high level of task motivation that can drive the quest for excellence.

Leading for Excellence

❝ What you get by achieving your goals is not as important as what you have become by achieving your goals. ❞

Zig Ziglar

At the beginning of the chapter, we noted that task and ego motivation are somewhat like personality characteristics. These motivational tendencies are relatively stable. Some people are drawn more to ego goals, whereas others get fired up by embracing task goals. However, these motivational tendencies can be modified. Different situations will encourage people to adopt one type of goal more than the other. The leader who is interested in promoting true competition would do well to create an environment that elicits and supports task motivation. When people are highly motivated by task goals, they more easily walk the path toward excellence.

The leader who adopts the goal of promoting task motivation, however, is immediately confronted with a challenge. Like catnip luring a feline, contests tend to elicit ego goals. The outcome of a contest, after all, is a declared winner. Unless you want to enter the winner's circle, it is unlikely that you will voluntarily enter the contest. Learning, growth, enjoyment, mastery—these goals are easily pursued outside of contests, but the quickest path to demonstrating superiority is to contest with others. Even for the person who is normally motivated by task goals, contests offer a seductive temptation to shift into ego motivation.

This is one of the reasons decompetition is the default approach to contests. To engage in true competition, you have to override the default setting so that you and your opponents can reap the benefits. Stated differently, to reach the summit of enjoyment and excellence, you have to climb the mountain of true competition. Doing so requires overcoming the gravity of decompetition. It requires maintaining high task motivation in a structure that pulls toward ego motivation.

Although contests have a natural tendency to prompt ego motivation, leaders can make quite a difference. Whether the setting is a home, a sport team, a classroom, or an organization, leaders (parents, coaches, teachers, administrators) can help to determine the types of goals that are pursued. They don't have complete control over the motivation of the participants, but they do have influence. To promote true competition, they need to use that influence to amplify task motivation and its connection to the pursuit of excellence and enjoyment.

To elicit or strengthen task motivation, leaders need to build what psychologists call a *mastery motivational climate*.[26] A mastery climate is simply one that pulls toward task motivation. How do leaders create such a climate? The short answer is by building a culture in which learning, improvement, growth, teamwork, and cooperation are highly valued. In a mastery climate, these outcomes are more prized than winning the contest.

Mike Krzyzewski, head coach of the men's basketball team at Duke University, presides over one of the most successful programs in college basketball history. He writes: "Our goal is not to win. It is to play together and play hard. Then winning takes care of itself."[27] Of course, Coach K cares about winning, but he is crystal clear about the priority: to play well.

A leader can use a number of strategies to create a mastery climate. We summarize them by using the acronym FAIR. The FAIR strategies are *focusing, appreciating, individualizing*, and *reframing*.[28]

To create a mastery climate, leaders can help *focus* attention appropriately, *appreciate* each athlete and his or her unique contributions, *individualize* expectations and goals for each person, and *reframe* the contest as an opportunity for contributing to personal fulfillment and growth in community. Focusing, appreciating, individualizing, and reframing are broad strategies that can be used across a range of situations, both in training and in actual competition. They are strategies for infusing the competitive experience with an emphasis on excellence and enjoyment. In the following sections, we elaborate on each.

FAIR Strategy 1: Focusing

We've all heard the old joke, "Don't think of elephants." Of course, uttering such a statement has the opposite effect: After hearing it, we cannot help but think of elephants.

Broad				Narrow
Excellence	Effort	Learning	Strategy	Specific
Enjoyment	Enthusiasm	Improvement	Technique	Cues

Continuum of focus.

One of the most powerful tools available to any leader is the ability to focus attention. In a contest, attention is easily drawn to results, to the score, to who is ahead of whom. Even in a practice, attention is often drawn to comparative performance. That natural tendency is part of a contest's gravitational pull toward decompetition. In most situations, it needs to be resisted.

The smart leader directs attention away from results, outcomes, and comparative performances, not by saying, "don't think about the score" (which will have the opposite effect), but by focusing attention elsewhere. The appropriate focus depends on the context. If we want to shed light on the broad goals of true competition, excellence and enjoyment are the appropriate foci. Often, however, we need to focus attention narrowly and help the person become fully absorbed in a highly specific dimension of the situation. Figure 5.1 shows a continuum of focus.

Starting from the left side, the ultimate goal of the true competitor is the enjoyment-rich pursuit of excellence in a valued activity or domain. Ideally, everything else that the competitor does flows from and serves that goal. But focusing on excellence and enjoyment is like bringing a lantern into a dark room; the broad panorama is revealed, but the eyes still don't know where to focus.

A narrower focus is provided by an emphasis on effort and enthusiasm. Elevating effort over outcome is a major key to unlocking the jewels of task motivation. Encouraging enthusiasm and mutual support also augments task motivation by underscoring the cooperative and fun dimensions of the context. Belief in the power of effort to improve our ability is central to staying

Effort and Outcome

Jim Thompson of the Positive Coaching Alliance suggests that coaches specifically look for opportunities to zero in on unsuccessful performances, not to criticize the outcome, but to praise the effort. It's good advice. If coaches (or teacher or parents or supervisors) want those under their guidance to focus on effort and enthusiasm, they must unambiguously communicate that these qualities are valued *above* outcomes. Praising effort when the performance is unsuccessful offers such an unambiguous message.

energized and enthusiastic. When the coach sees either effort or enthusiasm diminishing, it is time to focus the competitor's attention on them.

More specific than effort and enthusiasm are learning and improvement. To further support task motivation, the leader should help contestants focus on learning over performance, improvement over objective success. Learning, of course, is a central goal for those who are task motivated. A key advantage to focusing on learning and improvement is that they are much more within the control of the competitor than are outcomes. The winner of a contest may be decided by the skill of the opponent, by the officiating, by luck, or by a number of extraneous factors. In other words, contestants have only limited control over the contest's outcome, but they can control their effort and whether they learn something from it. Coaches should help athletes stay focused on what they can control: effort and enthusiasm, improvement and learning.

Learning and improvement, of course, are facilitated by a focus on specific strategies and techniques. These are the key components that comprise the fundamental skill sets relevant to success in the contest. Even decompetitive coaches will emphasize these. Leaders should continually help athletes connect mastery of the strategies and techniques to the larger goals and foci—learning and improvement, effort and enthusiasm, and ultimately the pursuit of excellence and enjoyment.

© Human Kinetics

Both competitive and decompetitive coaches are likely to offer a diver feedback about body alignment. How might they offer that feedback? Try to identify as many different ways as you can.

Finally, in the immediate situation, it is often helpful to focus attention quite narrowly. To avoid all internal and external distractions, attention may be directed like a pinpoint laser to a precise detail. When attention is concentrated in a very specific way, it can help the person stay absorbed in a task-relevant goal. For example, when Tim Gallwey coaches tennis, he often encourages players to focus on where the ball makes contact with the racket. He discourages them from thinking about the effectiveness of the hit, focusing only on the detail of where contact is made. Interestingly, he finds that learning tends to occur most rapidly when attention is directed not on the outcome, but on a relevant cue.[29]

FAIR Strategy 2: Appreciating

We have already mentioned how important it is to appreciate effort. Regardless of whether the effort leads to the intended outcome, the effort itself needs to be appreciated. Now we want to emphasize the importance of appreciating each individual, regardless of his or her level of skill. The two ideas fit together: When effort is celebrated, everyone is on an equal footing.

In a mastery climate, the bit player, the backup, and the second-stringer are appreciated and celebrated as much as the top performer. In any great team effort, the whole is always greater than the sum of its parts, and the performance of the whole rests on the respect and trust everyone has for everyone else. Although every group will have its stars, the effective leader highlights the interdependence of the whole and affirms each individual.

Appreciating each person's effort and contribution helps to infuse a spirit of cooperation within the team. Teams that sizzle in the heat of competition have long soaked in the marinade of cooperation. You can almost taste their effectiveness, drawing as it does from the spices of shared affirmation. In this, the leader sets the example by highlighting the importance of each person, each role, each skill, and the group as a whole.

But, you may point out, everyone is not the same. Some people are simply better than others. From one perspective this is obviously true. Not all members of a team will receive the same accolades from the public or external audience. That is OK. On a professional sport team, salaries will be determined by management's perception of relative worth. Endorsement contracts will be more lucrative for those with greater public appeal. That is fine. Even on a high school team, some will be starters; others, backups. The same principle is true, of course, in other contexts. On the job, some will get promoted over others.

Building a spirit of mutual appreciation and cooperation does not require distorting the truth of differential skills and contributions. In fact, hiding the truth is never helpful, but neither is focusing on one side of the truth. Although we may be unequal in talent, we are equal from a moral standpoint. And in a team effort, everyone is vital. Just because there is more flour in a pizza than cheese does not mean that the mozzarella is less important.

Appreciating everyone equally is the recipe for success; success in the whole-grain sense of true competition.

FAIR Strategy 3: Individualizing

Those in leadership roles also need to individualize their expectations about the quantity and quality of effort that each individual can make at any given time. High expectations are important—vital, in fact. However, it is equally important that those expectations be realistic and tethered to the unique circumstances and goals of each individual. A 10-year-old might be on a soccer team to enjoy time with friends, whereas her friend might be on the team because she is eager to develop her budding skills. The coach of both children should emphasize effort, while recognizing that the latter child is more likely to practice on her own than the former.

By mid-adolescence, a high level of devotion to the team and its goals is an appropriate expectation of every participant. Even then, though, goals need to be individualized. Developing goals with input from the athletes can focus attention on effort and learning.[30] Good goals are tailored to each individual, and progress is measured against that person's own previous performance. To be most effective in supporting task motivation, goals should be challenging but achievable. Goals that are either too easy or impossible to achieve are not helpful.

Individualized goals should also focus more on process than outcome. It is better to have a goal of completing the follow-through on jump shots than of making 40 percent of them. The goal should focus on an aspect of strategy or skill that needs improvement, but should not be tied to achieving a certain outcome. This is because outcomes focus the learner's attention on things that are not always within his control. Also, a focus on outcome can create stress that interferes with learning. The sailor can learn to trim the sails correctly, but she can't control how quickly she will make it across the lake.

When working to individualize goals, leaders should encourage learners to state goals positively rather than negatively. Like the instruction to stop thinking about elephants, goals that are stated in negative terms are often counterproductive. From a motivational standpoint, it feels better to accomplish something positive than to overcome something negative. This suggestion also fits with the frequent advice of performance gurus to build on strengths rather than focus on weaknesses.

Finally, leaders must not forget the team. Group goals help the team focus on working together. Such goals, of course, also need to be individualized to the unique strengths and characteristics of the team. Team goals, which should also be focused on process and stated in positive terms, can focus on performance, such as improved communication during huddles, or on improving team chemistry, such as encouraging every player who comes off the floor for a substitution.

FAIR Strategy 4: Reframing

Reframing is about changing the way a person thinks. This book is about reframing contests as a special form of cooperation in which opponents push each other toward excellence. We hope leaders will join in this effort to reframe how we think about the process of competition.

To help create a mastery climate, leaders must reframe the concept of making mistakes. Typically, we think of making a mistake as an occasion for embarrassment, a signal of incompetence. Most learners tend to view mistakes as negatives to be avoided. Mistakes, however, need to be reframed as positives. A very important part of unleashing the power of effort is to reframe mistakes as opportunities. They are to be welcomed. In all learning processes, mistakes are common and a natural consequence of trying hard to master something new.

John Wooden once said, "The team that makes the most mistakes will probably win."[31] Most likely, that observation was never tested empirically, yet it does highlight the important fact that mistakes are a valuable part of the learning process. Leaders and their charges should consider whether the mistake was a result of poor concentration, of focusing on the wrong thing, of a skill not yet mastered, or of a misunderstanding. Mistakes can be opportunities to promote learning. They should be treated seriously, even greeted with enthusiasm and support.

A final reframing strategy is an amplification of the one about mistakes: Make every defeat into a win. No one looks forward to defeats, but they do provide clear teaching moments. Leaders should find what went well when the team went down. This not only increases the likelihood of task motivation, but it is also a solid formula for success. Building on the positive is a more effective strategy for success than highlighting the negative. Although constructive criticism has its place, it is easier to overcoming shortcomings if one is confident and assured. Whether the team won or lost shouldn't determine the positive or negative tone of the leader's response. The leader should remain positive and focused on the effort and the benefit of the mistakes. Despite the letdown, the leader is in a position to lift up the opportunity for growth that the opponent has created. In the next chapter, we elaborate further on relations with opponents. ■

1   In this chapter, we limit ourselves to contests in which people are interested in achievement and in which outcomes are determined to a significant extent by participants' game-relevant effort and abilities. We are not considering, for example, games of chance.

2   Some of the more influential early works on achievement motivation include Duda (1987), Gill and Deeter (1988), Nicholls (1978, 1989), and Roberts (1989). A good summary of more recent work on achievement motivation within this same tradition can be found in Roberts, Treasure, and Conroy (2007).

3   We are not suggesting that every person who has a high dispositional tendency toward becoming ego involved in contest situations will necessarily be a decompetitor. However,

(continued)

(continued from previous page)

they are certainly at greater risk. We base this conclusion on the positive correlation that most researchers have found between ego orientation and a range of problematic moral variables, including approval of poor sport behaviors and aggression (for a review, see Shields & Bredemeier, 2007). Reflecting on this same literature, Glyn Roberts and colleagues (Roberts, Treasure, & Conroy, 2007) wrote: "Competitive sport often places individuals in conflicting situations that emphasize winning over sportspersonship and fair play. It would be wrong, however, to attribute this to the competitive nature of sport. The results just cited suggest that it is *not* the competitive context in itself that is the issue. Rather, it may be the salience of ego involvement in the athletic environment that induces differential concern for moral behavior and cheating, rules, respect for officials, and fair play conventions among young players" (p. 10). Despite extensive evidence that high ego motivation is associated with problematic attitudes and behavior, it is important to emphasize that task and ego orientations are orthogonal, and both are influenced by contextual cues. As a result, a person with a high dispositional ego orientation might sustain a truly competitive orientation if, for example, that person is also high in dispositional task orientation and situational cues support task motivation. These are conjectures that need further empirical investigation.

4   See Nicholls (1978, 1989).

5   Young children are more task oriented in their motivation than adults are largely because they conflate the concepts of effort and ability. An ego orientation becomes possible only with cognitive advancement, enabling them to distinguish and coordinate these two concepts (Nichols, 1978, 1989).

6   We side with those who suggest that the task and ego motivational orientations are orthogonal. Although this is the view of Nicholls, Duda, and Roberts, for example, others (e.g., Dweck, 1999) have argued that the two orientations are bipolar and that a person high on one must, of necessity, be low on the other (for a discussion, see Duda, 2001). We concur with those who see the motivational orientations as orthogonal, but we do see competition and decompetition as dichotomous. Thus, a person who is heavily committed to true competition will, of necessity, reject decompetition.

7   For a review of the antecedents and consequences of task and ego motivation, see Roberts, Treasure, and Conroy (2007).

8   See the reviews by Kavussanu (2007) and Shields and Bredemeier (2007).

9   An ability to engage in social comparison is a prerequisite for adopting an ego orientation. Just as important is the ability to distinguish among and coordinate the concepts of effort, ability, task difficulty, and luck. Young children, for example, conflate the concepts of effort and ability, which precludes adopting ego goals. By the age of 12, most children have gained the cognitive prerequisites for embracing ego goals (Nicholls, 1978).

10 There are multiple perspectives on the process of social comparison. For an excellent collection of readings, see Stapel (2007). For an influential early essay on how social comparison fits within the competitive process, see Scanlan (1978).

11 For a discussion of the motivational dynamics involved in avoidance goals, such as avoiding defeat, see Elliot (1999, 2005).

12 For a discussion of hedonic adaptation, see Lyubomirsky (2007), especially pp. 48-52.

13 Gallwey (2000), p. 223.

14 This connection of excellence, community, and service is not just fanciful thinking. Excellence requires optimal functioning, and optimal functioning requires appropriate activation of relevant regions of the brain. Though we still have much to learn about how human interactions affect the brain, evidence suggests that there may at least be a correlation between positive engagement with others and beneficial and differentiated activation. See, for example, Urry and colleagues (2004).

15   The quote from Michelle Kwan is from Gallwey (2000), p. 128. High-profile, elite athletes, of course, are well trained in the art of self-presentation, and their comments cannot be taken at face value. Whether Ms. Kwan was completely sincere, however, is not our primary concern. The truth of the insight that she expressed is independent of whether she fully believed in it herself (though she may have). We quote from her and other high-profile athletes and coaches not to suggest that they are ideal competitors, but simply to illustrate our points.

16   Armstrong is quoted in Mastrich (2002), p. 78.

17   Quoted in Nelson (1998), p. 274.

18   This story is also recounted in Thompson (2003), p. 20.

19   For more on the dangers of perfectionism, see Flett and Hewitt (2002).

20   Nelson (1998), p. 223.

21   Our point about *excellence* and *virtue* both being translations of the same Greek word is based on Clifford and Feezell (1997), p. 15.

22   My treatment of gender draws both from Nelson (1998) and Messner (2007).

23   In this section, we focus on masculinity and femininity. These, of course, are important aspects of a person's identity. It is also important to emphasize that other aspects of a person's identity and culture may sometimes give them a shove toward decompetition. The great American myth portrays the rugged, isolated individual. In reality, we are all part of groups. The groups to which we belong influence how we think about ourselves. All of us, for example, are influenced by our race and class, and we see ourselves as having a particular sexual orientation. Many of us have a particular religious identity. We may associate with a particular ethnic group, political view, or occupational category. All of these can influence how we approach contests. All have unique strengths and vulnerabilities. Caution needs to be exercised, however, in thinking about how culture and identity interact. A fine line often exists between stating a generalization about a cultural group and fostering a stereotype. No two people are identical in their cultural identities, and cultures are highly varied. Suffice it to say that effective leaders need to be sensitive to cultural issues, but they cannot follow a guidebook.

24   See Shields (1986).

25   Ibid.

26   See, for example, Ames (1992).

27   The quote from Coach Krzyzewski taken from Janssen (1999), p. 43.

28   Although we invented the FAIR strategies framework, the specific suggestions are derived from numerous works on motivational climate. For a good review of the construct, its implications, and how to implement a mastery climate, see McArdle and Duda (2002).

29   This is a central point in several of Tim Gallwey's popular books (e.g., Gallwey, 1974).

30   For a helpful discussion of goal setting, see Weinberg and Butt (2005).

31   The quote from John Wooden is taken from Thompson (2003), p. 29.

6

Opponents
Allies or Adversaries

Larry and Leroy are top contenders for the golden gloves title in their weight class.

Sam and Samantha are in the same 10th-grade biology class. Excellent students, they contest for top grades.

Working in separate real estate firms, Joe and Josephine are best sellers. They often vie not only for clients, but also for the regional title of top agent.

Ray is married to Rae. Both enjoy sharing stories with friends and, without even realizing it, often try to outdo the other in their storytelling.

> ❝ **An opponent is someone whose strength joined to yours creates a certain result.** ❞
>
> Sadaharu Oh

Competition is not a solo endeavor. Whether the setting is sports, school, business, or marriage—or a myriad of other contexts that range from war to love—opponents are part of the picture. As we have seen, however, opponents can be viewed as partners or enemies, as allies or adversaries. It all depends on whether we are contesting *with* or contesting *against* the opponent. As the etymology of the word suggests, in true competition, we contest *with* our opponents. Together, we seek enjoyment or excellence or both.[1]

To many, it may seem odd to consider opponents partners.[2] So let's be clear. By *partner*, we do not mean friend or companion or comrade. A partner is not a pal—not necessarily, at least. In fact, you do not have to like your opponent. On a personal level, it is entirely possible to dislike the opponent and still engage in genuine competition. Warm, fuzzy relations are not essential. But respect is.

We also want to emphasize that the metaphor of partnership is not necessarily expressed in "partnership" language. To be a true competitor, you do not have to talk about the opponent as a partner. In fact, use of the word *partner* is rare in competitive settings, even though the concept may drive much of what is experienced. We are using the word *partnership* to describe how true competitors think and feel about their opponents, not how they talk about them. The metaphor works whether or not the language is used. In fact, as we will see, competitors sometimes affirm the partnership relationship while using language that, at first blush, seems incongruent. We will have more to say on this later.

In this chapter, we deepen our discussion of opponents as partners. Later in the chapter, we also talk about a key threat to true competition—contesting against a decompetitor. Finally, we offer guidance for those in leadership positions, including league officials, coaches, teachers, and parents, with regard to how to nurture and sustain true competition. We begin by elaborating on what the partnership metaphor implies about the structure of true competition.

Structure of Competition

Both competition and decompetition take place within a contest. As we emphasized in chapter 2, how one thinks about the contest determines whether it leads to genuine competition or devolves into decompetition. Let us explore this a bit further. Within a contest, there are two sets of goals. On the one hand, everyone who participates wants to win. Let us refer to this as the structural goal of the contest. The goal may be to outscore the opponent, produce the best essay, gain the contract, win the election, or spell the most words. Regardless, the goal is to win.

The structural goal, however, does not exhaust the possible goals of contest participants. Although all want to win, people also compete for a variety of personal reasons. Some view their participation as primarily about enjoyment. For others, it's about personal growth; for still others, friendship. Let us refer to these as personal goals. So there is both a structural level to contests and a personal level.[3] In chapter 5, we elaborated on two major categories of personal goals: task-oriented goals and ego-oriented goals.

In contests, at the structural level, one wins while another loses. As such, people's goals are mutually exclusive. If I win, you lose. This analysis, however, applies only to the structural goal of contests. The same relation does not necessarily hold for personal goals. Personal goals are not inherently mutually exclusive. In fact, at the personal level, competitors often hold positively interdependent goals.

Our family enjoys playing board games, among other things, on "Family Days." Most of these games lead eventually to a winner and multiple losers. That's the structure of the game. But our goal in playing isn't just to see who will emerge victorious. In fact, that is a rather trivial dimension of our play. On a personal level, we all enjoy passing the time in a way that strengthens our family togetherness. Our goals are cooperative and interdependent. When one person—say, the one with the least Monopoly property—starts to get cranky and upset, it undermines everyone's enjoyment. On the other hand, when one person starts cracking jokes or even teasing a bit, we all have a more delightful time.

The diagram in table 6.1 reflects how competition and decompetition work within contests.

In both competition and decompetition, contests lead to winners and losers in the overt, scoreboard sense. However, in genuine competition, both the winners and losers at the structural level can "win" at the personal level. This is because many personal goals can be met regardless of the game outcome. In fact, some important personal goals may be advanced more by losing

TABLE 6.1

Everyone Can Win in a Win-Lose Contest

	Competition	Decompetition
Structural goals	Win-lose	Win-lose
Personal goals	Win-win	Win-lose

than by winning. Losing can help build resilience and perseverance; it can help identify weaknesses that, when addressed, strengthen performance. Losing can nurture humility. It can, for those who let it, foster empathy and compassion. Imagine a person who always wins—at games, at debates, at bets. Regardless of the contest or setting, this person is driven to win. The image that you conjure in your mind is unlikely to be a flattering one.

The partnership metaphor allows for a win–win orientation at the personal level. At this level, contests are cooperative. If my goal is to improve my ability to hit a clutch three-point shot in basketball, I can practice in isolation all I want. I can also practice with teammates offering a mock defense. However, there is nothing quite like a real opponent, especially if we are well matched. Opponents cooperate with me by offering their best effort. Ironically, their opposition to my success facilitates my learning and development. The same, of course, holds true for them. Like muscles that need resistance to strengthen, many of our personal goals, especially if we are task motivated, are facilitated by the resistance of the opponent.[4] Opposition, in true competition, is an important form of cooperation.

Respect

Decompetitors replicate the win–lose structure of the contest at the psychological level. To win is to be a winner, and to lose is to be a loser. All personal goals are subordinated to the prime goal of emerging victorious on the scoreboard. Because losing the contest tends to be equated with being a loser, an attitude of disrespect is an inherent part of the relationship between opponents. It is hard, after all, to respect someone that you think of as a loser. It is equally hard to respect someone you believe is trying to expose the loser in you. Is it any wonder that so many studies of "competition" have revealed that it tends to thrust people toward derisive and hostile relations?

True competition rests on mutual respect.[5] What does this mean concretely? It means, first of all, that you grant your opponent the same rights and privileges that you claim for yourself. It means that you give your best performance. It means that you don't gloat in victory or wallow in resentment when defeated. Most important, it means that you view the performance of your competitor as a gift because it is a challenge that stimulates you to grow and develop. How can you not respect and appreciate someone who is enabling you to call forth your best?

Respect for opponents is key to true competition.[6] But in competition, respect can be expressed in a number of surprising ways. Sometimes, of course, it is conveyed openly and directly. Following a game, athletes at all levels often go over to members of the other team, shake their hands, and express appreciation. Respect and appreciation for opponents, however, does not have to be expressed so directly. In the next two sections, we describe two other ways that respect for the opponent might be conveyed.

Shaking hands after a game is a common ritual. Sometimes it is genuinely felt; at other times it is an empty gesture. It can even be an occasion for expressing distain or hostility. Do you think the ritual should be kept? Why or why not?

Competing Against Yourself

Many athletes like to talk about competing against themselves. The great Dallas Cowboys' quarterback Roger Staubach, for example, once said, "Winning isn't getting ahead of others; it is getting ahead of yourself." Similarly, tennis great Arthur Ashe wrote, "You are never really playing an opponent. You are playing yourself, your own highest standards, and when you reach your limit, that is real joy." In a similar vein, Bud Wilkinson, one of the most celebrated college coaches of all time, said that "every game is an opportunity to measure yourself against your own potential."

In reality, you can't literally compete against yourself. Contests involve opponents. However, the concept of competing against yourself has real metaphorical meaning, and it often indirectly expresses a deep respect for opponents. One of the treasures of competition is its capacity to enable us to challenge ourselves to achieve new heights of performance. A great life lesson that sports and other competitions can teach is that real joy can be found in pushing our talents to their limits. Doing so, however, requires strong opponents.

You cannot "get ahead of yourself" if you are a tennis pro playing a novice. When opponents are tough, well-matched competitors, they provide us with the privilege of pushing ourselves as far as our talents and effort will allow. They enable self-discovery. They facilitate personal growth. When a person utters the phrase, "I am competing against myself," it can be translated as, "I have an opponent who is pushing me to the boundary of my competence." The phrase suggests that the opponent is presenting a worthy challenge, and both the opponent and the challenge need to be respected. In trying to defeat a skilled opponent, we are not trying to annihilate an enemy; rather, we are trying to call forth and expand our best inner resources.

If competing against yourself seems like an odd way to show respect for an opponent, the next one may seem stranger yet!

You Run Like a Sick Walrus!

In the introduction to this chapter, we said that even though the metaphor of partnership informs how true competitors think about their opponents, the language of partnership is often absent. We now suggest that a genuine sense of partnership can be expressed in truly paradoxical ways.

Imagine, for a moment, a neighborhood game of street basketball among friends. If you stood nearby and eavesdropped on the game, would you hear flowery talk of partnership? Probably not. You would be more likely to hear a volcanic barrage of teasing, with insults flowing like lava! The language you hear may, in fact, sound a lot more like the verbiage of decompetition than competition. And yet, the game may still operate as a genuine competitive experience. How can this be?

Humans are quite capable of appreciating subtlety, satire, and paradox. In fact, people tend to take delight in playing with words and meanings. When friends gather to play, they often play on multiple levels at once.[7] There is the formal game, of course, but people also play with language and the moral meaning of words. What might in another context be considered a vulgar slur may be viewed as a friendly overture in a game.

There is a close parallel in the animal kingdom to the harsh language of friendly combat among people.[8] Imagine two kittens playing. If you had never seen kittens play before, you might easily conclude that the two young cats are fighting. They snarl and snap and jab and tumble. Fangs are bared; claws are flashed. The kittens, however, are merely playing with their fighting tools. They act like enemies, but in reality they are maintaining strong bonds of affiliation. Appearance is not reality.

As we have seen, war is the root metaphor of decompetition. Despite this, people can play verbally with the war metaphor and remain competitive. People can talk about opponents as adversaries and yet still view them as partners. You can "talk bad" and still be good. What is critical isn't the language used, but the underlying attitude and intention.

In our academic research, we have found that people often use a kind of special game morality when they enter sport contests.[9] In everyday life, morality requires that a person consider everyone equally. But in a con-

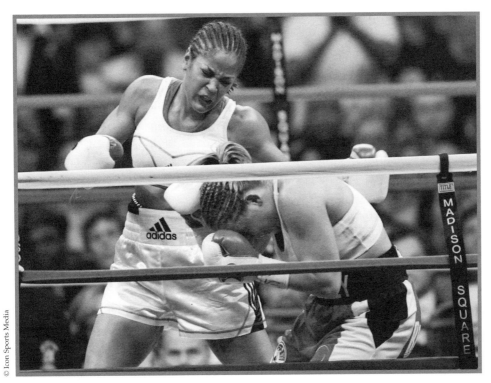

© Icon Sports Media

Athletes sometimes taunt their opponents. When is this consistent with true competition, and when does it reflect decompetition?

test, the contest structure itself requires that each contestant temporarily focuses only on what is in their own interest. Not surprisingly, then, sport participants frequently describe a kind of personal transformation that they undergo when they enter a game. Whereas they might be gentle and pleasant in everyday life, they become fierce on the playing field. Altruists at home, they become egoists on the court.[10] But it is all in a spirit of play. It is a kitten fight . . . *or is it?*

Among friends, when mutual respect is well established, people can temporarily act like moral egoists without really being egoists. People can talk as if they were at war when, in reality, their words are a moral spoof. However, considerable caution needs to be exercised. If the foundation of cooperation and respect is not solid, such language can easily lose its playful quality and rapidly slip into genuine disrespect and hostility.

Remember that contests feature a win–lose structure that requires each person to focus on his or her own gains and goals. Although friends may "fight" within this structure and still maintain an underlying attitude of deep respect, not all contestants who "playfully" speak the language of decompetition will be so successful. What may start as playful trash-talking can easily spin out of control. Egged on by the oppositional structure of the contest, a person may easily misperceive the intent of an opponent's teasing. The opponent can shift from a pretend enemy to a real one. When play hostility becomes real antagonism, competition slips into decompetition.

Playful trash-talk may increase the enjoyment of a game for some, but it should come with a warning label. If something should occur that saps the game of its playful character, even momentarily, what was initially intended as a tease can easily escalate into a genuinely hostile exchange.

Teasing is tricky business. As any good marriage counselor will bear witness, genuine hostility can be disguised under a cloak of humor. Although teasing can be an innocent expression of affection and respect, it can also be

---

Dear Authors:

I coach in an inner-city youth football program for boys 12 to 14. During both intra-team scrimmages and games, the kids are constantly bad-mouthing their opponents. I've confronted the kids about it, but they claim it's no big deal. They say, in fact, that they enjoy it. Almost all the kids on my team are African American, and I'm white. Is this just a cultural issue? What should I do?

— Coach Culture

Dear Coach Culture:

Culture has a big influence on language. Given our richly multicultural world, it is not surprising that miscommunications occur. What may sound disrespectful to a person raised in one culture may not be heard that way to someone from a different background. In your situation, it is important to understand the meaning that the language has for the kids.

On the other hand, verbal baiting has no place in genuine competition. Watch the kids. Does the language sometimes lead to someone becoming upset or agitated? Does it ever escalate into physical confrontation? Does it interfere with the kids' being able to return to positive, friendly relations after the scrimmage or game? If you answer yes to any of these questions, it is time to put an immediate stop to it. Hopefully, you can do this through persuasion. Have a team meeting; tell them what you have noticed. Talk about the benefits of a positive, supportive atmosphere.

If the kids are simply being playful, you may want to tolerate it. However, just as they want you to be culturally sensitive, it is important that you require them to be sensitive as well. During games, when they may not be totally familiar with the kids on the other team, your kids should keep their language unambiguously friendly and affirming. Help them appreciate their opponents as partners, and encourage them to talk in a manner consistent with that understanding.

a Trojan horse filled with subtle aggression. Similarly, in contests, a double paradox can occur: Respect can be expressed in the paradoxical language of insult, but the teasing, supposedly playful, can express hidden hostilities. And even if it isn't intended to, it may be mistakenly interpreted that way.

The reality is that most contests, whether in sports or other domains, are not among good friends. Even in sports, in which contests are called games and we talk about "playing," there is precious little genuine play.[11] To protect the integrity of true competition in more formal contest settings, it is usually best to avoid trash-talking. It is far better to keep the talk positive to reinforce a respectful and appreciative orientation to the opponent.

Respect is the glue holding true competition together, but it is a two-way street. What if your opponent exhibits disrespectful language or behavior? Does true competition become impossible? Yes, in its pure form. However, an alert competitor can still seek to approximate the conditions of true competition. We turn now to the threat to competition posed by the decompetitive opponent.

The Challenge of the Decompetitive Opponent

> ❝ Never let us do wrong because our opponents did so.
> Let us, rather, by doing right, show them
> what they ought to have done. ❞
>
> James Joyce

True competition is a tight-rope act that requires balancing a number of factors. In this chapter, we have emphasized how it involves balancing the cooperative and oppositional dimensions of contests. We have suggested that appreciating the cooperative underpinnings of competition helps to put the oppositional dimension in perspective. It helps us to appreciate that our opponents are partners.

To win a contest against a skilled opponent requires extensive preparation. Similarly, to sustain true competition, we need to be prepared. If we are unprepared, the tight-rope act can be easily upset, and competition can fall into decompetition. As we have seen, threats to true competition can arise from extrinsic rewards and internal insecurities. Now we focus on threats posed by our relationship with opponents.

In the introduction to chapter 1, I shared a story about being tackled by a boy we called Bull. Most of us who have played sports, competed in school, vied for votes, or fought for market share have had experience (probably too much) contesting with others who didn't play by the rules or who engaged us with open hostility. Contesting against someone who has adopted a decompetitive orientation is one of the most potent challenges

Opponents and Opportunities

One way to help sustain a respectful and appreciative attitude toward opponents is to continually remind ourselves that they represent opportunities. Here is how Mariah Burton Nelson put it in her book *Embracing Victory*:

> [Opponents] present you with a chance to learn who you are, to notice what you want. They give you a chance to rise to the occasion. This is what athletes learn: that opponents can make us swifter, wiser, more effective. We welcome them.[12]

Nelson goes on to point out that this view of opponents is not limited to the playing field. Gandhi, for example, viewed political opponents as teachers because they forced him to do his best. He learned from them about his own areas of weakness and grew through his efforts to address them. Similar reflections could be offered from the worlds of education, politics, and business. Opponents can make you study harder or campaign better. Opponents can make your company swifter, wiser, and more effective. However, in any of these realms, a focus on destroying the competition undermines these positive benefits.

to sustaining true competition. Consider how you would respond to the following sport situations:

- You're playing basketball. Your team is on defense, and you are guarding the other team's top-scoring forward. The ball has just been passed to the guard on the far side of the court. As the ref's eyes shift in that direction, the player you are guarding throws a sharp elbow into your rib cage.
- Every time you get near a particular opponent in a lacrosse game, you receive a deluge of crass insults about your mother, your ancestry, your sexuality, and your ability.
- You're playing soccer, and an opposing player keeps grabbing your jersey when the official isn't looking.

Incidents like these happen all the time.[13] Decompetitors deplete competition of many of its positive benefits; their efforts to win through intimidation or cheating disrespect the opponent and the game. What is a competitor to do when confronted by the behavior of a decompetitor? Although we cannot provide a comprehensive guide to restoring health to competition that has been infected with the decompetitive virus, three principles may be helpful. In brief, we suggest that you limit your vulnerability, deescalate the situation, and view the contest as an opportunity.

Limit Your Vulnerability

By *limit your vulnerability* we mean that you should not allow the decompetitor's behavior to risk your well-being or put you at a major strategic disadvantage.[14] Being a true competitor does not mean rolling over when confronted by the decompetitor. Seek to sacrifice neither ethics nor ground. Do not be a victim, but refuse to resort to similar tactics.

What can you do to limit your vulnerability? Several strategies might work. Of course, if the contest is optional, abandoning the game is a potent way to protect yourself and rob the decompetitor of power. When this is not possible or desirable, the goal should be to *respond with strength and moral force*. Of course, the force of argument is always the most desirable form of force. If there is an opportunity, try to persuade your opponent that everyone is better served by a fair, safe, and respectful contest. Challenge your opponent to beat you fairly.

In most situations, efforts at verbal persuasion will be impossible or insufficient. Your next best option may be to ignore the behavior of the opponent, if you can do so without being significantly disadvantaged. If the opponent

Dear Authors:

I'm a 10th-grade student. My geometry teacher grades on a curve, and several students in my class sneak in crib notes during tests. Frankly, I don't see how they are my "partners." You suggest that I should limit my vulnerability, but if I confront them, I'll be ostracized. Because you also say that athletes should sometimes respond to force with force, should I respond to cheating with cheating? To cheat or not to cheat; that is my question.

— Geo Student

Dear Geo Student:

No, we certainly do not condone cheating, even when fairness puts you at a disadvantage. You might suggest to the teacher that he or she adopt new monitoring techniques. Hopefully, the cheaters will eventually get caught. Even better, you might want to talk with other students who are similarly disadvantaged and together confront either the cheating students or the teacher. As to whether the cheaters are "partners," we suggest that they may not be the kind of partners that you desire, but it is still to your advantage to see them as partners more than enemies. By viewing them as partners, you can ask yourself: How can I grow through this situation? Focusing on how they can help you grow will be more productive than focusing on how you can get revenge.

is trash-talking or otherwise showing disrespect, a simple unnerving smile may be the best response. Stay focused on the game.

In many sports, physical violence, or the threat of violence, is often used to intimidate. In such circumstances, it is important to let your opponent know that such tactics will not work with you. Once again, the best way to do that is to simply stay focused. In fact, when opponents are seeking to intimidate, they are not fully concentrating on the game and there may be strategic openings. Like the judo expert, you can respond effectively to intimidation by turning it to your advantage.

What if the opponent's aggressive behavior is genuinely putting you at a major disadvantage? Ignoring it may only invite further aggression. If the opponent's behavior is illegal, one avenue of response is to quietly and respectfully alert the officials, or ask your coach to do so. It is the officials' job to enforce the rules, and you have a right to expect them to do so.

Rarely, your only recourse may be to respond with legal and limited force of your own.[15] If the officials are not doing their job and the opponent is being highly aggressive, you may need to respond assertively. Through your actions, you may need to let your opponent know that you and your teammates will not be rattled. The specific context will have to determine the best response, but you should seek to act without anger and within the rules. The point is not to get back at the opponent; rather, it is to communicate that the opponent's behavior will not succeed in distracting or intimidating you. Importantly, whenever such force is used, it should be done consistent with the spirit of the second and third principles, discussed next.

Deescalate the Situation

You do not want to let the power play of the decompetitive opponent put you at a disadvantage. On the other hand, it is important—vitally important—to avoid a tit-for-tat battle of revenge actions. Rather, without becoming a victim, seek to calm things down, to return to the spirit of true competition. Find your center of gravity. Keep your own composure, your poise, your focus, your values. By your actions, if not your words, let your opponent know that you are a tough competitor, but a fair and respectful one.

Take Advantage of the Opportunity

Finally, regardless of what your adversary does, *view the contest as an opportunity.* Although the actions and attitudes of the decompetitor can be aggravating and unpleasant, do not let them cause you to lose focus. Keep this in mind: The unfair, hostile, or disrespectful actions of the decompetitor provide unique opportunities to grow. Decompetitors challenge our creativity and character. In life, creative problem solving is often required, and many opportunities arise to excuse our own unethical behavior by blaming others. Staying true to your ethical principles is easy when situations are easy. Staying true to them when others are acting poorly can help you exercise

Three Principles
for Responding to the Decompetitor

1. Limit your vulnerability (don't be a victim).
   - Abandon the game.
   - Respond with the strength of argument.
   - Ignore the opponent's behavior.
   - Quietly alert officials.
   - Respond with limited and legal physical force.
2. Deescalate the situation.
3. Take advantage of the opportunity.

the muscle of character. So use the confrontation with the decompetitor as an opportunity to exercise your moral imagination and stay committed to what *ought to be* rather than give in to what currently is.

Responding appropriately to the challenges of the decompetitor is easiest when leaders consistently support true competition. Thus, we turn now to leadership guidelines for building and sustaining true competition.

Leadership for Cultivating Allies, not Adversaries

❝ Most important, leaders can conceive and articulate goals that lift people out of their petty preoccupations and unite them in pursuit of objectives worthy of their best efforts. ❞

John Gardner

We close this chapter with three leadership strategies for making opponents allies, not adversaries. Each recommendation will help leaders create an environment in which opponents are respected and true competition is nurtured. The three recommendations are to teach cooperation, teach about competition, and avoid the metaphor of war.

Teach Cooperation

Our first recommendation is that leaders *teach cooperation*. Because competition is a special form of cooperation, children, youth, and adults will be better able to appreciate true competition if they have ample experience with cooperation. Learning to cooperate is an important life skill, and it needs to be cultivated and developed. Getting children involved in competition before they have learned how to cooperate effectively is like teaching them algebra before they have learned basic arithmetic.

The majority of work on teaching cooperation has been done in conjunction with schools and education. Leaders in other areas, such as sports and business, can learn from the cooperative learning literature. In schools, cooperative learning is a proven and effective means of accomplishing academic goals and has the added value of preparing youth for true competition. Its use should become even more prevalent than it is.

In business and sports, teamwork is often a key to success. Another word for *teamwork* is *cooperation.* At the beginning of each season, coaches would do well to use a number of cooperative, team-building activities. Cooperative drills, for example, can be used to develop specific skills, advance conditioning, and promote team cohesion. Coaches should not only take advantage of cooperative strategies, but also emphasize to the team the importance of cooperation. They can then extend this idea to help everyone see the opponent as a necessary partner in the contest.

As part of teaching cooperation, leaders should talk openly about respecting opponents as partners. They should emphasize how opponents provide an opportunity to improve and enjoy the challenge of the contest. Even when opponents act as decompetitors, they provide a set of challenges by which we can improve ourselves. Leaders would do well to draw from partnership imagery in their discussion of opponents. This does not mean soft-pedaling the rivalry involved. But it does mean remaining appreciative of the opponent in word and deed.

Teach Competition

Second, leaders should *discuss competition* and distinguish it from decompetition. Every coach, player, student, and employee should know the difference between competition and its imposter, decompetition. Learning the mark-

Teaching Cooperation

Ted Wohlfarth, founder of EnTeam, has developed a number of creative ways to encourage the development of cooperation skills in sports and classrooms. In addition to developing games and exercises of his own, he has transformed a number of traditional games into cooperative games. Most intriguingly, he has developed scoring procedures that enable facilitators to "score" cooperation. For more information, check out the EnTeam Web site at www.enteam.org.

ings of competition and decompetition, which are summarized in the field guide of chapter 3, is vitally important. Like a gyroscope that is starting to wobble, the descent into decompetition has visible signs that one can learn to recognize and respond to. Negative comments about opponents are often one of the first telltale signs.

Here's a true story: Jim is a youth soccer coach in New Hampshire. After attending a coaching workshop in which the concepts of competition and decompetition were introduced, he taught the concepts to his boys' U-14 team. In the very next game, a player came to the sideline during a time-out and said, "Coach, number 26 is being decompetitive. He keeps grabbing my jersey." It gave the coach an opportunity to invite the player to stay focused. Jim then watched the offending opponent, and when he confirmed that the player was indeed violating the rules, he discreetly encouraged the referee to keep an eye on the situation. Sure enough, the next time it occurred, the whistle blew.

Avoid the War Metaphor

Finally, leaders should *avoid the language of war and battle*. Those in leadership positions should refrain from suggesting that the opponent is an enemy to be conquered or a foe to be subdued. They should avoid depersonalizing opponents, turning them into objects to be overcome in an effort to win. This includes avoiding in-group/out-group language. This suggestion, of course, is the flip side of the first (teaching cooperation), but it bears emphasizing.

Some coaches object to this recommendation because they believe it is helpful to "psych up" their teams by stirring up anger, resentment, or hatred—that is, by turning opponents into enemies. Anger and hatred are, indeed, strong emotions and can get players' juices flowing. However, such emotions are hard to channel appropriately, and they often lead to mistakes and misjudgments.

In the acclaimed book *Sacred Hoops: Spiritual Lessons of a Hardwood Warrior*, Phil Jackson wrote about the destructive impact of anger: "I realized that anger was the Bulls' real enemy, not the Detroit Pistons. Anger was the restless demon that seized the group mind and kept the players from being fully awake. Whenever we went to Detroit, the unity and awareness we'd worked so hard to build collapsed, and the players reverted to their most primitive instincts."[16]

Jackson went on to talk about how the Pistons' strategy was to raise the level of violence in the game. Clearly, they were embracing a decompetitive approach. Coach Jackson struggled with how to respond. Should he encourage his players to retaliate, to return violence for violence? Rather than just thinking strategically about the immediate challenge posed by the Pistons, Jackson reflected on the whole nature of competition. After rejecting an approach that would likely create an intensifying cycle of violence, he concluded:

> ❝ **There has to be another way, an approach that honors the humanity of both sides while recognizing that only one victor can emerge. A blueprint for giving your all out of respect for the battle, never hatred of the enemy. And, most of all, a wide-angle view of competition that encompasses both opponents as partners in the dance.**[17] ❞

Indeed, opponents are partners. They deserve our respect and appreciation. If we are motivated by the intrinsic benefits that we derive from competition, it will be easier to appreciate the positive role of opponents. It is also important, of course, to appreciate the officials and the rules that they seek to enforce. Examining the role of rules and refs is the topic of the next chapter.

By the way, the Bulls went on to win. ▪

1   Throughout the book, we suggest that true competition aims at excellence and enjoyment. In particular contests, however, one or the other of these may be more prominent. For example, we play games of chance primarily for enjoyment with little attention to excellence. On the other hand, there may be contest situations on the job in which we focus almost exclusively on excellence and experience little enjoyment. And, of course, in numerous contexts excellence and enjoyment are both highly salient.

2   To get at much the same idea, Warren Fraleigh (1984) discusses the opponent as "facilitator." Fraleigh suggests that considering the opponent as a facilitator leads to a view of competition as "an attempt to perform the same skillful actions better than opponents in order to express and develop competence." It also leads to a view of excellence as "a qualitative concept concerned primarily with how well the contest is played" (pp. 84-85).

3   The discussion of structural and personal goals is clearly a simplification of a much more complex set of conceptual issues. Our purpose here is not to render a philosophically adequate depiction of the purposes and goals structured into the contest itself nor of the imputed purposes of participants. Our more limited agenda is to offer an everyday language depiction of how all participants can gain through the value of contesting, regardless of outcome. For a classic description of the structural ends that are necessarily pursued in a contest, see Suits (1967).

4   Credit is usually given to Triplett (1897) for being the first investigator to examine the impact of competition on performance. His findings support the view that opponents are "facilitators." For his study, he obtained the official bicycle race records of the League of American Wheelmen. What he found was that racers in the unpaced races against time were slower than those in the paced races against time, and that those in the paced races against time, in turn, were slower than those performing in competition against opponents.

5   See Clifford and Feezell (1997).

6   In the economic realm, when "opponents" are not respected, it eventually increases costs to everyone. This happens because decompetition heightens distrust and increases the use of such tactics as coercion, deception, and threat. This, in turn, erodes the social capital that, under more optimal circumstances, enables commercial transactions to take place without undue legal constraints and regulation. As Robert Putnam (2000) notes, "Social capital of the right sort boosts economic efficiency, so that if our networks of reciprocity

deepen, we all benefit, and if they atrophy, we all pay dearly" (p. 325). The argument here is that within true competition, in which opponents are respected, community and mutual trust thrive, but decompetition interferes with "our networks of reciprocity" because it turns opponents into enemies.

7   See, for example, Johan Huizinga's (1955) classic study of play.

8   See, for example, Bateson (1972).

9   Game reasoning can be either legitimate or illegitimate. To stay legitimate, the "egocentrism" of game reasoning must remain playful and pertain only to game-limited actions. Injuring an opponent using the justification of the egocentric requirements of a contest would be illegitimate, for example, because the injury would persist beyond the bounds of the game. See Shields and Bredemeier (1995). For a popular treatment of this theme, see Bredemeier and Shields (1985).

10   The idea of game reasoning was recently expressed by Clem Davis, a former running back for the Oakland Raiders. "You have to have two personalities," he said, "One for football; one for your daily life." See Rhoden (2008).

11   According to a number of modern thinkers, many of the ills in today's society are related to our relative neglect of play. See the discussion in Kretchmar (1994), especially chapter 4. Sharing this view, we suggest that a neglect of play is a significant source of decompetition in many contest situations, both within and beyond sports.

12   Nelson (1998), p. 277.

13   The frequency with which negative behaviors occur in sports is hard to quantify. Nevertheless, we found alarmingly high rates of poor sport behavior in one survey of youth sport participants, along with their coaches and parents. See Shields, Bredemeier, LaVoi, and Power (2005).

14   Of course, the best way to minimize vulnerability is through more systemic change in the culture of competition. In the realm of sports, for example, the best plan would be for a whole league or conference to come together and talk about the norms of true competition and seek to affirm, build, and support those norms consistently at all levels.

15   Game theorists have long advocated a tit-for-tat strategy to address departures from cooperative behavior, based primarily on computer modeling of the famous prisoner's dilemma game. According to the tit-for-tat strategy, every act of aggression should be retaliated against, whereas every act of cooperation should be met with a cooperative response. It is a simple and elegant strategy that works exceedingly well in computer simulations. In the real world, however, numerous complexities and ambiguities undermine the effectiveness of the strategy. One critical problem is that what constitutes an aggressive action is often more a matter of perception and interpretation than objective fact. Two players who each believe they are applying a tit-for-tat strategy to overcome the aggressive behavior of the opponent can easily set in motion an escalating spiral of retaliations. To escape the "death spiral," one party must risk responding cooperatively to the perceived aggression on the opponent's part. This has been called a tit-for-two-tats strategy. For an introduction to game theory and its application to real life, see Barash (2003).

16   Jackson and Delehanty (1995), p. 131.

17   Ibid., p. 136.

Regulation

Upholding the Spirit
of the Game

I met Darryl through a mutual friend. I was 27 at the time, and Darryl was one of the first professional athletes I had ever met. Though he was in his third year as an NBA player for a West Coast team, he was down in the dumps. He was bemoaning the fact that he was not where he had hoped to be in his career. It was true that Darryl was not one of the marquee players, but he still saw plenty of floor time and I was surprised by his comments. Naively, I blurted out, "What stands in the way of you getting where you want to be?" Without a moment's hesitation he replied, "It's because of the three Rs: rules, refs, and rivals." He was only half-joking.

> **" If you don't cheat, you look like an idiot;
> if you cheat and don't get caught,
> you look like a hero; if you cheat
> and get caught, you look like a dope. "**
>
> Darrell Waltrip

Play fair. It's such a simple idea, isn't it? It applies to games, business, school, politics, and relationships. The theme of fairness reverberates deeply in the human psyche and echoes through every known culture.[1] Visit a preschool and one of the most common phrases you'll hear is "That's not fair." Everyone, everywhere, is concerned with fairness. And yet we cheat.

This chapter takes up the theme of rules and officials. As we will see, competitors and decompetitors adopt fundamentally different attitudes toward the regulations that govern contests. In brief, competitors embrace the *intent* of the rules and respect those charged with enforcing them. In contrast, decompetitors tend to play a game of cat-and-mouse with rules and officials. Sometimes decompetitors simply cheat. Other times they may follow the rules, but seek advantages in ways that depart from the spirit of the game. After discussing rules and officials, we address another trigger for decompetition, another wind that can blow a competitor off-balance: *perceived injustice,* the belief that one has been treated unfairly. We close the chapter with recommendations for leaders.

Rules and Regulations

> **" Rules are for the obedience of fools
> and the guidance of wise men. "**
>
> Douglas Bader, British World War II pilot

Here's a simple equation: No rules = no game.[2] If we are going to compete, we must agree on the rules that govern the contest. Some rules, such as what defines a touchdown in football, an A on a test, or a bankruptcy in business, are simply part of the definition of the game.[3] You can't play Scrabble without the rule that words used must be those found in the dictionary. Other rules proscribe or prescribe particular behaviors and identify penalties for violations. In basketball, rules define dribbling, and penalties are specified for violating them. In school, rules define originality, and there are penalties for plagiarism. In business, rules govern price fixing, and penalties are enacted for companies that collude.

Contests rest on the tacit assumption that each participant agrees to abide by the rules. Imagine a neighborhood game of baseball. Billy gets a crisp hit to right field and sprints to first. After tagging the base, he mysteriously turns and sullies back home. Everyone is confused. Undeterred, Billy proudly announces, "I scored a point." "No, you didn't," protests everyone else, including his befuddled teammates. But Billy insists, "Yes, I did. That's the way I'm playing it."

Decompetitors sometimes approach the contest the way Billy approaches baseball. They want to play by their own rules. Of course, they don't do this outwardly and obviously, like Billy. They are, to put it bluntly, sneakier about it. But the effect is the same. The real game dissolves and is replaced by a game imposter.

Several sports have halls of fame that celebrate the great athletes who have participated throughout history. Some athletes seem destined to be inducted into the hall of fame; that is, until it is revealed that they cheated, perhaps by taking performance-enhancing drugs. When their cheating comes to light, they are no longer considered candidates for induction. This is not just because they are considered poor role models, though that is true as well. The other reason for their exclusion is that they weren't really playing the game.

True competitors, who appreciate and value the *process* of competing, recognize that the game is destroyed by cheating. The outward shell may remain, but the real, living game has been killed. Because decompetitors are

© Human Kinetics

Some athletes argue that cheating is the only way to have a fair contest because their opponents cheat. What do you think of this argument? Is learning to cheat part of learning to play the game? What about contests outside of sport?

less interested in the game itself than in what they can derive from victory, killing the game is of little concern. They can still feast on its carcass.

Ben Johnson crossed the finish line first in the 1988 Olympics 100-meter final. He reaped the benefits of victory. In his case, however, the feast ended abruptly. When he failed to pass a drug test, he was stripped of his medal. Five-time Olympic gold medalist Marion Jones went much longer before her cheating caught up to her. She belatedly admitted to taking steroids before the 2000 Olympic games. The point here is not to demean these individuals. Whatever we may think of their behavior, the point is larger: The cheating reduced these races to shams.

Only the shell of a baseball game was played when eight members of the Chicago White Sox plotted to throw the 1919 World Series to the Cincinnati Reds. When basketball players from four New York colleges were arrested and charged with shaving points in the early 1950s, numerous so-called games were revealed to have been hollow imitations. Was a real Little League game played when Danny Almonte threw the first no-hitter in Little League World Series history in 2001? Not really. When it turned out that he was two years older than the rules allowed, the game that everyone thought they played turned out to have been a mirage.

> ❝ **We've got to find a way to win.**
> **I'm willing to start cheating.** ❞
>
> Tight end Marv Cook on the 0-6 New England Patriots

When Marv Cook said, perhaps tongue-in-cheek, that he was willing to start cheating to lift his team out of its slump, technically his words made no sense. *You can't cheat and win.* It's a logical impossibility. Once you cheat, you are no longer playing the game.

Cheating is typically done to gain a competitive advantage not allowed within the rules. This alters the fairness structure of the contest, a structure on which all legitimate contests stand. Cheating doesn't take a brick out of the wall of the contest; it destroys its foundation. The whole edifice collapses. What remains standing is simply a hologram, a shell, an illusion. The best a cheater can do is create the appearance of victory. Of course, sometimes that is all the decompetitor cares about. Less interested in developing mastery than in flaunting superiority, the decompetitor is often focused on appearances, not reality. Even if the contest is a charade, the victor's spoils may still be distributed. A win is still recorded in the record book. The paycheck still arrives. But let's be honest: You can't cheat and win. Not *really* win.

Although the effects of cheating are always the destruction of the contest, cheaters have a variety of motives. Usually, of course, the motive is simply to reap the benefits attached to victory. Most often, students cheat on exams to get better grades. A journalist may cite an unnamed source who doesn't really exist to grab a byline. A scientist may fudge a statistical analysis to get the research published. As we saw in chapter 4, the more valuable the reward for victory, the higher the temptation to fall into decompetition. However, reaping rewards is not always the motive.

What possible motive, for example, might Coach Bill Belichick of the New England Patriots have had for stealing signals from the hopelessly outmatched New York Jets when the teams played in September 2007? Sometimes the motive may just be the cops-and-robbers game of "what can I get away with?" Even wealthy people have been caught shoplifting low-cost items. Sometimes the motive is simply to see if they're clever enough to find a legal loophole. Human psychology is complex. Within a single decompetitor, a myriad of motives may be at work.

The true competitor finds enjoyment in seeking excellence through contesting. Enjoyment and excellence are values impossible to realize without a level playing field. Consequently, an orientation to fairness is built into the mental framework of the true competitor. Moreover, true competitors respect opponents and the game itself. Because they recognize opponents as partners, they take for granted that opponents should have an equal opportunity to succeed. Cheating is simply not an option for the true competitor; it would defeat the purpose of playing.

The Moral of the Rule Story

Rules, at least the kind we are considering here, are important because they codify fundamental moral principles. If you dig deep into the rationale for these rules, you will unearth such ethical concepts as fairness and welfare. Rules, whether in sports or elsewhere, usually promote equal opportunity, a fair distribution of rewards, and participants' well-being. If well-intentioned, they give concrete form to abstract notions such as justice and compassion.

Because true competitors recognize that rules serve moral purposes, they focus on the spirit as well as the letter of the rule. Let's amplify on those moral purposes. First, as we have said, many rules are designed to promote fairness. Though chance always plays a role, the intent of rules is to make the outcome of a contest dependent primarily on the mastery and execution of relevant skills and strategies.[4] Those who play better are supposed to win. It would not be fair, for example, to allow one baseball team to have four outs per inning, while the other team gets only three. Similarly, rules promote fairness by balancing offense and defense. To stick with baseball, the pitcher's mound is 60.5 feet (18.4 m) from home plate to balance the ability of pitchers and batters. This distance is considered fair to both sides. If, over time, people come to believe that the distance favors one side over the other, adjustments to the game will be made. Fairness is a foundational value in all legitimate contests.

A second major moral purpose of rules is to promote the safety and welfare of those involved.[5] Why are late hits prohibited in football? Because allowing

---

Dear Authors:

In sports, doesn't the frequent practice of handicapping contradict what you are saying? If the contest outcome is supposed to be decided by game-relevant skills and strategies, doesn't handicapping violate fairness?

— *Handicapped Golfer*

Dear Handicapped Golfer:

I see your point. Handicapping does provide a systematic boost to the less skilled or otherwise disadvantaged. But the purpose of handicapping is to correct a situation that is considered unfair to begin with. Yes, handicapping does compromise the general principle that the contest's outcome should be determined by mastery of game-relevant skills and strategies, but that compromise is outweighed by the gain in fairness. If anything, the practice of handicapping demonstrates just how foundational the concept of fairness is to contests. It tends to outweigh almost every other consideration. In somewhat similar fashion, many contests (such as lotteries and many children's games) allow for chance to play a significant role in determining winners. Despite the fact that chance, similar to handicapping, takes away from the role played by game-relevant skills and strategies, it is often valued because it provides an additional element of suspense and surprise. Again, however, fairness remains intact because chance is inherently unbiased.

---

them could easily lead to more injury. Although the rules of various sports tolerate greater and lesser degrees of risk, sports would degenerate into street brawls without rules protecting participants. Such rules are based on the moral principle that people's well-being should be respected and protected. Again, although we are using sports to illustrate, the same principle holds across all types of contests.

Although rules are designed to promote fairness and safety, they can create problems. Sometimes, by intent or accident, rules can be unfair. Such rules, of course, need to be challenged and changed. More important to the present discussion, however, is the fact that even the best of rules are only imperfect guides to the moral principles that underlie them. Rules simply cannot cover every possible contingency.

Just as laws, even the best ones, are only imperfect expressions of justice, contest rules only imperfectly guarantee fairness and safety. It is neither possible nor desirable to adopt laws or rules to cover every possible circumstance or to spell out every possible interpretation. Rules have inherent ambiguities.

Rule books and legal codes start out thin yet soon become thick. If you look at the rules and regulations that now cover college sports and compare them to those in existence 50 years ago, you will see astonishing growth. This is because we keep adding rules and amplifying old ones to cover new situations and new ways that sly people have invented to get around the intent of the rules.

True competitors recognize that rules are essential. More important, they recognize that the moral purpose of the rules provides the guiding light. Good competitors will even go beyond the literal requirements of the rule if doing so will help maintain a fair, safe, and respectful contest. In the 2001 Tour de France, no rule required Lance Armstrong to slow and wait for his arch opponent, Jan Ullrich, to catch up after the German rider missed a left turn and crashed off the road.

In February of 2006, Canadian cross-country skier, Sara Renner, won a silver medal in the Winter Olympics despite the fact that her left pole broke during the race. When her pole broke, the coach of the Norwegian team, Bjornar Haakensmoen, immediately gave her his, despite no rule requiring him to do so. Although his action disadvantaged his own skier, it upheld the spirit of fairness. In Canada, he was hailed as a hero. Coach Haakensmoen, though, brushed off the praise, suggesting it was no big deal. Perhaps the coach did not realize what a rare bird true competition has become.

Rules: Floor or Ceiling?

Competitors recognize that upholding the rules is a minimal requirement for a true contest. It is a floor below which they will not descend. But rule obedience is not all that competitors seek. Rather than look for loopholes in the rules or places where the rules can be violated without detection, good competitors are constantly guided by the moral intent of the rules. They follow the spirit of the rules, even if doing so results in a competitive disadvantage. If a situation arises in which fairness requires going beyond the rule, fairness takes priority. To summarize, upholding the spirit of true competition—even when not required by the rules—is the essence of being a good competitor.

Decompetitors see rules simply as conventions. If they refrain from outright cheating, they believe they have fulfilled all the requirements of fair play. For decompetitors, rules are the ceiling, not the floor. Of course, they do not always reach that ceiling. Cheating is not uncommon. Because the contest is a war and the goal is to win, stretching the rules is to be expected. Fairness may be shrunk to what one can get away with. Thus, although decompetitors may recognize that rules are needed conventions, they may circumvent the rules when detection is unlikely.

The "Good Sport" Decompetitor

Even though decompetitors are unlikely to follow the example of Coach Haakensmoen, they are not necessarily bad sports. Most decompetitors are neither villains nor cheats. It is important not to reduce the decompetitor to a caricature. Most decompetitors do not embrace a ruthless "anything goes" mentality. And remember, we all slip into a decompetitive mind-set from time to time.

The old notion of being a good sport is as relevant for decompetitors as it is for competitors. Many decompetitive athletes, for example, want to be, and believe they are, good sports. However, because they do not focus on the cooperative and moral underpinnings of the contest, when they take interest in being positive athletes, they tend to focus on superficialities.[6] Decompetitors may conform to the minimal demands of politeness, civility, and rule obedience. They may abide by the conventions of decorum in their sports. The "good sport" version of the decompetitor will gladly shake hands with opponents after a game or perhaps even stretch out a helping hand to a fallen opponent. These things are good, but they miss the major point. For the decompetitor, they are "extras" done out of graciousness.

By and large, decompetitors do not acknowledge the centrality of ethical judgment in contests. Their thinking is guided more by convention than by the basic principles of fairness, respect, and responsibility.[7] For the true competitor, showing respect for the opponent and upholding the spirit of the rules are not extras. They spring from the very meaning and purpose of the contest. This may be a subtle distinction, but it is an important one.

Officials

" I wanted to have a career in sports when I was young,
but I had to give it up. I'm only six feet tall,
so I couldn't play basketball. I'm only 190 pounds,
so I couldn't play football. And I have 20-20 vision,
so I couldn't be a referee. "

Jay Leno

" Officials are the only guys who can rob you
and then get a police escort out of the stadium. "

Ron Bolton

Every official who puts on a striped jersey is crooked, biased, or blind. At least that's the conclusion a visitor from Mars would reach if she listened to locker room postgame talk, especially if she visited only losing teams.

The antagonism between players and officials often erupts into the kind of sarcastic humor captured in the preceding quotes.

The disrespect shown to officials, however, is no joke. According to the U.S. National Association of Sports Officials (NASO), two or three physical assaults against umpires or referees are reported each week.[8] Some of these incidents end up in court. Although some attacks occur at professional and college events, many are perpetrated by parents at games for kids as young as five and six. Teenagers, seeking to earn a few bucks after school, may referee a soccer game for elementary children only to end up hospitalized. The problem has become so severe that NASO now provides assault insurance, and 20 states have enacted laws requiring penalties against those who assault sport officials.

Physical violence, however, is only the tip of the iceberg of the abuse suffered by officials.[9] This highly disturbed behavior of a few rests atop a much larger problem of verbal assault and abuse. Some coaches view it as simply part of their job to puff themselves up with righteous indignation and spew an acidic stream of venom at an official who makes a call that goes against their team. Many fans seem to believe that buying a ticket buys them the right to demean and degrade officials through vulgar and obnoxious speech yelled at the top of their lungs.

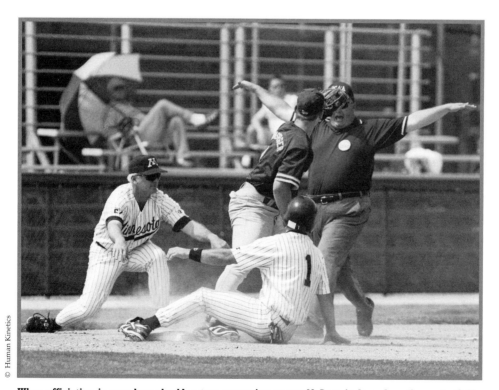

© Human Kinetics

When officiating is poor, how should a true competitor respond? Does it depend on the context? If so, how?

Sports, of course, mirror the larger society. They also help shape it. The rampant attitude of disrespect for sport officials draws from a societal pattern of disrespect for those who arbitrate contests. Consider judges. Judges are attacked from all sides when they make rulings based on their interpretation of the law. Yet laws are unavoidably ambiguous and in need of interpretation. Those who disagree with a particular ruling often accuse the judge of prejudice or legislating from the bench.

In organized sports, officials are an important and vital part of the game. They are part of what makes the game possible. As sport philosophers Craig Clifford and Randolph Feezell note in their book *Coaching for Character*:

> ❝ Officials are guardians of the spirit of the game. For that reason, respect for officials is closely related to respect for the game. Officials enforce not only the explicit rules but also the traditions and customs of the sport, the unwritten rules. . . . Officials in sport are somewhat like police, somewhat like parents enforcing habits of etiquette and good manners at the dinner table, somewhat like orchestra conductors interpreting traditions and establishing aesthetic rhythms.[10] ❞

Most sport officials take their obligation to neutrality seriously. Sure, some act with bias, intentionally or not. Some cops are crocked. Some judges

Challenging Officials

There is no place in sports for spitting on umpires, kicking referees, or unleashing a verbal tirade. However, at times it is appropriate to challenge an official. Just because I respect you doesn't mean I can't disagree with you. If an official has made a bad call, the coach has a right to ask for clarification, unless communication with officials violates the rules. If serious errors are made, a coach can certainly file a grievance with the governing body.

When challenging an official, it is important to be sensitive to his or her developmental level. Athletes become good athletes through practice. The same is true for officials. We would be upset by someone jumping all over a second-grader who drops a ball. Similarly, it is inappropriate to get on a 17-year-old official who is also learning the trade. Officials, like players, cannot learn without making plenty of mistakes along the way. But they learn best in a positive atmosphere. If you are a coach and you see a young official consistently making a mistake, privately and quietly share your perception. Helping someone learn is a form of respect.

approach the law with a close-minded philosophical slant that predisposes them to certain outcomes. Nevertheless, the larger bias usually comes from the partisans. Following a game, players and fans on both sides often believe that the officials were biased against their team. We have yet to see a coach screaming red-faced at an official for a call that went in his or her favor.

Not surprisingly, competitors and decompetitors adopt different attitudes toward officials. Just as the decompetitor may seek to bend the rules to gain an advantage, she may also seek to manipulate the official with the same aim in mind. She may view the referee as just one more obstacle to overcome in the pursuit of victory. In the mind of the decompetitor, the mental categories for officials and opponents tend to blur. Opposition to success comes in the form of "rules, refs, and rivals," all of which occupy the same mental space. When opponents are considered enemies not deserving of full respect, disrespect for officials is to be anticipated.

The attitude toward officials is quite different for the true competitor. Foremost, competitors respect the humanity of officials. Officials are neither objects to be overcome nor enemies to be manipulated or conquered. They are people with an essential role to play in the contest. Recognizing their vital function in the game, competitors extend respect, even appreciation, to the officials. They also recognize that they themselves are more likely to be biased than the officials. Consequently, they take a more charitable and humble stance in their approach toward questionable calls than decompetitors do.

The Reality of Injustice

Thus far, we have been talking about contests, rules, and officials as if *the system* is generally fair and just. Under such an assumption, it is reasonable to expect true competitors to adopt a respectful attitude toward the rules and a humble stance in relation to officials. Respect for legitimate authority is an important part of character.

Unfortunately, sometimes the deck is stacked. Sometimes the rules, rather than upholding fairness and welfare, diminish them. In both sports and society, the idea of a level playing field may be honored more in language than in practice. The reality of injustice should not be ignored or swept under the proverbial rug. Wherever there is real injustice, vehement protest and challenge are called for. Rocking the boat can be a moral act; protest a moral virtue. The true competitor is not a passive conformist who will sit silently by when discrimination rears its ugly head.

But what about the smaller injustices that occur everyday in contests? To be sure, sometimes coaches and leaders don't have our best interest in mind. Sometimes opponents cheat and officials look the other way. Again, protest can be legitimate. Still, in the heat of a contest, it is vitally important to recognize that taking matters into your own hands is rarely a good idea. While it is important to respond to systemic injustice (doing so though thoughtful, organized strategies), it is often a mistake to try to redress immediate, context-specific injustices. This is because the perception of injustice can exert a strong tug toward decompetition, just as strong as that exerted by such forces as decompetitive opponents, extrinsic rewards, unfulfilled ego needs, and rigid gender roles. Let's take a closer look at this.

The Role of Perceived Injustice

> **"** Thou shalt not be a victim. Thou shalt not be a perpetrator. Above all, thou shalt not be a bystander. **"**
>
> Inscription, Holocaust Museum, Washington, D.C.

Most of us, at least occasionally, feel like victims. We believe someone has done something unfair or hurtful to us—*and gotten away with it*. We believe we are subjected to rules or practices that are unfair. Perhaps we haven't gotten the rewards that we believe we rightly deserve. Or perhaps we see others take credit for something we did. What these situations have in common is a perception of injustice.[11]

When we believe that we have drawn the short straw of injustice, we naturally want to set things straight and restore equality. This is a natural impulse and one that can affirm and reinforce the moral principles of equality, justice, and fairness. Injustice, wherever it is found, should be challenged. When Jackie Robinson defied the color barrier in baseball, he was challenging a real injustice. He was right to do so. Those who fight to end gender apartheid within the Olympic programs of some countries are fighting a noble and worthy fight.[12] The list of injustices is indeed long.

Unfortunately, however, the desire to restore justice can also rapidly guide us down a spiral staircase into decompetition. Perception can play tricks. In this section, we address two sources of perceived injustice: the actions of opponents and the actions of officials. In both cases, the perception of injustice exerts a pull toward decompetition.

The Problem of Escalation

In chapter 6, we noted that one force pushing us toward decompetition is the presence of decompetitors. When we see an opponent cheat or throw an illegal elbow, we are mightily tempted to retaliate. Strategically, retaliation is rarely a good idea, especially if we are interested in promoting true competition. But the temptation is real. Cheating does create injustice; so does aggression. Responding in kind, however, is not the answer. In fact, responding in kind may be what the decompetitors we face believe they are doing.

If you're a teacher or a parent, you've probably sat two kids down who were arguing or fighting and asked them: "Who started it?" Invariably, each child points to the other. Although sometimes the perpetrator is clearly identifiable, more often it is impossible to untangle who really got the argument going. The origins are lost in a web of charges, countercharges, and ambiguities. So, in frustration, you may have simply responded, "It takes two to fight," and sent the kids to separate rooms.

We like to believe that events follow a neat cause-effect, stimulus–response logic. Event A causes event B, and so on. In many situations, however, just what causes what is open to variable, and often equally valid, interpretations.

Consider Pedro and Steve, two boys who are best friends. Sometimes, their friendship is derailed by a consistent argument. Pedro gets upset with Steve's tendency not to share things. Whenever Steve starts to become stingy, Pedro pushes him to share. Looked at through the framework of stimulus–response, Steve's stinginess is a stimulus. That stimulus leads, quite naturally, to Pedro's response of pushiness.

Now look at the following sequence of letters:

$$... S\ P\ S\ P\ S\ P\ S\ P\ S\ P\ S\ P ...$$

Each "S" represents an act of stinginess and each "P" an act of pushiness. The dots at the beginning and end of the sequence of letters simply suggest that there is no definable beginning or ending point to the sequence of events.

Pedro and Steve each look at the sequence differently. Pedro experiences the above chain of events as consisting of a series of "S → P" chains. By this we mean that Pedro sees Steve's stinginess (S) as causing his pushiness (P). Thus Pedro mentally "punctuates" the above sequence of events like this: ...S→ P, S→ P, S→ P, S→ P, and so on.

Steve, on the other hand, experiences the exact same series of events, except that Steve sees a different pattern. Steve sees: P→ S, P→ S, P→ S, and so on. Steve thinks he is stingy only in response to Pedro's pushiness. What Pedro sees as "stimulus," Steve perceived as "response," and vice versa.

Who is right? It is impossible to say. What is labeled "stimulus" and what is considered "response" is largely arbitrary; it depends on the vantage point. In the language of communications theory, *it depends on how you mentally punctuate the sequence.*[13] The important point is that each child firmly believes that he is only responding to a provocation on the part of the other. Such cycles, once set in motion, tend to escalate in their intensity. This is shown graphically in Figure 7.1.

Our example is rather trite. The reality it refers to, however, is rampant in sports. A baseball pitcher hurls the ball toward the head of the batter. Angered, the batting team's dugout empties as players charge the field. Who started it? If you are on the team that was batting, you will point to the pitcher who hurled the ball at the batter's head. But the pitcher says, with righteous indignation, that he was only retaliating for an earlier offense against his team, and that, in turn, was caused by [fill in the blank]. It's like

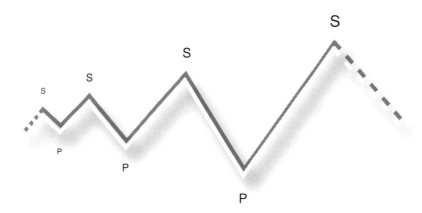

Corrective escalation; each act of stinginess (S) leads to an act of pushiness (P).

Pedro and Steve. Such sequences, which tend to grow and escalate, rarely have a clearly identifiable beginning point. Yet each side strongly believes that the other side was at fault.

What happens in sports also occurs, with tragic consequences, on the world stage every day. Take the Israeli–Palestinian conflict. As we write this, Israel just conducted a military incursion into the West Bank. Several civilians were killed. The raid was justified as a response to the firing of homemade rockets by Palestinians. The Palestinians, in turn, saw their rocket attacks as justifiable responses to earlier Israeli heavy-handed tactics. No doubt, they will seek to retaliate. What is the stimulus and what is the response? Who is acting offensively and who is acting defensively? The answer depends on which side of the fence you stand on. Each side can always go further back in history to identify an injustice that they were seeking to correct.

In numerous international as well as intergroup and interpersonal conflicts, the answer to the question of who is being belligerent and who is being defensive depends on whether you see "S → P" or "P → S." Stated differently, the answer depends less on objective facts than on where your sympathies lie.[14] Each side often feels quite passionately that it is correct.

The point is that contests encourage us to "punctuate" an ongoing sequence of events so that we see the opponent as the provocateur and ourselves as the party that must push back. Regardless of the origins of a conflict (which can rarely, if ever, be determined with precision), each side sees the other as the initiator. Stated more broadly, we have a strong tendency to see the opponent as deviating first from the norms of true competition; we see ourselves as just responding.

In sports, school, business, and politics, to name a few places where contests are frequent, people often believe they have been disrespected, violated, or treated unfairly or aggressively. That perception leads them to respond in an effort to correct the injustice. From the vantage point of the other party, however, their effort to "right the balance" is a provocation or escalation. What one person perceives as a response the other may perceive as a stimulus. Again, what is stimulus and what is response depends on how you mentally punctuate the sequence of events.

How do you get out of such an escalating cycle? The best strategy is to stay focused on your motive for competing in the first place—the pursuit of excellence and enjoyment. You will never get to excellence or enjoyment by responding to cheating with cheating or aggression with aggression. A better idea is to break the cycle, embrace responsibility, take the initiative in restoring balance, not by retribution or by retreat, but by simply giving your best.

Will this strategy put you at a disadvantage? Occasionally. If an opponent cheats and gets away with it, they are advantaged. But it is important to remember this: Staying focused on your own performance is itself an advantage. All other things being equal, there is an advantage to being a true competitor. Retaliation is a distraction that undermines optimal performance. So forget seeking to redress minor injustices (they may be just perception bias anyway), and keep your head in the game. Even if they aren't doing it perfectly, let the officials do their job. They are the ones who have the primary responsibility for enforcing the norms of fairness.

But what if the officials are unfair?

Bad or Biased Officiating

Perceived injustice often comes about through a questionable call on the part of an official. We've all been there. The game is tight. Tensions are high; emotions are steaming. The clock is winding down. Suddenly our team makes a brilliant play only to be erroneously flagged by an official. Rotten call! And it's going to cost us the game.

Bad calls are one thing; biased calls are quite another. That's what really gets our blood boiling. That gymnastics judge keeps doling out higher scores to favored gymnasts. The official from the Big Ten is favoring a local team. That high school ref officiating at my daughter's soccer game overlooks offsides by his niece but calls my daughter for them every time.

Of course, concerns about bias extend far beyond sports. Why did the teacher give me a C when my paper was just as good as Tom's, who got a B? Why did that cop pull me over? I wasn't going nearly as fast as that red Porsche that sped by me five minutes ago. Why did the boss give Cassandra a raise and not me? Moving to a much larger and more systemic picture: Why are women still paid less than men for the same work? Why are African Americans jailed more frequently than whites for similar offenses? You can fill in the blanks: Why is group ___ treated one way, while group ___ is treated more favorably?

There are a great many real injustices in the world, genuine tragedies. We don't want to diminish the importance of fighting against them. In the big economic "contest," for example, biases are built into the foundations of the game: the way we allocate resources, govern financial institutions, regulate commerce, and practice commercial interchange. The economic rules themselves are not always fair, which can lead to predictable and systemic discrimination against some and unfair advantaging of others.[15]

Our focus here, however, is much more narrow and modest. It is limited to situations in face-to-face contests in which we believe we are being treated unfairly by officials. Sometimes we are. Officials are human. They can have hidden loyalties and biases, sometimes knowingly but more often, unintentional. So, yes, we are sometimes wronged by officials. Much more often, however, we only believe we have been wronged. Yet that belief is a powerful incentive to slip into a decompetitive mind-set. When we believe the officials are against us, we are tempted to take matters into our own hands. That is almost always a mistake.

There is no easy remedy for distorted perception, but here's our recommendation: *Assume the best.* Recognize that you are more likely biased than the official. Act charitably. At a minimum, wait until you are calmer and can evaluate the situation more dispassionately. If you still believe that you have been treated unfairly, take action. File a protest. Talk to the person. Go public. Do whatever is within your legitimate power to remedy the situation. But first make sure that you are not simply seeing what is to your advantage to see.

Leading for Responsibility

> ❝ I ask our players to follow three basic rules.
> Do what is right. Do your very best. Treat others
> like you'd like to be treated. Those rules answer the
> three basic questions we ask of every player, and every
> player asks of us. The questions are: Can I trust you?
> Are you committed? Do you care about me?
> People might think this is corny, but I don't care.
> This is what I believe. ❞
>
> Lou Holtz

The field of ethics can be rather abstract. When an ethical issue arises in the heat of a contest, however, it is anything but abstract. It is pulsating with blood. It is in your face. It is down in the mud of life. Nothing is more real than a decision about whether to retaliate against an aggressive opponent, blast an official who seems to be having an off day, or take advantage of a loophole in the rules. Because many people first learn about competitive ethics through the medium of sport, the moral vision that we develop in sports may well carry over to realms far beyond the playing fields.[16]

If a child learns that it is OK to bend the rules in sports, he may well ask, Why not in school? Why not, years later, when filling out a tax form? If a child learns that opponents are there to be exploited, that officials are there to be berated, and that rules are there to be bent, such attitudes are unlikely to take a time-out when the game is over. Whether we are on the playing field, in the gym, or in a corporate boardroom, we are always playing the game of life.

Leaders need to help those under their influence develop a keen sense of personal responsibility. The way leaders perceive and respond to rules and officials can have a profound impact on the attitudes and values of those they lead. In this section, we talk about two kinds of rules: those set up within the team and formal game rules. We also talk about fostering an attitude of respect toward officials.

Team Rules

In chapter 4, we suggested that all team members should be involved in the creation of team rules. This helps give everyone a sense of ownership. Similarly, personal responsibility is reinforced when rule enforcement is seen as everyone's job. Because the well-being of the team affects everybody, everybody must take responsibility to ensure that the team's rules are upheld.

The focus, however, should not be on the rules themselves, but on the values that the rules seek to embody. Duke University's basketball coach, Mike Krzyzewski, recommends that coaches have as few rules as possible. He has observed that the more rules you set, "the more you become a slave to the rules. . . . You become an administrator of rules rather than a leader. So the first thing is to not have too many rules."[17]

When it comes to team rules, you do not want to travel the same path that happens with more formal rules. You don't want to keep proliferating more rules to address new situations and new contingencies. It's better to have just a few basic rules that all members understand and agree to. This also has the important advantage of focusing attention not on the letter of the rules, but on their spirit. The leader's goal should be to encourage each team member to take responsibility for upholding the intent of each rule, recognizing how it serves the common good.

If the team has come to consensus that they like the rule "Be on time to practice," the leader's goal should be to foster a commitment to a spirit of punctuality that carries beyond arriving at the appointed time. The team needs to become clear, through discussion rather than lecture, about the underlying value and its importance beyond the immediate context.

Developing a sense of responsibility for the spirit of team rules moves easily into the second focus: game rules.

Game Rules

We advocate a democratic leadership style. Nevertheless, players should be crystal clear that the coach never, under any circumstances, expects them to cheat. That's a floor below which they cannot descend. Even within a highly democratic coaching style, there is plenty of room for saying that some things are simply out of bounds. Cheating is one of these because it destroys the game. It makes it impossible to realize the key values of excellence and enjoyment. It has no place in true competition. So, before the season even begins, coaches should talk to their teams about cheating, bringing everyone on board to a full commitment against it.

The situation can be more complicated than external observers might realize, however. Like laws, rules need to be interpreted and applied to specific situations. Invariably, there are gray areas. Through countless interaction across extended periods of time, players develop unstated, informal norms that help define how the formal rules are interpreted. For example,

Dear Authors:

I think there is a problem with relying too heavily on sports to illustrate ideas that you suggest apply beyond the artificial world of games. In much of life, we compete for real resources, not ones that are artificially scarce such as goals in ice hockey. If my child is starving and so is yours, are we going to follow the same "fair" rules in contesting for food? Are there things that trump rules?

— Hungry for Insight

Dear Hungry for Insight:

It is true that competition looks different in different settings and that many of our ideas need to be thoughtfully adapted to different contexts. Certainly in the extreme situation that you describe, seeking excellence and enjoyment through contesting is irrelevant. In such a situation, outcome matters more than process, and you are unlikely to be concerned about rules. If a person must steal to survive, we'll side with the thief. But such extreme situations are not very illuminating because they don't capture the reality most of us face on a daily basis. Even when outcomes are important, following the rules (assuming they are just and fair) and upholding the moral principles on which they are based is ethically required. True competitors recognize this.

The existence of an informal culture of rule interpretation can complicate the issue of fairness. Is every intentional rule violation an act of cheating? What criteria can a leader use to identify what counts as cheating?

rules prohibiting certain types of body contact in basketball may come to be interpreted quite loosely, as might some forms of holding in football. This loosening of the formal rules can be done not to undermine fairness, but to make the game more enjoyable and flexible.

Over time, the informal norms evolve and change, partly in response to the evolution of athletes' skills and partly in response to changes in the broader culture. The same formal rule may be applied quite differently at various points in history, at various competitive levels, and in various geographical locations. Some technical rule violations may be universally accepted, even by officials, within the culture of a sport as practiced by a particular league or group. Taking a strictly legalistic stance toward the rules is not the solution.

Here's the key problem with the informal culture: Over time it has a tendency to drift away from the moral underpinnings of the rules.[18] One major purpose of the rules is to make the outcome of the contest dependent primarily on the mastery and execution of specified game-relevant skills and strategies. The informal culture drifts toward adding: "plus our cleverness in getting away with whatever we can get away with." Most often, athletes push for a looser interpretation of rules, rather than a stricter one. Without becoming rigid and legalistic, leaders need to apply the brakes to this tendency before the informal culture drives off the road of fairness.

The moral norm of fairness is the key definer of cheating, even more than the literal rule. Seeking an unfair advantage, whether within or outside the rules, is cheating. An unfair advantage is created by any action that deliberately increases the likelihood of victory apart from the execution of mutually accepted game-relevant skills and strategies.

Focusing on excellence and enjoyment minimizes the tendency toward cheating. Within true competition, there is little temptation to cheat because the mind is fully absorbed in game-relevant skills and strategies. Pushing to transcend oneself in the executive of those skills and strategies is a source of enjoyment and satisfaction. For the true competitor, cheating is simply not considered. Not usually, at least. However, even the true competitor can be tempted to cheat in response to the cheating of others. Cheating may seem like a way to right the balance. However, it is a temptation that needs to be resisted.

Leaders need to provide opportunities to practice resisting such temptations. In addition to talking about it and collectively thinking ahead about how to respond, it may be helpful to actually rehearse it. In a scrimmage, for example, the coach might huddle with one side and tell them to deliberately violate a specific rule. When the rule violation occurs and the other side has had a chance to respond, the coach can stop the action and discuss it. If the noncheating side reacted in kind or inappropriately, the coach can talk about how responding to cheating can unleash a spiral of tit-for-tat exchanges that leads away from the team's goals. She can also talk about who they are as a team and the moral values they uphold, as well as the importance of character. Ten minutes of practice can sometimes drive the point home more clearly than an hour of talk.

A similar strategy can be used in responding to bad calls from officials, our next theme.

Officials

Kids can't learn to dribble without dribbling. They can't learn an offensive scheme without running through it repeatedly. Yet we often expect them to act with good character without practice. Although character is not reducible to good habits, it is important to have the opportunity to rehearse appropriate behavior. Perhaps no place is this more true than in relation to officials. At all levels of competition, people need the opportunity to practice respect for officials.[19] Everyone needs experience on both sides of the relationship.

Everyone who competes should have the opportunity to take the role of an official. In youth sports, for example, kids should have the opportunity—and the responsibility—to officiate during their own practices. Once someone has had the experience of being an official, it is much easier to understand the importance of respect for officials.

How do you want your team to respond to a bad call? Hopefully, by keeping focused on the game. So practice that. When you are officiating at a scrimmage, for example, deliberately make a really bad call. How does the team respond? If they have not yet learned to ignore it and stay focused, stop the action and talk about it. Practice it until the appropriate response is automatic.

Finally, a valuable life lesson that can be learned in sports is to take responsibility. As a leader, you can nurture responsibility by discouraging any effort to blame officials for an unfavorable outcome. Sure, officials may sometimes play a role, but rarely—very rarely—is a bad call or even a series of bad calls the primary determinant of the outcome.

Respecting rules and officials and accepting personal responsibility are important components of true competition. In the next chapter, we expand on the relationship between the value of winning and the values that come from the process of contesting. ■

1   Numerous individuals have suggested that fairness may be a universal moral concern. See, for example, Haan, Aerts, and Cooper (1985).

2   Clifford and Feezell (1997) put it this way: "The internal goal of an athletic contest is to win the game. But what counts as winning is determined by the rules of the game. To play a sport is to engage in an activity that is defined in terms of the rules that have been created to make the activity possible. Because a game is essentially a rule-governed activity, the game itself is possible only because of an implicit agreement on the part of each participant to play by the rules" (p. 63). Because all formal contests are rule-governed activities, the same requirement of rule adherence applies. Even informal contests are typically rule governed, though the rules are less formalized.

3   Various types of rules have various moral and conventional implications. Linguist John Searle (1969), for example, distinguishes between "constitutive" rules and "regulative" rules. For a discussion of how game rules function similarly to and differently from social-conventional rules and moral rules, see Weston and Turiel (1980).

4   See Fraleigh (1984).

5   Ibid.

6   Jim Thompson (2003), founder of the Positive Coaching Alliance, makes a similar point: "Sportsmanship has a passive feel about it—it's a minimum. It seems like it is mostly about not doing something bad: 'don't yell at officials. Don't break the rules.' PCA believes 'Honoring the Game' is a powerful proactive concept" (p. 102).

7   Many game rules serve both conventional and moral functions (Shields & Bredemeier, 1995). As conventions, they enable the social regulation of the activity; as moral regulations, they point beyond themselves to ethical principles that they partially encode. Because contests are often "mixed domain" (Turiel, 1983) activities, participants may orient more to one domain of thought than the other. Because competitors view the contest as a partnership enabling excellence and enjoyment, they are more likely to orient to the moral function of the rules. This focus is consistent with viewing the contest in light of the ideals it can nurture. Decompetitors are less interested in such ideals and, viewing the contest as a battle, are more likely to orient to the minimal requirements of the rules. This lends itself to a more conventional approach.

8   Still (2002).

9   Prejudice and discrimination often reflect something of a pyramid. At the top of the pyramid are the most ugly and vicious acts that are perpetrated by only a small minority. However,

(continued)

(continued from previous page)

as one moves down the pyramid to less overt and intense forms of negative action, larger and larger numbers of people are involved. Shields (1986) states the pyramid principle this way: "The latent antipathies of the many will be amplified in the overt actions of a few" (p. 166).

10   Clifford and Feezell (1997), p. 52.

11   The concept of perceived injustice is important in numerous fields of investigation (e.g., Azzi, 1998). For example, in sport psychology it is seen as a significant contributor to aggression and violence in sports (e.g., Scholtz & Willemse, 1991).

12   The reference to gender apartheid is based on the fact that many countries still do not allow women to participate in sports altogether or restrict their participation in significant ways. The International Olympic Committee charter states that "any form of discrimination with regard to a country or a person on grounds of race, religion, politics, sex or otherwise is incompatible with belonging to the Olympic Movement." Despite its charter, the Olympic Committee has failed to address the refusal of some countries to allow women to join their Olympic teams. Countries with "men only" policies include Brunei, the United Arab Emirates, and Saudi Arabia. Numerous other countries have various restrictions that limit women from full participation.

13   See Watzlawick, Beavin, and Jackson (1967), especially pp. 54-59.

14   Watzlawick (1976).

15   See Rosenau (2003). It is important to emphasize that (a) capitalism is not built exclusively on the idea of competition and (b) unfettered competition in the marketplace is rejected by virtually all modern economists. Moreover, an inherent tension exists between our democratic tradition, built on an egalitarian ethic that supports the widest possible dispersion of political power (one person, one vote), and the structural dynamic of capitalism, which works at counterpurposes—namely, to concentrate power and control. As economic power and control become more concentrated, the foundations of genuine democracy are eroded, even as the formal structures of democracy are left in place. See, for example, former secretary of labor Robert Reich's (2007) book on the pitfalls of "supercapitalism."

16   This statement is difficult to prove empirically and rests, instead, on numerous autobiographical accounts. Building on his own experience in sports, for example, President Gerald Ford (1985) famously said, "Broadly speaking, outside of a national character and an educated society, there are few things more important to a country's growth and well-being than competitive athletics. If it is a cliché to say athletics build character as well as muscle, then I subscribe to the cliché" (p. 247).

17   The quote from Mike Krzyzewski is found in Janssen and Dale (2002), p. 43.

18   The tendency of the informal culture to drift away from the spirit of the rules is evidenced, for example, in Gary Fine's (1987) excellent ethnography of a Little League baseball team.

19   Clifford and Feezell (1997) also suggest having officials visit the team and talk about the role of officials.

8

Playing and Winning
The Pursuit of Victory

Ever heard of the sport Q-ball? No? Well, imagine you have. Now imagine you are an exceptional Q-ball player and that your team is about to compete in a major tournament. You and your teammates arrive at the tournament site and go over to a large board where the brackets are laid out. You discover that the Horned Cupids will be your opponent in the first round. They're a pretty tough team, but not so tough that you can't defeat them if you are at the top of your game. The contest begins in an hour.

As captain, you take your team through some warm-ups. By the time the opening gong is sounded, your adrenaline is flowing; your mind is focused like a laser; your body is as responsive as a finely tuned piano. Early in the contest, the Horned Cupids surge ahead. But soon the tide turns and your team comes roaring back. You take the lead. Twice more the lead changes, but when the final gong sounds your team is up by 1 to claim the victory.

After several minutes of celebrating, your team hits the showers. You then gather to go out and see who your next opponent will be. You arrive at the big board and are stunned. Your team is not listed for the next round. Instead, the brackets indicate that the Horned Cupids will advance. Sure that a mistake has been made, you go to the tournament director to protest. The director patiently explains that there has been no error. The tournament, he says, is based on the principle that winning teams are eliminated. Only the losing team moves forward.

> **❝ We play with enthusiasm and recklessness.
> We aren't afraid to lose. If we win, great.
> But win or lose, it is the competition
> that gives us pleasure. ❞**
>
> Joe Paterno

The Q-ball tournament is totally bizarre, right? Yet Tim Gallwey describes a tennis tournament set up in just such a manner in his book *The Inner Game of Work*.[1] Of course, it wasn't part of college sports. Rather, it was a tournament set up during a national sales conference for a large American corporation. And it was set up to make a point: It's not all about winning.

In the film *White Men Can't Jump*, Rosie Perez says to her boyfriend: "Sometimes when you think you win, you haven't really won. And sometimes when you think you've lost, you haven't really lost."[2] Victory can come in the guise of defeat, and failure can stumble out of triumph. Although scoreboards declare winners and losers, the distinction is often without any real depth of meaning. Whether the scoreboard tracks individual or team points, test scores, sales, salaries, promotions, factory output, publications, or any other so-called objective measure of success, the same principle applies. Reality does not lend itself to the simple and often superficial duality of winner and loser. True competitors recognize the profound truth of Rosie's words. Decompetitors cling to the scoreboard to define what's real and valuable.

This chapter examines the role of seeking victory. No doubt, there can be very good reasons for wanting to win. Jobs can depend on it. So can self-esteem. In a contest, however, there are benefits to be had regardless of where you end up on the scoreboard. Though it sounds cliché, appreciating the intrinsic values inherent in contesting makes you a winner, regardless of the outcome. To tap into those values, we must maintain a balance between an outcome focus and a process focus. After discussing values that can enrich the experience of the true competitor, we once again identify forces that can knock competitors off balance and into decompetition. We conclude the chapter with reflections geared to leaders.

Playing to Win

No one plays to lose. Well, actually, some people use the contest as an opportunity to confirm their sense of inferiority, but they are the exception. They subvert the contest's meaning. When we compete with others, we sign an invisible contract to seek victory. This is true whether we are talking sports, politics, or business. A contest in which people aren't trying to win is like bread without flour, an omelet without eggs. It ceases to exist.

People compete to win. This is not a distortion of true competition; it is part of its essence.

So, then, do problems in competition arise because people are trying to win at any cost? No doubt, competition can turn sick with symptoms such as cheating, taunting, aggression, showboating, and other forms of disrespectful behavior. But is *trying to win at any cost* the correct diagnosis? Probably not. We have yet to meet a person who wants to achieve victory regardless of the costs to himself or others. This diagnosis would suggest that problems in contests are a rare disorder, yet in reality they are as prevalent as the common cold. Clearly the phrase *win at any cost* is hyperbole. More importantly, it is misleading.

When we claim that problems arise because some people seek to win at any cost, we divest ourselves of responsibility, finding it easier to blame a few people with highly distorted priorities. This diagnosis encourages us to look outward, rather than acknowledge that we all share in responsibility for the problems that too often infest contests. Moreover, this diagnosis totally misses the larger picture.

In our view, decompetition arises neither from a desire to win, nor typically from a desire to win at any cost. Primarily it arises from the contest

© Icon Sports Media

Children can exert considerable effort to meet a challenge and have fun at the same time. If hard work does not undermine enjoyment, what does? Can an overemphasis on winning detract from the positive benefits of sport?

structure itself. Because contests are set up to designate winners and losers, the very structure of the contest exerts a gravitational tug toward decompetition, and it exerts it on all participants. *The contest structure itself encourages people to define winning as the most important goal.* However, just as we can walk upright on the earth despite the pull of gravity, we can engage in true competition despite the pull toward decompetition exerted by the contest structure. Doing so takes effort, knowledge, and balance, however. Maintaining our balance in competition requires that we appreciate why the desire to win is important in the first place.

The Q-ball tournament creates a dilemma for participants. If losing is rewarded, if only the losers continue in the tournament, what is the purpose of playing hard? Why try to win? In stark fashion, the topsy-turvy tournament structure poses the question of whether effort and striving have value independent of the outcome. Those who think in terms of scoreboards alone may as well sit down on the field with their arms folded. But if winning is defined in terms of enjoyment and excellence, then striving for victory in the game is still the best course of action.

The question is not how much a person wants to win, but how well that desire is integrated with a desire for the fuller experience available. Importantly, these desires are not in a zero-sum, trade-off relationship with each other. A person can have a great desire to win simultaneously with a deep appreciation for the value of the contest itself, regardless of the outcome. In fact, top competitors often have burning desires in both dimensions. A strong desire to win can enrich the process.

Although a true competitor can feel both desires strongly, there is a proper priority between them. Yes, we play to win. But even more important, we play to improve, learn, have fun, enjoy, and seek excellence We compete to test and improve ourselves in body, mind, and character. Ultimately, the value of our striving to win is found in the contribution that such striving can make to our happiness and that of others. Such goals extend beyond the self and are grounded in a vision of a larger purpose and meaning. At least that's the orientation of the true competitor. In contrast, like a reader who sees in poetry only the literal meaning of the words, the decompetitor reduces the contest to the scoreboard, collapsing all values into the single goal of defeating others.

A fine line exists between competing hard and hardly competing. When one is hardly competing, one is slipping into decompetition. The goal has shifted from the pursuit of excellence through questing for victory to seeking victory in and for itself.

For those who work with youth, conveying this insight can be challenging. Kids can easily act out their immaturity and lose control if they think winning is the most important goal. In both word and deed, adults need to help children learn that it is important to strive to win, yet not because winning matters most. Adults often have trouble with this insight, so it is not surprising that children do. How can adults teach it to children? Briefly, they need to model it and talk about it. Eventually, children need to have experiences in which hard work blends with enjoyment in the pursuit of worthy goals. Such experiences pave the way for being able to fully grasp this idea. In chapter 9, we discuss in more detail how we can set up conditions, especially in sports, to nurture the spirit of true competition in children.

To summarize, the structure of a contest requires winning and losing. When a person enters a game, he must adopt the goal of winning if the game is to be played in the way it was intended. What matters isn't how much a person wants to win. Really, the stronger the desire to win, the better. What matter is the relative priority of winning. We don't need people to value winning less. We need them to value the process more. Ironically, the value of *striving to win* isn't found in winning. Winning is great when it happens, but what's most important is the striving. If we want to foster true competition, we need to encourage *competing hard* rather than *hardly competing.* To do so, we need to help all participants experience the contest as a deep well of values from which they can drink.

Values of the Game

❝ Each time a father takes his son or daughter to the playground to shoot baskets for the first time, a new world opens—one full of values that can shape a lifetime. ❞

Bill Bradley

We have mentioned several times that competing is beneficial regardless of who emerges victorious. Just what are the benefits of competition? If the process of competing is of utmost significance, what values are nurtured in that process, that striving? Broadly speaking, they are values stemming from excellence and enjoyment, but can we be more specific?

Answering that question is always provisional. Bill Bradley identified several values, including passion, discipline, selflessness, and respect.[6] Read the autobiographies of other great competitors, and you will find that each identifies a somewhat different list of the values that they learned through competition. There is no definitive, or correct, list. Competition is a great banquet. In that banquet, some will taste fish; others, chicken. The vegetarians among us may taste tofu.

The specific values that a true competitor discovers or strengthens through competition cannot be identified in advance; not completely, at least. Each person will benefit differently, and each competitive context is likely to nurture somewhat different values.

The Game of Life

Phil Jackson once remarked, "There's more to life than basketball, and there's more to basketball than basketball." Basketball, like all sports, is as much about life as it is about physical skills. In *Values of the Game*, Bill Bradley reflects on the qualities he nurtured through playing basketball.[3] Specifically, he talks about developing passion, discipline, selflessness, respect, perspective, courage, leadership, responsibility, resilience, and imagination. It's a great list. He also tells a number of moving and poignant stories about how his career in basketball prepared him for his career beyond the court.

The learning curve bends in both directions. Games can teach for life, and life can be rendered more manageable and enjoyable when viewed as a game. For 16 years, Madelyn Jennings served as senior vice president of human resources for Gannett Company, the largest newspaper publisher in the United States. In an interview, she recalled that when faced with the most serious business decisions, some CEO would often say, "Just remember, it's all a game."[4] The point was not to diminish the importance of the decision. Rather, it was to say that we often do our best when we lighten up, appreciate the process, and see things in a broader perspective than simply through the lens of outcomes.

When confronting serious issues in life, we can benefit from thinking playfully. All competition, whether in sports, school, business, or elsewhere, requires finding the balance between seriousness and playfulness, between work and pleasure, between effort and enjoyment. Sometimes we may need to lighten up. Other times, we may need to get serious. Like finding the right station on an old radio dial, to experience true competition we may need to dial up toward seriousness or down toward playfulness.[5] When you find the right balance, you can enjoy the music of true competition.

In general, we suggest that people may discover values that guide personal growth, support a sense of community, and put them in touch with the transcendent, however they may envision that.[7] These, of course, are overlapping categories. Nevertheless, we will use them to illustrate some of the benefits of participating in competition.

Personal Growth Values

Some of the many values that competition can nurture and support under the broad umbrella of personal growth include passion and enthusiasm, optimism, self-understanding, and self-control. The reader may recognize that these values are connected with character development. We begin by reflecting briefly on enthusiasm.

Ralph Waldo Emerson once wrote, "Enthusiasm is the mother of effort and nothing great was ever achieved without it." Only when we have a strong desire can we pursue our goals with energy and commitment. Passion is one of the most important elements of a happy and meaningful life. Those who are truly happy have allowed their deepest desires to guide their life choices. They have discovered their passion and allowed it to bloom into enthusiastic action. Competition can help clarify our desires and enable us to act on them.

Clearly, no one can maximize their abilities in all areas. We may wish to expend a great deal of effort on some pursuits, but somewhat less on others. You may enjoy golf and yet not want to devote five hours a day to perfecting your game. Although lasting happiness is found in the dedicated pursuit of excellence, seeking excellence in everything is self-defeating. It is also overwhelming and exhausting. I'm OK with not becoming the best mathematician I'm capable of becoming.

Competing raises such questions as these: Is it worth the effort? Do I enjoy the process? Do I want to push further? What is my level of commitment to this goal? Am I finding enjoyment? Reflecting on these questions can help us clarify our desires and values. As we tap into them, our lives are energized with passion and enthusiasm. Of course, even when we are engaged in activities that are important to us, we still will not be passionate all the time. That brings us to a second area of personal growth.

Another growth dimension that competition can nurture pertains to the willpower, or what we call *skill power,* component of our character. To pursue excellence and enjoy a sense of personal fulfillment, our initial commitment must be sustained through time. We must hone the capacity to overcome obstacles, work through frustrations, and stay focused despite distractions. We must recognize that enthusiasm can wax and wane and that we must sometimes work through an apparent lack of desire. Others, referring to similar ideas, might talk about developing discipline, courage, resilience, self-control, dedication, persistence, or perseverance. These are not identical virtues, but they all bear a close family resemblance. They all require an ability to manage emotions and stay focused on goals despite challenging circumstances.[8]

Because of the heightened emotions they arouse, contests also provide an opportunity to practice other aspects of self-regulation, including controlling temper, managing fear, and regulating arousal level. The hot-tempered athlete, for example, can learn from contesting how to manage her temper successfully. That may be a vital life lesson with benefits far beyond the playing field. The student who experiences disabling anxiety during tests can learn to face his fears by mastering the techniques of anxiety management. Perhaps he will be able to extend his courage to other domains in which anxiety or fear has hampered his pursuit of goals.

Competition contributes to skill power in other ways as well. For example, success in sports or other competitive endeavors requires keeping long-term goals in mind while simultaneously breaking those goals down into a sequence of manageable, short-term objectives. Competition invariably involves surprises that require flexible thinking and an ability to adapt quickly. These are skills that improve with practice and with deliberate effort; with guidance, such skills can also be transferred beyond the immediate arena within which they were learned.[9]

Importantly, competition also involves temptations to take shortcuts. Staying true to one's values and principles requires not only moral clarity but also, once again, skill power. The athlete tempted to cheat, the salesperson tempted to lie to a customer, the politician tempted to slander the opponent are all offered an opportunity to build their skill power.

Optimism might be considered part of skill power, but it is worth highlighting as a key value of its own. A wealth of scientific evidence suggests that optimism is a crucial contributor to a healthy and happy life, and contesting can enable a person to hone this skill-based value.[10] Contests naturally have their ebbs and flows. They provide a rich opportunity to practice rising above the ups and downs, neither descending into despair when things go badly nor taking benefits for granted when all is going well. Within competition, participants can discover and experience the benefits of composure and levelheadedness, of hope and confidence. What sport enthusiast cannot recall a great comeback when most fans had given up? The great comeback is a powerful metaphor, a potent mental model, for approaching challenging circumstances.

Let's be clear: Optimism does not require turning a blind eye to reality. We are talking about *realistic* optimism, not indulging in groundless flights of fantasy. But optimism does require seeing possibilities that others may miss or dismiss. Hope is powerful and can help bring about the reality hoped for. We will have more to say about learning optimism in chapter 9. For now, it is simply important to indicate that it is a value that can be learned and practiced through competition.

Finally, contesting can also be a guide on a journey of self-discovery.[11] How do you handle stress? Why do you feel competitive with some people and not others? How tied is your self-esteem to outperforming others? How disciplined are you in pursuing a goal? What is really important to you? Competition can help provide answers to these questions and many others. Such answers, of course, are always provisional. When we find answers that are troubling, we can make changes. That's the beauty of life. We can modify the script we are living. One purpose of this book is to help readers act from a different script when they enter a contest, a script based on a metaphor of partnership rather than of war.

Community Values

Contests also provide people with an opportunity to gain in the arts of friendship and community.[12] On the team, people learn to work together, to build bridges across various skills, interests, and backgrounds. As the team works hard toward common goals and endures the trials of the season, friendships tend to deepen. If all goes well in the team chemistry, members discover the life-enriching values of trust, loyalty, commitment, and respect. The intrinsic enjoyment of friendship, of course, is not dependent on winning. In fact, enduring loss and hardship together can actually strengthen the bonds of friendship.

Bill Walton, winner of the NBA's most valuable player award in 1978, said he was never interested in being a star. He just wanted to be part of a great team. For many, both in business and sports, competition is all about camaraderie. It is about friendship and loyalty. It is about giving oneself to a team effort.

Giving oneself to a team effort opens us to the idea of the common good. Participating on a team can provide experiences of interdependence in which everyone relies on everyone else. Such experiences of mutual benefit, of dedication to the whole, can also lay the foundation for an appreciation of the broader values of citizenship.

There is much to gain from relationships with teammates, but relationships with opponents are also important.[13] Sometimes opponents are strangers and offer the opportunity to learn to approach unfamiliar people with

© Icon Sports Media

Contests tend to generate antagonisms and hostilities. How can positive relationships with teammates and opponents be fostered within true competition?

openness and affirmation. Sometimes we compete with people we know and we can learn to embrace confrontation within friendship. In all cases, opponents are in *opposition* to us—as far as the game goes. Although true competitors recognize that all genuine competition is built on a foundation of cooperation, there is the constant temptation to treat the partial truth of the game as the full truth of the relationship. We can ask no greater favor of a friend than to help us become the best we can be. That is a service that a good opponent provides. Learning to accept opponents with understanding, respect, and appreciation is a critical value of the game.

Self-Transcendence

We all want to be part of something larger than ourselves. Ultimately, we find meaning not by trying to pull our egos up by our bootstraps, but by dedicating ourselves to purposes that are nobler, more worthy, and better than we are. As Ralph Bunche, winner of the 1950 Nobel Peace Prize, once said, "Hearts are strongest when they beat in response to noble ideals." Whereas decompetition is driven by a desire to enhance the self by demonstrating superiority over others, competition involves commitment to larger purposes. For some, competing can even become a means of communing with the ultimate author of excellence and enjoyment.

Peter Schultz tells the following story: Three people were at work on a construction site. All were doing the same job, but when asked what the job was, the answers varied. "Breaking rocks," the first replied. "Earning a living," the second said. "Helping build a cathedral," said the third.

The true competitor enters the contest to build a cathedral. Inside the cathedral are the great values of humanity: compassion, friendship, fairness, respect, responsibility, justice, excellence, spirituality. The decompetitor, by contrast, just breaks rocks. Decompetitors don't connect their striving in the contest to the rich and noble pursuits of humanity. Maybe they are just seeking the external rewards, like the worker who is focused on earning a living. Maybe they are just seeking to demonstrate superior strength, like a worker who wants to break more rocks than others. In either case, the true meaning of the work is lost. Self-transcendence is one of the great values that can be found in striving for victory, but not when victory itself is the ultimate goal.

Sports and Spirituality

Readers interested in thinking more about the possible spiritual and ethical values connected with sport competition may find the Center for Sport, Spirituality, and Character Development at Neumann College a useful resource. Visit them at their Web site: www.neumann.edu/mission/sscd.asp.

Kids participating in sports can learn that giving themselves to the ideals of their sport and their team can be personally rewarding in ways that self-serving behavior can never be. Few experiences can be as enriching as being part of a selfless team that is motivated by a shared commitment to values-based goals.[14] Sports raise not only the question, Who am I? but also, Who are we? Implicitly or openly, team members ask themselves, What values do we share? Hopefully, they are values that transcend the scoreboard.

Winning and Losing

" Winning is great, sure, but if you are really going to do something in life, the secret is learning how to lose. Nobody goes undefeated all the time. If you can pick up after a crushing defeat, and go on to win again, you are going to be a champion someday. "

Wilma Rudolph

Such values as enthusiasm, skill power, optimism, knowledge, relationships, and self-transcendence are connected to the pursuit of victory. They are tied to process more than outcome. But the outcome is important too. Winning *is* important. Actually, so is losing. Whereas winning is far more enjoyable and often carries in its wake tangible benefits, losing has its own benefits. Before we turn to a reflection on what might throw us off balance and into decompetition, let's briefly reflect on values that the true competitor might find in winning and losing.

Perhaps the most important value to be learned through both winning and losing is a sense of perspective. Most of the time, the real consequences of winning and losing aren't as critical as we make them out to be. Lose a game and you can still eat the next day. Lose a tournament and you still have a roof over your head. Lose the championship and the same people still love you.

I often hear people express concern about others' attitudes toward winning. Sure, some people may experience an inner compulsion to win that pushes them into decompetition, yet the bigger problem may be people's attitudes toward losing.[15]

Marvin Berkowitz, a colleague of ours at the University of Missouri at St. Louis and a leading expert on character development, was one of the founders of an improvisational troupe called Comedy Sports. They had a motto: "We play to win but don't care if we lose." Perhaps that goes a bit too far. Most of us, in most contest situations, indeed care when we lose. Yet their motto captures an important point. Winning is desired more, but e true competitor embraces an orientation to loss that sees within it the otential for growth and gain.[16]

Disappointment can be very real and quite painful following a significant loss, but resilience is an important life skill. Even in the shadow of loss, hope is essential. Learning to navigate emotions in the wake of defeat, without tossing optimism overboard, enables the true competitor to chart a constructive response. This is true not only in sports, but also in other arenas of competition. Five contractors bid for a construction job. One wins. Life goes on for the others. When a company is driven out of business by competitors, the pain to the employees may be quite real. This is contesting with serious consequences and hopefully there are adequate social programs in place to aid in the transition. But even in this situation, the real meaning of winning and losing isn't found primarily in the consequences that follow, but in how we respond to them.

Losing is usually a temporary setback at most, and on the positive side, there is often real value in losing. If we don't get caught up in resentment, envy, or excuse making, it can be turned into an opportunity to learn so as to return to the contest with new skill and determination. Losing, if we let it, can also build humility, empathy, and compassion. Although often undervalued, these are important virtues at the core of good character.

The specific gains relevant to any defeat depend, of course, on the circumstances. Imagine, for example, that your team has just lost a critical game because of a badly blown call by an official. Of course, you're bitter. It feels like an injustice. You may need some time to regain your balance. But what can you learn? What virtues can you nurture? For starters, let's consider empathy. You might reflect on the fact that some people live their whole lives under a boot of injustice. Ideally, your unjust loss can awaken a desire to fight back—not against the relatively inconsequential injustice of a bad call, but against the real injustices that entrap people in dire circumstances. Perhaps this is an extreme example bordering on the absurd, but it does illustrate how losses can be transformative. Every loss is a learning opportunity.

Don't get us wrong. Whether you are a coach, a parent, an athlete, a student, a businessperson, or anyone else who competes, you should seek victory with your whole heart. Loss is not the goal, but when it comes, learn from it. Let it be the irritating grain of sand that becomes the pearl.

What about winning? Of course, there are values to be gained in winning as well. In true competition, winning can be appreciated as an enjoyable outcome that confirms the value of the effort. It feels good, and there's nothing wrong with celebrating a victory. Winning sometimes carries rewards and—so long as you won fairly—there is nothing wrong with enjoying them. Winning is not cruelty against the defeated. Giving your best performance is a gift to the opponent regardless of who wins. But gloating in victory is callous. It is a sure mark of decompetition. One of the great values that can be learned in victory is, once again, humility. Win with grace, and allow your opponent to lose with dignity.

Winning a contest is not the same as being a winner. Many things contribute to victory: skill and determination, yes, but also luck, circumstances beyond anyone's control, teammates, support networks, previous opportunities, and the list goes on. True competitors invariably share credit with a broad range of others. They recognize that they are indebted to others even for their own talents. If, for example, they've previously had the opportunity to compete against worthy opponents, they owe some of their skill to those opponents. Recall that Gandhi referred to his opponents as teachers. The key point is that human accomplishments are never based on individual effort alone. Every victory is a shared win; every defeat, a shared loss. And both winning and losing are temporary ebbs and flows that are less important than the river itself. Speaking of rivers, we turn now to a discussion of some of the dangerous currents that may capsize our efforts at true competition.

Pressures and Loyalties

> ** Winning is the name of the game.
> The more you win, the less you get fired. **
>
> Bep Guidolin

True competition is like paddling a canoe upstream. Built into the oppositional structure of competition is a current that will drift you into decompetition if you stop paddling in the desired direction. Sometimes the river is fairly calm and it is not too difficult to maintain your forward momentum. Other times, rapid currents may threaten your stability. Decompetitive opponents, extrinsic rewards, personal insecurities, and rigid gender roles, for example, can create dangerous whitewater in the river of contests. In this section we identify two additional sources of danger in the river: external pressures to win and misplaced loyalties. In both cases, focus is easily diverted from the values that come from the process of competing, and undue focus is placed on winning.

Outside Pressures

One of the most insidious forces pushing toward decompetition comes from people outside the contest. We live in a culture that idolizes winning. Those who are vested with leadership often experience tremendous pressure to provide tangible results in the form of victories. In his book *Raising a Team Player*, Harry Sheehy reflects on this reality:[17]

> ** The need to win to please outsiders who aren't
> interested in the personal development of the team's

> **players is what makes a lot of coaches change their priorities for the worse. In fact, one reason I decided to stop coaching the men's varsity basketball team in favor of becoming the athletic director at Williams was that wining was becoming too important. Losing had never stolen the joy of the game from me, and I didn't want that to change. 🙶**

Pressure can come from a number of sources. In the world of college sports, alumni and fans can put tremendous pressure on their universities to produce winning teams, especially in the high-profile sports. Pressure can also come from regents or directors who are concerned about the institution's public image. Feeling the pressure, college presidents pass it down the line. Athletic directors know they must produce, and they turn the fire up under the coaches. Finally, coaches, knowing their own jobs are at risk, overtly or implicitly threaten their athletes to produce.[18] Change the names and titles and you have the same flow of pressure in many corporations, offices, and schools.

Those on the front lines of competition, feeling the heat, drift toward a view of the opponent as the enemy. This is quite reasonable, given that their jobs may be on the line. If not their jobs, maybe promotions. Or maybe just their sense of self-worth. Regardless of where they come from, external pressures to win create considerable whitewater for those paddling their canoes toward true competition. But is giving in to that pressure inevitable?

Here's an important point to remember: Decompetitors are no more likely to win than true competitors.[19] In fact, adopting a decompetitive mind-set can interfere with optimal performance. Throughout this chapter we have emphasized that striving to win is important. Indeed, it is essential. But striving to win is not the same as focusing on winning. The most effective striving comes by focusing your full attention not on the outcome, but on the moment. Thinking about how important it is to win is a distraction. External pressures to achieve victory rarely translate into better performance. This is true in sports, school, music and art, and jobs. Although external pressure can be felt as a very real threat, the best and most effective response is to sustain a truly competitive attitude.

There is one circumstance, however, in which becoming decompetitive may increase the likelihood of standing atop the victory stand: cheating. Unfortunately, the old adage that cheaters never prosper is not always true. Sometimes, from the narrow perspective of the scoreboard, cheating does pay a dividend. When there are strong external pressures to win, the temptation to take shortcuts can be quite alluring. Add to that the possibility that the opponent may cheat, and that temptation doubles.

Contests often pose this stark question: What is more important to you, your character or winning? Sometimes you can have both, but sometimes you may have to choose. True competition is an ethic as much as a process. Being ethical is easy (but meaningless) when it comes at no price. Character is necessary only when there are temptations to overcome. For some, the temptation to cheat (in self-talk this is usually called bending the rules, finding a loophole, or just doing what everyone does) is enormous, especially when there are external pressures to win. Unfortunately, once you start down that path, it is hard to get off it.

Misplaced Loyalties

In addition to external pressures to win, decompetition can come from misguided internal pressure to achieve victory. This pressure can stem from a positive value: loyalty to those who depend on us. Loyalty can get us to focus unduly on winning, distorting the process of competition. It can lead us away from appreciating the values intrinsic to the process.

But isn't loyalty a virtue? It can be, of course; but it isn't when it undermines fairness and integrity. Take a high school coach who has a skilled athlete on the margin for a college scholarship. Should the coach seek to artificially beef up that athlete's stats to impress a college coach? Is that loyalty?

The problem of loyalty is common in the business world.[20] We have all read about the massive scandals that have plagued large corporations, affecting millions in the process. Companies such as Enron, WorldCom, and Arthur Anderson have become household names, and not for the good work they do. Of course, they are just the tip of the iceberg. Typically, we assume that greed is the primary motivator driving these scandals. Indeed, that is often the case. But sometimes a more subtle motive is at play: loyalty. Even compassion.

In his popular book, *The Fifth Discipline*, management guru Peter Senge states that of all the responsibilities of a leader, being a steward is the most basic.[21] It is a sound principle. Being a steward means recognizing that the ultimate purpose of leadership is not found in self-benefit. It is found in benefiting those led. As CEO, I may want to increase profits not just for myself, but also for shareholders and those who work for me. But poor decisions can come from good motives.

Imagine a small business. As the owner, I know all my employees. I know that Audrey has two kids with health problems; she desperately needs the insurance we provide. But recently, my company has been losing business. So, in an effort to maintain profits, I cut some corners. I violate a few rules. I don't do it for greed; I do it because I genuinely care about Audrey and my other employees. At one level, my motive is good; still, I have slipped into decompetition. A better strategy would be to help all my employees see the challenge posed by competitors as a spur to product or service improvement. If sustaining profitability is still impossible, it is time to give employees advance warning and ease the transition as much as possible. No matter what the form of contest, if you can't win fairly and you can't afford to lose, it is time to get out of the game.[22]

We noted earlier that competition can build camaraderie and friendship. These are positive values indeed. But team loyalty can also pave the road into decompetition. The team gets a significant emotional boost from winning, but after a loss your teammates feel down. It is a small step from that recognition to feeling like you want to do whatever it takes to help the team achieve victory, not because it is so important to you, but because it is important to the morale of the team, to your friends. In fact, a willingness to violate moral norms can even be interpreted by some as a measure of group loyalty.

In sum, loyalty is a double-edged sword. Appropriate loyalty, such as standing up for a friend falsely accused, is a virtue. Self-sacrifice for others is good—if the cause is just. But loyalty is not a free bird; it needs to live within the cage of moral principle. Loyalty should be geared to supporting the best in others. Blind loyalty is loyalty distorted. Just as it is not loyalty to let a friend drive intoxicated, loyalty is no excuse to resort to decompetitive tactics in a contest. Confronting a friend when she is tempted to violate her best ethical intuitions is a form of loyalty. Loyalty to friends is simultaneously loyalty to the values and ideals you share. One of the goals of leaders should be to nurture a shared commitment to the norms and ideals that support true competition. That brings us to the final section of the chapter.

Leaders as Culture Creators

> " A community is like a ship;
> everyone ought to be prepared to take the helm. "
>
> Henrik Ibsen

Most of the time, we think of peer pressure as negative: A kid goes along with a hazing ritual because he feels pressure to do so; a 15-year-old attends a party and is pressured to drink. We also tend to think about peer pressure in the context of adolescence. Yet peer pressure is exerted on people of almost any age. In this chapter, we have emphasized the importance of pursuing victory with vigor while simultaneously prioritizing the more intrinsic values that are largely independent of winning or losing. A key goal of any leader, whether in the home, the school, the sport environment, or the world of work, is to create a culture that supports this orientation. It is to make peer pressure work for him, rather than against him. The leader who is interested in promoting true competition needs to build a culture that supports the values, norms, and orientations of true competition.[23]

There is no magic formula for building a positive peer culture, but there are some reliable steps that can be used as approximate guides. We present them as steps because it may help to think about them that way, but they are not really so neatly sequential. In practice, they are overlapping and mutually reinforcing.

Step 1: Know Yourself

The place to begin to build a positive peer culture is to become rock sure of your own core beliefs and values. What do you stand for? What are the guiding lights in your life? In their study of highly successful and credible coaches, Jeff Janssen and Greg Dale found that such coaches were self-consciously character based.[24] They understood their principles, were able to articulate them, and were not willing to sacrifice them for wins. As Coach K said, "A lot of our success at Duke Basketball has to do with character. And at the heart of character is honesty and integrity."[25]

In the business world, moral clarity is equally valuable. For example, David Luban, the Frederick Haas Professor of Law and Philosophy at Georgetown University, provides an illuminating discussion of a number of notorious corporate ethical meltdowns, elaborating on the legal, cultural, economic, and psychological underpinnings of such business scandals. He laments the fact that "everyday morality does not have settled principles for hypercompetitive, highly adversarial settings."[26] Stated differently, many business leaders are confused about the moral principles that govern contests. If business leaders are going to build cultures supportive of true competition, they must begin with clarity about, and commitment to, the core values and principles that define competition as distinct from decompetition. That such moral courage and leadership is possible in the sometimes ruthless world of business is evidenced by numerous examples of successful companies that operate in full compliance with such core values.[27]

Step 2: Focus on Relationships

If you want to build a positive, character-based culture, then a second step is to focus on the three Rs: relationships, relationships, relationships. Building a character-based culture is all about building positive, affirming, values-reflecting relationships—relationships of trust, relationships of compassion, relationships of commitment.[28]

Of course, this is easier said than done. Relationships take time to build. Before you can enjoy the boat of trust, there must be a lake of supportive experiences. Those you lead must know that you are genuinely *for them*, that you have their best interests at heart. Even when you have tough things to say, they need to know that you will be both honest and compassionate. They need to know that you care about them as people, not just as cogs in the machine of team performance.

How you build positive, affirming relationships depends considerably on your own personality. A few guides, however, can be identified. Leaders with effective relationship skills consistently demonstrate that they care, act with integrity, communicate effectively, and express genuine interest. They are clear in their overall philosophy and direction, yet responsive to the individuality and needs of each team member. They handle conflicts with openness. They both inspire and empower those in their charge (see chapter 4).

Building positive relationships requires a balance between inviting appropriate intimacy and respecting boundaries. Most athletes, for example, don't want the coach to be their best friend. Even if they did, that's probably the wrong type of relationship to nurture. Leaders are mentors. Although both intimacy and trust are important, trust is paramount.

Here's an unfortunate but unavoidable truth: Relationships of caring and trust take months or years to build, yet they can be destroyed in an instant. The coach who blows up at a player who errs in a clutch situation demolishes the credibility of her thousand statements about winning not being the ultimate value. The accountant who cooks the books once may never be trusted again. True, we all err, and we are capable of giving and receiving forgiveness. When we make mistakes, it is best to return immediately to the virtue of honesty and forthrightly admit those mistakes. Rebuilding trust, however, takes far longer than building it in the first place.

Step 3: Build Enthusiasm

Earlier, we indicated that enthusiasm is a key value that can be nurtured through competition. Enthusiasm tends to unleash positive emotions. Moreover, it is often a potent antidote, as Harry Sheehy noted, to negative peer pressure.[29] Of course, if you work with youth, then you know that they often believe it is "uncool" to be enthusiastic. Despite this, enthusiasm is highly contagious. People like and want to be enthusiastic; they just don't want to stand out from the crowd. To overcome the culture of cool, give permission to fake enthusiasm. Once you start to fake it, you start to feel it.

Of course, it is vitally important to direct enthusiasm, to help those you lead be enthusiastic about the right things. To support true competition, focus the enthusiasm on effort and mutual support. In a game, for example, when one player substitutes for another, the whole team should greet the player returning to the bench with enthusiastic high-fives regardless of the game circumstances. In practice, when a player makes a great effort, especially when it is unsuccessful, it should be rewarded with enthusiasm from coach and teammates. Effort is what counts.

It is also helpful to support enthusiasm in a way that simultaneously affirms the team culture. When someone exhibits honest enthusiasm, praise her with "Yes! That's the way we do things on this team!" Stay positive as much as possible. But even when someone acts contrary to expectations, you can point to "the ways things are done here" as a mode of reinforcing the culture.

Step 4: Build Shared Values

It is not enough for the leader to know her own values. Nor is it sufficient for the leader to express them clearly. It is vitally important to build a shared commitment to core values. *This is the heart of building a culture.* Shared values pump the blood of moral dedication into the veins of every member of the group.[30] They turn a collection of people into a genuine community in which everyone feels needed, cared about, and empowered. The leader needs to build the team into a close, enthusiastic community with a culture of shared values.

We are using the term *shared values* as an abbreviation for shared beliefs about what is good, shared moral principles, shared ideals, and shared norms. A team has shared values when everyone knows that certain behaviors are expected, that certain commitments are held in common, that certain ethical goals and ideals guide the group. Shared values are part of a group's collective identity. They help to define what it means to be a member of the team. Shared values are expressed in *we* language. This is what *we* believe. This is how *we* behave. These are the ideals that guide *us.*

What are those shared values? Answers will vary, but the values and norms that structure true competition can be a guide to developing a positive, values-based culture. *We,* on this team, think about opponents as people who help us become the best we can be. *We,* as members of this group, do what we do because we love doing it. *We* also work incredibly hard because we believe in the value of effort, and we seek our own personal forms of excellence. For further ideas, review the list of values intrinsic to competition in earlier sections of this chapter. Variations on such values as enthusiasm, skill power, optimism, knowledge, relationships, and self-transcendence (often expressed in different words) are core to the identity of competition-affirming groups.

Another strategy for identifying the values that should be at the core of the team's culture is the "virtues to norms" strategy. Think about what character traits are important to you. Let's say you list honesty and perseverance. Your job, then, is to communicate to your players that you value honesty and perseverance not just in individuals, but in the group. If you want honest players, then develop a team culture in which honesty is prized and expected and becomes part of the team's collective identity until everyone expects it of everyone else.

How do you do this? It is important to recognize that shared values and norms cannot be created by the dictate of authority. They cannot be commanded into existence. The role of the leader, as a guide and mentor, is twofold. Although the leader cannot force his values on the team, he can inspire the team to share his commitment to his values. The leader can, and

Coaches can make a big difference in the attitudes and values of their players. But there are also larger, more structural, influences on all who participate in sports. Are there policy changes that you can think of (such as awarding college athletic scholarships on the basis of financial need rather than performance) that would help support true competition?

should, present a compelling vision that awakens ideals within the membership; and not just once, of course. The vision, in myriad forms, needs to be presented and processed continuously. There are many ways to share the vision. Leaders can tell stories that embody the ideals, show films, relate personal experiences, and invite speakers.

Even more important than inspiring a vision is fostering a discussion among the team members about the team's values, ideals, and norms. The vision must be processed by every member through genuine dialogue. Everyone must have a say and feel heard. In the team dialogue, the leader is one among equals. She can and should advocate for positive, prosocial norms, but if the norms are to genuinely shape the team's culture, they must belong to everyone.

If you are a coach, the beginning of the season is the time to start building the team culture. We often encourage holding a "benchmark meeting" devoted entirely to a discussion of team values. What do we stand for? That's the essential question. A budding culture, however, will take lots of reinforcement. Throughout the year, look for opportunities to stimulate discussion about key values and ways to reinforce them. If someone makes a derogatory remark about an opponent, raise it up for discussion at a team meeting. Rather than dictate the appropriate attitude, let the team discover it through guided discussion.

Step 5: Build Shared Responsibility

In the spring of 2007, six Penn State football players were arrested and charged for crimes stemming from an off-campus fight in which at least 15 Nittany Lions were present.[31] If you had been in Coach Paterno's shoes, how would you have handled the situation? To his credit, the coach saw immediately that the problem was not limited to just those players directly implicated. For such behavior to have occurred, there also had to have been a more widespread problem in the team's culture. If the team had a strong culture centered in shared values, those players would not have acted that way because they would have known how upset and disappointed their teammates would have been.

We like to think that each person is responsible for his or her own behavior. There is certainly truth to this. We are all accountable individually. However, most of our behavior is heavily influenced by the expectations that others have of us. The stronger those expectations are, the more our behavior conforms to them.

Why is it that when I teach a class on a hot day I don't show up in a swimsuit? Why don't I eat spaghetti with my fingers? I don't even consider such things. There's nothing illegal about them, but I've internalized a set of social expectations that would make such choices unthinkable. When I shop in a department store, I don't bellow out a song. I save that for the shower! When I enter a bus, I sit. When I enter a theater, I'm quiet. These and countless other everyday behaviors conform to social expectations without my ever even considering alternatives.

To this day, in some towns and communities no one bothers to lock their cars or homes. Why aren't they fearful of losing property? The reality is that no one in town would even consider stealing from another. Over time, norms of trust evolved, and as people live within that culture, they come to embrace those norms. One of your goals as a leader is to create such strong social norms that no one on your team would even think of deviating from the team's core values.

Coach Paterno devised a plan to address the culture of the Penn State team. He let the legal and student judicial process handle the students involved in the fight, but to prevent his team from being viewed as trash, he involved the whole team in a cleanup effort. After each home game that fall, the entire Penn State football team cleaned up Beaver Stadium. The players gathered garbage, swept stairs, and hosed the place down.

Was Coach Paterno's response fair? Wasn't he punishing students who had nothing to do with the incident? At most, this is a half-truth. In reality, everyone *was* involved. Everyone was partially responsible for what happened. Everyone shared responsibility because everyone is responsible for the team's culture. Every member of a team bears responsibility for the relative strength or weakness of the team's collective norms.

If a team has a strong, shared culture that affirms a core set of values, then it is highly unlikely that anyone will violate them. Doing so would be like singing in a store or attending class in a swimsuit. The Penn State athletes who got in the fight did so for their own reasons, but fighting was an option because they did not anticipate strong disapproval from their teammates. When individuals act out, it reflects on the whole team. It shows that the team has not yet taken full control of itself and its culture.

Coach Paterno's collective punishment recognized that the whole team shared in the responsibility. However, we're not big fans of authority-imposed collective punishment. An even better response would have been to turn responsibility back over to the team. Because it is the team's culture, the whole team should be responsible for figuring out how to uphold it. To

Dear Authors:

I'm the president of our regional youth soccer league. After we had a few disturbing incidents in which coaches had to be disciplined for poor sport behavior, we held a mandatory "sportsmanship summit" in which all the coaches came together and wrote a sportsmanship code for the league. Do you think this is a good strategy for dealing with decompetition?

— League President

Dear League President:

We definitely commend you for taking the step that you did. Most likely, it will help for a time. To build on your effort, let us offer two suggestions. First, it is important to keep in mind that true competition is an entirely different concept than being a good sport. A decompetitor may be able to follow your ethics code completely and still think of the game as a battle and the opponent as the enemy. The concept of true competition is much deeper and broader than simply sportsmanship. So our first suggestion is to launch training programs that educate coaches, parents, and players in this broader understanding of true competition.

It is also important to recognize that the greatest benefit of ethics codes accrues to those who were involved in developing them. We're skeptical regarding the value of plastering "sportsmanship codes" on locker-room or gym walls or requiring people to sign an ethics pledge. However, there is considerable value in getting people together to talk about the values and norms that will guide your program. So our second suggestion is that you add an expiration date to your code. Every two or three years, start from scratch and develop a new one. This is especially important if the turnover in personnel is high. Involving people in the process of creating such a document is much more effective than using such a document to tell people how to behave.

take full responsibility for its shared values, the team needs to decide how to handle violations of shared expectations. Enforcement of the team's culture belongs to the whole team. That is a big part of what makes it *our* team, not the leader's team.

If someone is goofing off in practice, you might solve it individually. Better yet, have the team discuss what it means to be committed to a goal. If a player is continually showing up late, raise the issue for discussion. If an athlete commits an abundance of fouls, present it as a problem for the team to solve. These actions should not be done as a means of collectively dumping on specific individuals. Rather, they should be focused on how to clarify the shared expectations and strengthen the culture. Whenever possible, have the team take responsibility for building and enforcing its own culture, hopefully a culture of true competition.

Step 6: Ritualize Team Norms

The last step in creating a positive peer culture is to build rituals that reflect and reinforce the team's culture. Rituals crystallize the values of the team and help members sustain them over time. For example, if you want punctuality to be a core team value, announce an odd starting time, for example, 3:04 P.M., and stick to it religiously.

Rituals are powerful means of reinforcing a group's culture, exemplified by the New Zealand All Blacks performing the Maori haka before a match. If a team wants to embrace a culture of true competition, what rituals might it develop to reinforce the norms and values of true competition?

Symbolic words or gestures can also become part of your team's ritual life, reinforcing its culture. Such words and gestures are abbreviated ways of expressing big ideas. For example, Jim Thompson, founder of the Positive Coaching Alliance, suggests using a hand motion that looks like flushing a toilet whenever someone makes a mistake. The idea is that we should "flush" mistakes and quickly move on. The flushing gesture can be a very effective way to add a touch of humor to lighten up a tense moment following a mistake, refocusing attention where it needs to be.

Creative leaders think about important times in their groups' lives and build in rituals that will help reinforce key values. Obviously, for a coach, the first day of practice would be one such time. Handing out uniforms could be done in a ritualized way. For example, older players could hand them to younger players to symbolize that they are there to help. Be creative and invite the creativity of your team.

Rituals that involve domination and submission, such as hazing, are to be assiduously avoided. Keep the rituals uplifting and focused on the positive values you want at the core of the team's culture.

In sports, awards ceremonies can be a great way to recap the season and build on the positive things that happened. Think carefully, however, about what is communicated by the awards you present. Sometimes awards ceremonies undermine the values coaches have been trying all season to build. The most valuable player award is usually given to a high-profile person who scored the most points or something similar. It is certainly not based on effort, or enthusiasm, or ethics. Recognizing effort, enthusiasm, and ethics, when it occurs at all, is typically relegated to a clearly second-tier set of awards. What really is "most valuable"? The thoughtful coach needs to carefully consider the signal that is sent when offering awards.

Similarly, by selecting a few players to "win" awards, the majority are relegated to the status of "losers." This can be disheartening and demotivating. Additionally, the rivalry that it sets up can undermine the spirit of cooperation that is core to an effective team. These problems are amplified when the leader selects the award recipients. A better strategy would be to have the players make the nominations and anonymously vote on the recipients. The team, after all, is really theirs.

A team culture that supports true competition will have respect as a core value. Respect is at the heart of true competition. In chapter 9, we expand on other qualities of an ideal contest. ■

1   Gallwey, T. (2000). The story of the tournament is described in the preface.

2   The quote from the film *White Men Can't Jump* is recorded in Nelson (1998), p. 260.

3   Bradley (1998).

4   See Nelson (1998), p. 61.

5   Philosophers Craig Clifford and Randolph Feezell (1997) make a similar point: "Ultimately, the principles of sportsmanship are based on the delicate balance of playfulness and seriousness that is at the heart of sport" (p. 11).

6   Bradley (1998).

7   We do not claim any scientific evidence for the particular list of values that we identify with the process of competing. The list is designed to be heuristic, provisional, and illustrative.

8   Evidence suggests that participation in sport can increase a person's self-management abilities. For a discussion of this literature and how it fits within the construct of character, see Shields and Bredemeier (2008).

9   The issue of transference is an important one, both theoretically and practically. Often learning is domain specific, meaning that it does not transfer from one area (e.g., sports) to another (e.g., school). Because insights gained in one domain do not automatically transfer to another, the teacher or coach should help scaffold the transference by helping the learner make connections across domains.

10   For a good yet brief discussion of the importance of optimism and how to cultivate it, see Lyubomirsky (2007), pp. 101-111.

11   On a similar theme, Harry Sheehy (2002) writes: "There's so much passion and intensity inside young people; by giving them an arena in which they can strive for success, sports facilitates the thrill of self-discovery" (p. 44).

12   Mo Weiss has been a leader in investigating the role of friendships within sport settings. See Weiss and Stuntz (2004) and Weiss and Williams (2004).

13   Hyland (1978).

14   The potential of sports to contribute to the dispositions and skills needed for democratic citizenships is often overlooked. Because sports are often one of the first places beyond the family where children learn to subordinate personal interest to a search for the common good, they can be a valuable context in which to learn democratic skills. Of course, sports might also teach more authoritarian approaches to group governance.

15   The analogy to economic competition is rather weak here in part because economic competition is rarely true competition. One of the problems with contests apart from games and sports is that the results of winning and losing are continuously carried forward. It's as if winning teams get to takes their points into the next game. Over time, this leads to predictable winners and consistent losers, an outcome that distorts the process. The process then becomes distorted even further when the big winners—large corporations—gain the power to write the rules. The revolving door between government and regulatory agencies reflects this problem.

16   Mariah Burton Nelson (1998, p. 60) relays how she likes to repeat the ironic Zen Buddhist phrase, "Oh, happy blessed opportunity!" whenever confronted by loss, difficulty, or crisis. As Nelson notes, the humor comes from the recognition that difficult and painful situations do offer opportunities, often unique and important opportunities, to learn and grow.

17   Sheehy (2002), p. 9.

18   For a good discussion of how this pressure distorts college sports, see Shulman and Bowen (2001).

19   Our important assertion that true competitors are likely to outperform decompetitors of parallel skills needs further empirical examination. It is based, in part, on evidence that those who are task involved tend to experience a performance boost, either immediately or over time (e.g., Sarrazin, Roberts, Cury, Biddle, & Famose, 2002; Theeboom, De Knop, & Weiss, 1995; Van Yperen & Duda, 1999; Vealey & Campbell, 1988). See, also, Pensgaard & Duda (2002, 2003). Further indirect support can be found in the extensive literature on

(continued)

(continued from previous page)

how "competition" (which is usually decompetition in our terminology) negatively affects performance. For a somewhat dated but still valuable review, see Kohn (1992), especially chapter 3.

20   See, for example, Luban (2006) and Price (2006).

21   The three primary tasks of leadership, according to Senge (1990), are leader as designer; leader as steward, and leader as teacher. Of these, stewardship is most important.

22   This comment assumes that the contest itself operates with reasonably fair rules that are impartially enforced. In situations of structural injustice, different responses may be called for.

23   Carol Alberts (2003) has written a helpful book for coaches that offers lots of practical advice and tools for developing a character-nurturing environment in sports.

24   Janssen and Dale (2002). Although the identification of credible coaches was purely a matter of subjective appraisal and convenience, rather than any scientific criteria, the coaches identified are likely sound exemplars relative to the points being made.

25   The quote from Coach Krzyzewski is taken from Janssen and Dale (2002), p. 73.

26   Luban (2006), p. 59.

27   William Damon (2004), for example, tells the stories of 48 business executives who achieved great success by adhering to moral conviction.

28   It is not surprising, for example, that the first three chapters of a recent text on the social psychology of sport are focused on coach–athlete relationships. See Jowett and Lavallee (2007).

29   Sheehy (2002), pp. 127-137.

30   Throughout our discussion of developing shared norms and shared responsibility, we draw from Power, Higgins, and Kohlberg (1989). For a recent summary of this approach, see Power and Higgins-D'Alessandro (2008).

31   Charges against all but two of the Penn State football players were eventually dropped; see Ryan (2007) for a discussion of the story and its aftermath.

The Ideal Contest
Embracing the Challenge

The point of a contest is to win, right? Move in close now, because I've got a secret for you. If the goal is to win, I can give you a master key to unlock victory. I can turn *YOU* into a game winner every time. And I do mean *every* time. *Really!* Would you like to know the secret to an uninterrupted flow of victories? Do you want to know how to come out on top in every contest? It's not by cheating. I can tell you how to play by the rules and still always win. Would such a secret be worth the price of this book? Well, read on.

> **“ It doesn't matter
> if you win by an inch
> or a mile.
> Winning is winning. ”**
>
> Unknownn

Here's the secret to winning every contest: Compete only against weak opponents. Hopefully you found that brilliant piece of advice about as appealing as mice find snakes. If you were to take it, it would devour the whole purpose of competing. This is because the goal of the contest (to win) is not the same as its purpose. To play the game, we need to pursue its internal goal (winning), but that's not the reason for playing.

At this point, our daughter might say, "*Duh!*" Both competitors and decompetitors recognize that the reason to play isn't just to win. For decompetitors, the ultimate purpose of contesting may be to demonstrate superiority. Although the primary focus of the decompetitor may be on the outcome, the whole contest can be turned into a platform for ego enhancement. I can flaunt my superiority every step along the way, unless of course I'm a college student playing a second-grader.

The true competitor, as well, recognizes that winning really has little to do with the reasons for competing. For the true competitor, competition is foremost about the benefits derived from the process of contesting.

In this chapter, we look at selected characteristics of the ideal contest. What makes a particular contest a good one? As we will see, having well-matched opponents is a fundamental requirement of a good contest. In addition, good contests balance work and play; they also are characterized by a favorable balance of positive emotion over negative emotion. Following these discussions, we go on to identify additional threats to true competition.[1] These can come in the form of lopsided contests, emotional intensity, and fans who have lost their own sense of balance. All these upset the aesthetics of the ideal contest and encourage a decompetitive orientation. Finally, we conclude the chapter with reflections for leaders, especially those who are initiating young people into the art of competition.

Before we leap into our topic, however, we need to clarify what we are addressing when we talk about the ideal contest. We are not asking what makes baseball a better game than tiddlywinks, assuming it is. Certainly, game designers need to consider the structural features of contests. However, that's not our concern. We are interested in the *quality* of play within existing contests. Once again, we will use the context of sports to illustrate, but with due adaptation, similar comments apply wherever contests are employed.

The Art of Competition

❝ Competitions are for horses, not artists. ❞

Bela Bartok, Hungarian composer

The central theme of this chapter is that good competition, despite what Bela Bartok thought, is an art form.[2] Hans Ulrich Gumbrecht, a Stanford University professor of comparative literature and author of the acclaimed book, *In Praise of Athletic Beauty*, said it well when he wrote, "The most obvious explanation for the widespread popularity of sports is their aesthetic appeal, as powerful as the experience of a beautiful work of music or art."[3] What is true of sport is also true of other well-contested contests: They have aesthetic qualities. A good contest is like a jazz improvisation or an unscripted dance. It has movement, power, and grace; beauty and energy; flow and rhythm; freedom and structure. It is also like a suspense novel or a dramatic play. As the contest progresses, tension mounts and startling twists occur. Also, just as a great novel reaches a climax in the concluding pages, the ideal contest is decided in the concluding moments. Whether the competition is for a contract or a league title, the play of the game—the good game, as least—is an aesthetic experience.

Keeping the Present Tense

Tension is important to most art forms.[4] Whether captured by the use of musical counterpoint, subtly jarring images or color schemes, or secrets that come only slowly to light, artists play with the themes of tension and release, frustration and fulfillment. In contests, tension is created when well-matched opponents come together in opposition.[5]

Well-matched opponents keep the contest open, the resolution in doubt. When great competitors contest, the competition is packed throughout with anxiety, tension, and mystery that is only resolved in the final frame.[6] Throughout most of the contest, the present is pregnant with clash, strain, and doubt. The uncertainty stimulates each participant to dig deeper into his or her personal reservoir of commitment to tap new levels of energy, skill, insight, and focus. It pushes people to their personal boundaries, and beyond.

If the tension of a contest is eliminated or resolved too soon, the value of the contest is diminished. The mismatching of opponents is probably the most common mode of robbing contests of their tension.[7] If the St. Louis Cardinals baseball team were to add a high school team to their schedule, few fans would show up for the game. There would be no tension, no uncertainly. In fact, it would be a bore. The only reason to show up might be to get an autograph.

Although hopelessly mismatched opponents destroy the artistic quality of a contest, appearances are sometimes deceiving. When the mismatch is not

Do you find it more enjoyable to watch a close contest or a blowout? Why? What are the values connected with each?

too great, tension is created by the possibility of the underdog triumphing. A team that is far behind may have a dramatic comeback. Great contests can be created by the triumphal underdog or the come-from-behind victory. Such contests, which appeared doomed to insignificance, vividly reverse our expectations and reveal the contest to be balanced in an unexpected way. The tension of a contest arises partly from the uncertainly of whether hidden dimensions are concealed under appearance.

In a limited sense, the ideal contest is a battle. True, throughout this book, we have emphasized that true competition has a cooperative dimension. Indeed it does. Competition is fundamentally a partnership, but one that works its magic through opposition and contention. During the game, and for the purposes of the game, the structural interests of the competitors are diametrically opposed. I want to score; you want to stop me. I want to cross the finish line first, but so do you. This structural antagonism creates the hidden pressure toward decompetition, but it also creates the positive tension necessary for art.

Tension itself is neither good nor bad. Just as tension in a household can either tear a family apart or open up new paths of communication and creativity, so the tension of a contest can lead to the ugliness of decompetition or the beauty of a contest well played. The outcome depends on how people address and handle the tension.

True competitors recognize this reality. Although they want to win, they also know that an easy win is rather meaningless. Consequently, true competitors want their opponents to do their best. They take delight in the closely contested contest. They want to be pushed toward excellence by both challenging the opponent and responding to the best that the opponent has to offer, even if doing so ultimately results in defeat.

The decompetitor, in contrast, hopes to release the tension early by knocking the opponent out quickly. It is not that the decompetitor wants to contest against an obviously inferior opponent. That would prove nothing. However, the decompetitor is often satisfied with appearances. If for some reason the opposition is unable to marshal their best effort on a particular occasion, so much the better. As long as the opponent appears to outsiders like a worthy opponent, jumping to an insurmountable lead early is ideal. For the remainder of the game, the conquered opponent becomes a platform for an extended victory dance. Less concerned with excellence than exhibiting superiority, decompetitors view the ideal contest as one that reveals their supposed superiority.

Of course, both competitors and decompetitors try to leap ahead. The true competitor, however, rather than feeling elated by a lopsided lead, typically experiences a sense of letdown. Although there are still benefits to be gained, growth that can occur, lessons to be learned, and enjoyment to be experienced, such a contest falls far short of the ideal for the true competitor. In sports, this experience of letdown during a triumphal blowout may be more common than some believe.

Back in the 1980s, Professor Robin Vealey of Miami University of Ohio wanted to know whether athletes cared more about winning or playing well. To find out, she developed the Competitive Orientation Inventory (COI). In the COI, respondents are presented with a grid containing the16 combinations that result from joining four qualities of performances (very good, above average, below average, very poor) with four possible outcomes (easy win, close win, close loss, big loss). Respondents then rate how satisfied they would be with each combination. Interestingly, she found that for most athletes the quality of performance matters more than the outcome. In fact, contrary to what many believe, most athletes appear to focus less on outcome than do nonathletes.[8] For the true competitor, a close win brought about through a very good performance is the most prized combination. For the decompetitor, on the other hand, a blowout is best, and an ugly win is preferable to an excellent performance that results in a loss.

Developing Plot and Character

We have noted that appearance does not always match reality. The apparently weaker opponent, for example, may have hidden strengths. We often like to cheer for the underdog, and not just in sports. We enjoy seeing the small, scrappy company make headway in a market dominated by giants.

Superficially, our affinity for the underdog would seem to violate a desire for parity in competition. To have underdogs, after all, requires that the opponents not be on par. However, rooting for the underdog stems, in part, from a desire to see balance restored.

Another reason we cheer for the underdog is that it gives the contest a familiar and cherished story line. Good contests have good plots. The triumphal underdog reenacts a beloved cultural archetype. Just think of Disney movies: Aladdin rises from poverty to gain the affections of Princess Jasmine. In *Annie,* based on the Broadway musical, the little orphan girl, through wit and determination, wins her way into the heart of Oliver Warbucks. In *Mulan,* a young girl rises from obscurity and gender bias to save China. Scrawny and disvalued, Wart becomes King Arthur in *The Sword in the Stone.* And, of course, we all know what happens to Cinderella. We love the ugly duckling who becomes the swan; the pauper who becomes the prince; the boy from the wrong side of the tracks who wins the affections of the girl from the right side; and the unschooled kid whose brilliance outshines the educated.

The ideal contest has an appealing plot that is rooted in a question. *Can the underdog overcome the odds?* That is one plot played out time and again, but there are many others. Listen to the sport commentators before any major game or event and you will hear a number of plot questions posed. What is more important: power or speed? Strength or agility? Teamwork or individual ability? Strategy or execution? Experience or enthusiasm? The same thing happens in political contests. The pundits narrate a political race much like sport commentators narrate sport events. What is more important: Money or message? Organization or charisma? Change or experience? The questions frame the contest as a particular type of story. The ideal contest has an intriguing plot.

For contestants, the story lines created by commentators are often viewed as artificial and simplistic. No doubt they are. Participants create their own stories, typically with much more nuance and detail. Viewed from one angle, game plans (or business plans) are plots. They are stories about how the contest will unfold if all goes well and what role each participant will play. They are stories about strengths and vulnerabilities, about strategies and leverage. The game plan is a story written on the minds of each contestant. It is centered on a plot—one that ends, of course, with victory. Of course, the opposition is seeking to enact a different story. They seek to follow a contrasting game plan.

Once the contest begins, interest is heightened by the interplay between anticipated plots and what actually happens. Stories quickly change and evolve, new themes emerge, and the plots thicken. That's part of the delight of the contest. The aesthetic contest doesn't conform strictly to a script. It is part well-rehearsed play and part brilliant improvisation.

True competitors take delight in the stories of the contest, even if they are

Dear Authors:

You talk about the triumphal underdog as a popular cultural script. Another one is the successful scoundrel who gets ahead through trickery and conniving. When someone wins, we tend to overlook the means they used to get there. Doesn't this contradict your point about the importance of character to the good contest?

— *Script Scoundrel*

Dear Script Scoundrel:

It is true that we often enjoy the story of a devious individual who shrewdly manipulates his or her way to the top. The media often celebrates the colorful yet ethically challenged personality. However, we tend to enjoy such people from a safe distance: in fiction or on the screen. We would not want them as neighbors, lovers, or teammates. Nor are they desirable in true competition. Although they may at times be culturally celebrated, they invariably create a downward thrust toward decompetition, sapping the contest of many of its positive benefits. Again, there can be a gap between appearance and reality. Some may appear successful, but in reality they have been unsuccessful at meeting the real challenges posed by true competition.

disappointed in the outcome. Shakespearian tragedies are still great plays. Sometimes sad movies are still enjoyable. For the true competitor, the outcome does not erase the good story of the contest. But decompetitors relish only story plots that reveal their supposed superiority.

Great novels have engaging plots. They also rely on well-developed characters. The ideal contest, too, rests on well-developed characters, now understood as people with well-developed *character*. The tension of the contest puts people's character on trial. The contest is a grand stage on which the great virtues can dance or fall. When a team is down, who has the resilience, determination, and drive to come back? When up, who has the poise and confidence to stay focused? Throughout it all, the contest poses questions of ethics: Who will act with respect, grace, and dignity? Who will succumb to the temptation to cheat or boast or aggress or retaliate? In the ideal contest, the contestants rise not only to the skill challenges of the contest, but to the character challenges as well.

Balancing Play and Work

Art is spontaneous yet disciplined; at once both playful and serious. To compete well likewise involves blending work and play. In reference to sport, the philosophers Craig Clifford and Randolph Feezell said it well when they wrote in *Coaching for Character:*

> ❝ **Coaches usually do not need to be reminded that sport is competitive, but it is crucial to remind some that it is competitive *play*. Sport is by its very nature paradoxical. It demands that we compete as hard and as fairly as we can, yet that we do this while realizing that sport is play, a set of captivating and intrinsically valuable activities that do not matter in the larger scheme of things. I must play my sport as if nothing matters more, . . . all the while realizing that it doesn't really matter.**[9] ❞

What Clifford and Feezell note about sport has resonance wherever contests exist. Although in many contests the outcome matters, the ideal contest, whether in sports, the office, or school, combines work and play, struggle and joy, excellence and enjoyment. It balances intrinsic motivation with extrinsic motivation, fun in the moment with strenuous goal pursuit. The relative importance of each may vary by context, but even in the most serious contests levity, play, and enjoyment have an important role.[10]

The precise balance required for true competition may vary depending, in part, on the importance of the outcome, but decompetition arises when seriousness, work, and discipline are given too much emphasis. The decompetitor takes the contest too seriously. This leads to an overemphasis on the outcome and a diminishment of the intrinsic values. It leads to seeing the opponent as the enemy. It may also lead to a disregard for the rules or at least the spirit of the rules. When contests are drained of play, real competition is also drained out and replaced with the ugly emergence of decompetition.

Yet contests must be taken seriously. Everyone must be motivated to win and to strive to his or her maximal capacity for victory. Contests that are not taken seriously do not lead to decompetition, but to poor competition. Poor competition, unlike decompetition, does not emanate from an underlying war metaphor. Nevertheless, it cuts the participant off from the values of the process just as much as decompetition does. It leads to frivolous competition with no real purpose or value. The ideal contest, the aesthetic contest, rests atop a precarious balance of seriousness and play. On the one side, it is in danger of toppling into decompetition. On the other side, it is in danger of falling into silliness. One of the major factors that can push the contest off its precarious balance is the emotion of the moment. Emotion, too, must exhibit an appropriate balance.

Playing With Feeling

> ❝ A positive mood jolts us into an entirely different
> way of thinking from a negative mood.
> A negative mood activates a battle-station
> mode of thinking. A positive mood buoys people
> into a way of thinking that is creative, tolerant,
> constructive, generous, undefensive and lateral. ❞
>
> Martin Seligman

There are two basic types of human emotion: positive emotions such as joy, ecstasy, delight, bliss, glee, enchantment, contentment, serenity, hope, and amusement; and negative emotions such as anger, fear, sorrow, sadness, despair, anxiety, depression, and guilt. Contests invariably elicit a range of emotional responses, just as a good novel or piece of music or art does. No doubt, winning will be accompanied by more positive emotion than losing. However, regardless of outcome, true competition requires a favorable balance that tilts toward the positive emotions.

Before we talk about the balance of emotions in the ideal contest, however, it might be helpful to take a slight detour and reflect on the role of these emotions in the human psyche. In his book *Authentic Happiness*, Martin Seligman, former president of the American Psychological Association, suggests that these two types of emotion have deep roots in our evolutionary history. As our species evolved, negative emotions were important survival-enhancing mechanisms that alerted us to danger. They activated our fight or flight responses. For our present purposes, it is important to note their connection to win–lose situations. Seligman explains:

> ❝ Negative emotions . . . are our first line of defense
> against external threats. . . . In evolution, danger, loss,
> and trespass are all threats to survival itself.
> More than that, these external threats are all win-loss
> (or zero-sum) games, where whatever one person wins
> is exactly balanced by a loss for the other person. . . .
> Negative emotions play a dominant role in win-loss
> games, and the more serious the outcome,
> the more intense and desperate are these emotions.[11] ❞

From an evolutionary standpoint, negative emotions have been valuable because they narrow our cognitive focus and trigger our self-defense mechanisms. As a species, we would not have survived without them. No doubt, they continue to provide a useful function in our overall mental and physical well-being, helping us deal with the various hazards we face.

Did positive emotions also have such an important evolutionary function? Seligman, based on the pioneering research of Barbara Fredrickson, suggests that indeed they did.[12] Whereas negative emotions tend to narrow our thinking in response to threat, positive emotions broaden our thinking in response to opportunity. Researchers have shown, for example, that when people are experiencing positive emotions, they are more likely to take on new challenges, pursue more difficult tasks, and be more open to novelty.[13] These responses, no doubt, were equally vital to our evolutionary development. Negative emotions arise from the perception of threat within a win–lose context; positive emotions, on the other hand, arise in response to situations that we perceive as win–win.

Seligman's analysis is sound as far as it goes, but it tends to underplay the two-way causality between emotion and perception. Seligman talks about how the perception of a win–lose situation leads to negative emotions, but the cause–effect cycle goes both ways. The more a person experiences negative emotion, the more likely she is to see her situation as threatening. When you are in the grip of a negative emotion, you are much more likely to interpret your situation through the lens of win–lose. You may perceive danger or threat where none exists. Positive emotions tend to have the opposite effect.

What do positive and negative emotions have to do with the ideal contest? As we have noted continuously, true competition is multilayered. It is structurally a win–lose contest that simultaneously allows for win–win at the personal level. Consequently, it is likely to encourage a wide range of both positive and negative emotions. This is one reason the root metaphor is so important. If one's primary perception of the contest reflects a metaphor of war or battle, the perception of threat will activate negative emotions. These negative emotions, in turn, will amplify the perception of danger. Ambiguous actions on the part of opponents will be interpreted as threatening actions. The accidental bump may be viewed as an intentional affront calling for retaliation. It is easy in such a situation to let emotions spin out of control.

Negative emotions are triggered by the perception of threat and, in turn, often lead to an exaggerated view of the dangers of the situation. In reality, what is most threatened by spiraling negative emotions is true competition. Negative emotions increase the salience of the war metaphor. Also, because negative emotions narrow perception and trigger the biologically rooted fight or flight response, it is hard to break out of their grip once they start to cycle into higher intensities.

Contests invariable produce a certain amount of frustration that can lead to anger, hostility, resentment, and aggression. From one vantage point, contests really are threatening. You are threatened with loss, with embarrassment, with at least a transient feeling of incompetence. Contests are not safe ground if you take them seriously. Consequently, the fact that negative emotions arise is not at all surprising. The true competitor is not immune from experiencing negative emotions, but is also poignantly aware of the danger that lurks within them.

Although contests are structurally win–lose events, the true competitor focuses on the potential win–win embedded in the opportunity for everyone to move toward excellence and enjoyment. Responding to the opportunity of the win–win dimension, true competitors experience heightened positive emotions that keep their thinking flexible, open, and responsive. When people feel good, they tend to see still more win–win opportunities. Positive emotions help them experience contests as partnerships in which everyone can benefit through striving for excellence. Within the partnership metaphor, the threats embedded in contests are looked at through a wider lens. They are the grains of sand that create the pearl, the chisels that help shape the diamond. Even great art is created through resistance.

The ideal contest draws on an emotional balance that favors the positive. Negative emotion is not eliminated; doing so would be neither realistic nor desirable. Negative emotions have their place. Joy is meaningless unless one has experienced sorrow as well. Just as enjoyment draws from both intrinsic motivation and the higher forms of extrinsic motivation, it can encompass both positive and negative emotion. However, the accent needs to be on the positive. Positive emotions will keep the true competitor rooted in the partnership metaphor.

As anyone who has tried to ride a unicycle knows, balance can be difficult to sustain. The ideal contest requires engaging in multiple forms of balance at once, such as work and play, positive emotion and negative emotion. The balance can be hard to achieve, but riding the unicycle of true competition can be exhilarating. In the next section, we look at threats to maintaining the appropriate balances needed for true competition and the ideal contest.

Threats to Balanced Competition

> **The tougher and closer the competition, the more I enjoy golf.**
>
> Jack Nicklaus

In previous chapters, we identified a number of threats to true competition. Decompetition becomes more likely, for example, when substantial rewards are offered for winning, when there is outside pressure to win, or when opponents act in decompetitive ways. Decompetition is also more likely when people feel an inner compulsion to win, internalize rigid gender roles, embrace overextended loyalties, or perceive themselves as victims of injustice. Building on what we have said about the ideal contest, in this chapter we add three more threats to true competition: the out-of-balance contest, the emotionally off-balance contestant, and the unbalanced fan or observer.[14]

The Out-of-Balance Contest

The ideal contest features well-matched opponents performing at the peak of their abilities. The outcome remains uncertain until the final moments. In reality, of course, such contests are the exception; most fall far short of this ideal. Sometimes the opponents are simply uneven. Sometimes, even when there is rough parity among the competitors, one side or individual, as a result of chance or circumstance, achieves a nearly insurmountable lead long before the end. Such a contest, although not ideal, can still reflect true competition. Sustaining true competition in such a circumstance, however, is a real challenge to participants and leaders alike.

Watching the informal games of children can be instructive.[15] When adults aren't running the show, kids spontaneously respond to lopsided events by tweaking the conditions. They may pick new sides. They may modify the rules, giving an advantage to the less-skilled team. They may spot one side a few points. They may ask the unusually gifted child to play with some form of handicap. Although kids want to win, they also recognize that the game is reduced if the outcome is all but predetermined. There's wisdom in the way kids play, yet their specific solutions are rarely applicable to more formal contest situations.

Competition between ill-matched opponents reveals with unique starkness the reality that the purpose of competition isn't just to win. It is to seek excellence and enjoyment. Let's look at the lopsided contest from both sides.

View From the Top

You're ahead, far ahead, and there is virtually no chance the opponent is going to catch you. Not in this lifetime, anyway. So what do you do? Continue to run up the score? Ease up? This is a controversial issue, even among ethicists. Some recommend reducing effort, but we find that advice unsatisfying. Part of the ethic of true competition is that you always give your best. To give less than your best is to disrespect yourself, the opponent, and the game itself. On the other hand, it is also disrespectful to the opponent if you just continue to run up the score.

Giving your best does not necessarily mean leading with your strength, however. You can give your best under self-imposed constraints. When sitting on the upside of a blowout, you are in an ideal position to strengthen areas of weakness. It is an opportune time to work on less-developed skills or strategies. If you're playing basketball and you're not as skilled with your left hand, why not focus on dribbling and shooting left-handed? In a game that uses substitutes, the coach can give less-skilled players needed practice.

In the spirit of true competition, what should a coach or player do when the team is far ahead?

In a high school debate, contestants might be coached to make their closing statements without notes. The point is to restores a degree of balance to the contest by relying on less-developed skills or players, while simultaneously keeping effort high. Of course, this needs to be done in a manner that will not further embarrass the opposition.

View From the Bottom

The contest can appear pretty ugly if you're the one being creamed. You may be tempted to just give up, resign, passively accept defeat and move on. You may choose to blame the officials, or just bad luck—anything to escape the embarrassment and humiliation of being out-classed. Yet sustaining true competition is possible by focusing on the aspects of excellence and enjoyment that are still within your grasp.

When I was a youngster, I liked to watch Popeye cartoons. The host of the show was an artist. Before starting the cartoons, he would often engage in a contest with a child. He would invite a youngster to take a marker and draw a squiggle on a large sheet of newsprint. The child was given the challenge to draw a squiggle that the host could not turn into a meaningful picture. Week after week, I was amazed at how he could take the cragged and random squiggles of his guests and render them into beautiful drawings, all within a minute or two! It was a great example of creating order and beauty out of chaos.

Contestants are artists. Sometimes an impending lopsided defeat may seem to provide little opportunity for beauty. But the true competitor—especially when guided by a talented coach, parent, or partner—can reframe the situation and learn something meaningful from it. To be sure, the leader needs to provide guidance with sensitivity, empathy, and compassion. A crushing defeat is no time for a lecture. However, both during the contest and afterward, there are prized teachable moments for those ready to grasp them. Here are four suggestions for how to gain even in such situations.

1. *Practice optimism.* Psychologists have documented numerous advantages of an optimistic orientation. People who have an optimistic disposition are generally happier, accept greater challenges, and even live longer. Optimism, however, is not an outgrowth of good fortune or outward success. Rather, optimism reflects a way of perceiving and interpreting events, regardless of how often we experience positive and negative occurrences. Importantly, optimism can be cultivated and learned. Being on the less desirable side of a lopsided contest is an ideal time to practice the skills of optimism.

First, it is important to learn that, despite outward appearances, *hope is warranted*. Although positive outcomes are far from guaranteed, dramatic comebacks in contests and life do occur. However, they occur only when we refuse to give up hope.

To support optimism, it is also important to learn that defeat stems from causes that are temporary and limited. Martin Seligman talks about the importance of learning to "decatastrophize" events that go wrong.[16] When things go poorly, we tend to pile insults on ourselves, many of which are based on a morbidly distorted view of reality. We feel like total failures in response to specific, limited failures. When we have experienced a lopsided defeat, we can learn to step back and consider negative experiences from a more positive framework. We can learn that bad events usually have temporary and specific causes that can be addressed or transcended. They are not permanent and fixed. Defeats, even by a large margin, are not catastrophes. Losing doesn't transform us into losers. Learning to sustain a positive, optimistic mind-set even when experiencing setbacks can be a life-enriching skill.

2. *Always give your best, regardless of the circumstances.* When we enter a contest, we take a silent pledge to give our best effort. That pledge carries to the end of the contest whether we are ahead or behind, regardless of the score. This important lesson can serve us well far beyond the playing fields, and even beyond contests. It is a character virtue that can enrich our whole lives. There is intrinsic value in working hard for worthy goals. We need to use our gifts to their fullest, even if they are not immediately successful in accomplishing what we hoped.

3. *Focus on gains in mastery.* Ask a great competitor whether she would prefer to compete against a superior opponent or an inferior one and she will most assuredly pick the former. This is because playing against a more talented opponent can help us improve far more than contesting against someone we can easily defeat.

When victory is out of reach, it is still important to give your best effort. But you may want to focus your effort on a learning goal that is achievable regardless of game outcome. Perhaps your goal may be to execute a particular skill well. And keep in mind that the skill need not be physical. Perhaps it is to master a dimension of teamwork, or to maintain poise and integrity. There is always something to learn. Build your level of mastery. Build your character.

4. *Embrace responsibility.* When things go badly, we all have a tendency to look for someone or something to blame. We have a natural tendency to look outside rather than inside. Yet accepting—even embracing—personal responsibility is one of the core foundations of moral character. In fact, it is better to err on the side of taking more responsibility than reality dictates than less. Learning to accept responsibility, without sliding into dysfunctional guilt or shame, is something that can be gained in a losing effort. Acknowledge to yourself and others that you could have done better, and dedicate yourself to doing so. Again, this is beneficial only if done in a spirit of honesty, openness, and humility. Wallowing in guilt or shame is a sign of self-absorption, not sound character.

In sum, the true competitor is always focused more on process than outcome, and in a lopsided match this becomes all the more crucial. Competing is about finding enjoyment in the pursuit of excellence. Neither excellence nor enjoyment need to be sacrificed, not totally, even when buried beneath the opponent's landslide. True: It is more fun to win than to lose. False: There is no learning and enjoyment available in defeat. To find the learning and enjoyment, however, requires emotional control. And that brings us to a second threat to the ideal contest.

The Emotionally Off-Balance Contestant

The ideal contest is not destroyed by negative emotions. Frustration, disappointment, and sadness are normal parts of contesting. Even more strident emotions such as resentment and anger can have their place. However, the ideal contest is destroyed, as is true competition, by negative emotion, particularly anger, run amuck. For example, the emotional intensity of contests is certainly no excuse to let frustration or anger boil into aggression.

In old-school Freudian thought, sports were seen as helpful outlets for aggression. They were thought to provide a catharsis whereby aggression was safely released. The thinking went like this: Everyone has an inner impulse to aggress, and pent-up aggression needs a safe place to vent. Sports provide a release. If aggression is not released in a safe place such as sport, it will explode in less desirable ways, such as in domestic violence or public rage. Conclusion: It is good to be aggressive in sports. At the very least, it is tolerable.

The only problem with the cathartic view of aggression is that it is totally false. Overwhelming research points to the opposite conclusion. When aggression is expressed in one setting, it does not "release" pent-up aggression and thereby make it less likely to occur in other settings. The opposite is true. Acting aggressively in one context increases the likelihood that the person will act aggressively in other contexts. Aggression begets more aggression. If sport is going to provide any help at all, it is simply as a place to learn to control one's temper.

Contests are emotional hothouses. Unfortunately, what often grows in these hothouses is a tendency toward decompetition. Generally speaking, the more emotionally intense the contest, the more fertile the environment is for decompetition to grow. Emotional intensity, after all, can bring to the fore any difficulties that a person may have in emotional regulation. When emotions spiral out of control, true competition is lost in the tornado.

We all have issues with emotional regulation. We either tend to overly express or overly repress certain emotions. Contests are likely to exaggerate our tendencies, especially as they become more tension packed and suspenseful. It is no accident that the heightened tension necessary for the ideal contest is also a threat to true competition. Top performance in any area is always against the backdrop of resistance and threat. However, the true competitor must recognize the threat that emotional intensity contains and prepare for it accordingly. The true competitor should also be ready to resist the influence of the out-of-control fan, which is the final threat to true competition that we will discuss.

The Unbalanced Fan

In sport settings, fans sometimes play a destabilizing role in the emotional climate. Loud and consistent booing and heckling can create a hostile environment not only in the stands but also on the field.

Coaching in the Media

The media tends to portray a distorted view of leadership. If you were to believe what you see on the screen, you would think that most coaches spend half their time heatedly lambasting officials and players. This is far from the reality. Although there are a few loose cannons on the sidelines, most coaches are highly disciplined and keep their emotions within a normal range. Especially the good ones. Letting anger move into the upper registers is rarely helpful from a strictly performance standpoint and is clearly counterproductive for building a values-based team culture. Moreover, it quickly destroys true competition. There is nothing like escalating anger to turn a contest into a battle.

Even professional athletes occasionally respond with anger and aggression to obnoxious fans. However, they have considerable experience tuning fans out and have usually rehearsed doing so. Many coaches create training exercises that help athletes practice maintaining focus despite crowd interference. Of greater concern is the influence of fans at the younger end of the spectrum. Research has shown, for example, that when kids perceive fans as exhibiting poor sport behavior, the young athletes themselves start to act more poorly.[17] When spectators at youth sport events loudly boo, disparage officials, mock players, taunt other fans, and argue with coaches, the young athletes' own behavior starts to degenerate.

If you ask youth sport coaches about their greatest headaches, they usually don't talk about the kid who can't make the play. They talk about parents who want to coach from the sidelines, who yell at them because Johnnie isn't

© Human Kinetics

What is the appropriate role for fans at a sport event? What are the characteristics of competitive and decompetitive fans?

playing enough, who goad opponents and try to influence officials through verbal nastiness, and who fight with other parents. If you are a parent of a child in youth sports, remember this: *The games are for the kids.*

The competition–decompetition distinction applies not only to the contestants themselves, but also to those who participate in the contest vicariously. Decompetitive fans are there to boost their own egos by vicariously triumphing over opponents. By psychologically identifying with a team or athlete, decompetitive fans feel a sense of superiority when their team or athlete triumphs. Because such fans are released from the need to actually face the opponent or experience the sanction of the official, their emotions aren't tempered by these constraints. They can quickly get carried away in the emotion of the moment, a tendency that can be augmented further by an aroused crowd.

Part of the fun of going to a sport event is to get caught up in the excitement, to identify with a side and let emotions rise and fall with the twists and turns of the contest. However, this is not a license to suspend the ethical requirement to respect others. Although some may believe that their shouted taunts are excusable because the player at whom they are directed cannot possibly hear them, the atmosphere created is toxic. It is also possible, particularly in smaller venues, that the player's friends or family are within ear range.

The fan who embraces a spirit of true competition wants what the true competitor on the field wants—to experience excellence. The greatest joy of the true fan is to be present at those moments when human capacity is stretched. Such moments provide an experience of awe and wonder. Similarly, witnessing a child discovering new capacities within herself that she never thought possible fills us with hope and exhilaration. Experiences such as these are far richer than those arising from the shot of adrenaline our egos get from a victory that we really had no role in achieving.

For both contestants and fans, positive emotions should lead the way. Leaders need to help those under their sway keep this positive focus. This brings us to the final section of the chapter.

Guiding Youth Into Competition

> ❝ Leadership is much more an art, a belief,
> a condition of the heart, than a set of things to do. ❞
>
> Max Depree, leadership consultant

Leadership is an art. Like a talented choir director, effective leaders help each individual perform at the top of his or her ability while simultaneously building harmony among the various contributors. The art of leadership involves dealing with potential challenges. Certainly within the realm of competition, there are many potential threats to the ideal contest. If the leader has built a positive culture dedicated to true competition, many potential pitfalls and problems will be averted or addressed already.

In this concluding section, we address a specific leadership issue: how to initiate young people into the art of true competition. Once again, we will use sport as our primary example, but what we have to say may apply to other youth-oriented competitive activities, such as Junior Achievement or competitive scholastic clubs. After outlining some of the trends in contemporary youth sports, we consider how we organize, govern, and structure youth sports. Finally, we offer suggestions for working directly with youth in various structures.

Competition in Youth Sports

Over the past several decades, youth sports have experienced almost explosive growth. More kids now participate in sports than in any other voluntary, adult-organized activity. Youth sports have expanded dramatically, not only in terms of offering more sports to more kids, but also in terms of the intensity of the competition. The growing trend has been for kids to start younger, specialize earlier, travel farther, and compete in extended seasons. The 14-year-old who tries out for his high school's basketball team may come with a resume boasting 10 years of basketball experience, including hundreds of games played in all parts of the state, if not the country.

Believing they are investing in their children's future, parents often fork out money for elite coaches and programs. They may get caught up in a dizzying array of expensive trainers, camps, travel budgets, and equipment. Meanwhile, the children, who in previous generations enjoyed playing in the streets and vacant lots with neighborhood friends, are now thrown into a system that is often designed to maximize performance, while sifting and sorting them by ability. Many kids feel squeezed out of sports before they even hit puberty.

The increased pressures of youth sports take their toll on everyone involved. News accounts of parents brawling at their children's games are an almost daily occurrence. Coaches sneak overaged kids onto team rosters to gain an advantage. High school coaches roam the middle school sport camps secretly trying to recruit talented kids to their schools. Refs are bribed. Children snarl insults at opponents under the approving eye of supervising adults. Parents push kids to practice longer and harder.

Teachers would be fired if they ranted and raged at kids in their classes, yet coaches seem to get away with such antics on the playing fields. Most people would be offended by a librarian who uses sexual slurs and innuendo to motivate kids to read, yet locker-room raunchiness is part of the modus operandi of some youth coaches. A parent who angrily swears at her child may be looked on disapprovingly, yet a coach yelling profanities at players is often overlooked. When kids fight in school, they may be expelled. When they fight on the ice or playing field, they may be given a starting role.

Are we painting an exaggerated picture of the problems? Perhaps. There are many excellent youth sport programs that are free of open displays of cheating and aggression. The majority of coaches are well intentioned and provide quality experiences. Yet there is no disputing the fact that youth sports are too often plagued by decompetitive coaches, parents, and players.[18] Is this how we want to introduce young people to contesting?

Reformers have offered a variety of recommendations. To make sports more kid-friendly, many argue that we need to replace a high-performance model of sport with a more educational or recreational model.[19] Many suggest reducing the emphasis on winning, replacing it with an emphasis on fun, friendship, and skill building. To accomplish this, many advocate that leagues not keep standings or discontinue postseason play. Other suggestions include eliminating extensive travel, tryouts and cutting, and early specialization; many believe there should be rules for equal playing time and that team memberships should be shuffled periodically. Some suggest that score should not be kept at the younger grades.[20]

Should leaders who believe in true competition back such ideas for reform? In the following section, we reflect on some of these proposals for changing the structure of youth sports. We then turn to leadership strategies that can be helpful, regardless of the overall sport structure.

Modifying the Structure of Youth Sports

In youth sports, the central importance of seeking victory is sometimes minimized by those who want to protect children from the negative consequences that flow from decompetition. Many who write about youth sports suggest that the emphasis should be on having fun rather than trying to win. We agree that these reformers have a point. When winning overshadows enjoyment, it is time to change what's going on. On the other hand, trying to win is a central feature of competition and gives the contest much of its energy, its zest. Athletes of all ages should try to win, just as businesspeople should seek to make a profit. Honoring the process of competition involves taking the challenge to seek victory seriously.

As soon as children are old enough to meaningfully contest, there is nothing inappropriate about teaching them that pursuing victory is important.[21] In fact, it is essential. The goal, in our view, should not be to eliminate the competitive elements from youth sport, only the decompetitive ones. We see nothing wrong, for example, with keeping score, even with youngsters. Some may not yet comprehend what the score is about, and that's fine. They'll learn soon enough. The emphasis, however, should be on enjoyment and doing their best. It should be on learning to both win and lose with grace and humility.

Trying hard and having fun are not incompatible. Is the problem, then, that some people simply want to win too badly? Do they desire victory too much? As we discussed in the previous chapter, not necessarily. Great desire begets great hope; great hope beget great effort; and great effort begets great achievement. Let's keep the "begetting" going. But let's also not try to impose it. In most youth sport contexts, it is the adults, not the kids, who first get carried away. It is most often the adults (parents or coaches) who are overly focused on performances, standings, and outcomes.

Again, the problems that arise in youth sports stem more from decompetition than a desire to win. Of course, in decompetition, the desire to win overshadows the intrinsic reasons for participating. However, the problem is not with the desire to win *per se*. The problem is with a lack of appropriate emphasis on the intrinsic values of contesting and of the gains that come from both winning *and* losing. The goal should be to teach children about true competition and initiate them into its values and norms. These include an emphasis on winning, but an even greater emphasis on excellence and enjoyment.

Of the two key values of competition—excellence and enjoyment—we believe the latter should take priority in youth sports. Here we tend to agree with most reformers. Children are developing rudimentary skills, are in the early stages of clarifying their desires, are in need of a broad range of experiences, and lack the maturity to make extended commitments that require weighing multiple priorities. They do not yet understand what is sacrificed by a dedicated pursuit of limited goals. Nor do they have the cognitive sophistication to carefully consider the *opportunity costs,* to use a business term, associated with extensive sport involvement. Given their inability to engage in hypothetical thought—to equally consider options that are not tangibly present—preadolescent kids are unable to make informed decisions regarding the various possibilities for their time and commitment.

We also agree with those who want to discourage early specialization, eliminate cutting, and reduce travel. Children are not miniature adults, and they have specific developmental needs. All children should have the opportunity to explore a wide variety of sports, as well as other achievement activities. They also need ample time for enjoyable activities that are not about achievement at all. Children should never experience the pressure of believing they must perform as a payoff for their parents' investment of time and money.

In educational contexts, there is a great hullabaloo about the benefits of "high expectations." It is certainly true that many children have suffered from low expectations, especially children from disadvantaged backgrounds. However, the helpful dialogue about high expectations, when translated into practice, often degenerates into external pressures to perform. The predictable result is an undermining of children's intrinsic motivation. Similarly, when we affirm excellence as a core value of competition, we do not mean to suggest that adults should impose on children high demands to meet adult-engineered standards. Excellence, in the way we are using the term, springs from inner desire more than external pressure.

The problem with elite travel teams, tryouts, cutting, and postseason tournaments is not that they are competitive. It is rather that they impose a particular understanding of what excellence is all about.[22] It is a narrow understanding not based on a developmentally sensitive form of excellence that recognizes the need for children to be multidimensional, playful, cooperative, and experimental. It treats children as though they have already gone through a wide range of experiences, tested their interests in a host of diverse activities, developed an appreciation for cooperation and mutual support, and resolved issues of identity and commitment. Only after such childhood experimentation are most people ready for the kind of sustained commitment to excellence that is envisioned in elite forms of youth sport.

The issue of playing time is one of the most controversial. Supporters of the traditional model suggest that competition requires that everyone commit to the goal of seeking victory. Accordingly, a coach has an obligation to field his best team. On the other hand, reformers suggest that youth sports are less about competition than having fun and learning skills. Based on these values, everyone should play.

In our view, requiring that teams give all players equitable playing time is an appropriate accommodation. It does not really undercut competition. Competition, after all, entails trying to achieve the goals of the contest within limitations set by the rules. A rule that all players should be fielded according to a prescribed schedule that is set in advance, for example, does not reduce the competitive element. At a time when children are growing and maturing at uneven rates, it is especially important that everyone be given the opportunity to experience competition, benefit from playing, and learn about the dynamics of true competition.

Coaching for True Competition

The coach has no more important job, in our view, than promoting true competition. And it won't be easy. The voice of the coach will need to stand out against a background clamor for decompetition that comes from many quarters. Some parents will be bellowing for it. The coach on the other sideline may be modeling it. Many young people will see decompetition celebrated on the small screen, and when they go to the movies with friends, they'll see it, in all its vivid colors, on the big screen.

Structural changes can be made to youth sports that will help, and we have discussed some of these. However, most coaches are unable to make such fundamental changes. So how can the coach promote true competition regardless of the structure? Hopefully, this book has provided a number of guidelines. It is useful, for example, to talk about true competition and how it differs from decompetition. Building a foundation of cooperation is also advantageous. External rewards can be minimized and a values-based culture built. Coaches can help children tap deeply into the values of the process. And, of course, it is always important to set a good example. It can also be helpful to look for examples in the larger world of sports.

A while back, we read about a college softball game between Western Oregon and Central Washington. The two teams compete in the Division II Great Northwest Athletic Conference. When they met in April 2008, the two teams were vying for the conference lead. Then, in the second game of a double-header, with the score tied and two runners on base, Sara Tucholsky came to the plate. Having gotten only three hits in her last 34 at-bats, she was an easy target for the hecklers. After taking a strike, Tucholsky swung and hit the ball sharply. It sailed over the center field fence. It was the senior's first home run ever. However, the overly excited young woman missed first base on her home run trot. When she doubled back to tag the base, her right knee gave out. Because she was unable to move, the umpires confirmed that her team's only option was to replace her with a pinch runner. Her three-run

© AP Photo/Blake Wolf

When you are competing, are there times when you should set aside (at least temporarily) the goal of winning?

homer would be recorded as a two-run single. Any assistance from coaches or trainers while she was an active runner would result in an out.

Then a voice called out, "Excuse me, would it be OK if we carried her around and she touched each bag?" The voice was that of Mallory Holtman, a four-year starter from Central Washington. Risking her own opportunity for a postseason appearance, Holtman and a teammate, shortstop Liz Wallace, lifted Tucholsky off the ground and supported her weight between them as they began a slow trip around the bases. Western Oregon held on for a 4-2 win. The sacrifice made by the two Central Washington players was real. Central Washington did not go on to postseason play.

Would this be a good story to share with children? Would it help them understand true competition? Some may say no. Mallory Holtman and Liz Wallace, they might point out, acted against the spirit of competition. Competitors, after all, are supposed to seek victory. It is true that these two athletes violated a central premise at the heart of competition. Yet, from our perspective, it is an excellent story to share.

The point that a coach might make is not that we shouldn't care about winning. The two women who helped the fallen runner were elite college athletes and, no doubt, wanted to win a great deal. Yet even in the heat of the contest, they intuitively recognized that contesting and winning are not what matter most. Really, no contest value comes before simple human compassion and basic decency. That's the real lesson of the story.

The best way for coaches to initiate children into the art of true competition is to help them adopt core human values. Contests need to serve those values rather than supersede them. In most situations, striving to win can drive a commitment to excellence and bring enjoyment in its wake. However, this will be true only if contests are not given greater importance than they actually deserve. In the end, they are not all that life is about. Seeking excellence is vital, but excellence of character is the most important of all forms of excellence. ■

1   As Fraleigh (1984) writes, "Well played contests are seen and felt qualitatively as an aesthetic event" (p. 85).

2   For a discussion of the importance of beauty to the athletic contest, see Gumbrecht (2006a).

3   The quote is from Gumbrecht (2006b), p. B11. For examples of contrasting views, see White (2006) and Sack (2008).

4   For an excellent classic treatment of the role of tension in art, see Dewey (1934).

5   Unlike sports, in which individuals or teams start off from a point of equality, competition in the economic realm is typically under highly uneven conditions. Viewed at the individual level, people enter the "game of life" with highly skewed resources. At the corporate level, most new companies must contest against large, well-established institutions. Although CEOs often verbally praise competition, their actions often reflect anticompetitive practices. There is certainly little interest in contesting against well-matched opponents, yet

the market works best with numerous relatively well-matched companies contesting for business. Although overregulation of the market creates its own set of problems, regulation is often needed for at least marginally moving toward the "ideal contest."

6   On a similar theme, Kaelin (1968) writes, "The game itself considered as an aesthetic object is perceived as a tense experience in which pressure is built up from moment to moment sustained through continuous opposition, until the climax of victory or defeat. The closer this climax occurs to the end of the game, the stronger is our feeling of its qualitative uniqueness" (p. 25).

7   For a discussion of the importance of well-matched opponents, see Hyland (1984).

8   Vealey (1986).

9   Clifford and Feezell (1997), p. 66. See also, Schmitz (1976).

10 The reader is likely to wonder how the proper balance of seriousness and play can be determined and assessed. There is no easy answer to this question. The heuristic guidelines are these: If the contestant is slipping into thinking of the contest through the war metaphor, if opponents are becoming enemies, then he or she is probably taking the contest too seriously. If, on the other hand, the contestant is not striving hard because the outcome doesn't seem important, than the contest is likely to be devoid of sufficient seriousness.

11 Seligman (2002), pp. 30-31.

12 Ibid, p. 35.

13 Ibid., pp. 35-44.

14 Nelson (1998) observes, "To compete well is rarely easy. Even the best, most well-intentioned competitors lose their balance, lose their perspective, lose their commitment to fairness. Since many jobs depend on bottom-line victories, it's easy for both employers and employees to engage in 'minor' ethical violations. Since cheating is so commonplace as to be socially acceptable in many contexts, it's easy for many of us to cheat in subtle, imperceptible ways. Since our society is so greedy for gold, it's easy for athletes to push past ability and into disability, never learning to respect their own physical limits" (p. 34).

15 See, for example, Coakley (2007), pp. 132-137.

16 See Seligman (1995).

17 Shields, LaVoi, Bredemeier, and Power (2007).

18 For an illustrative survey of problems plaguing youth sports, see Shields et al. (2005).

19 Some of the more prominent voices of reform are coming from such organizations as the National Alliance for Youth Sports and the Positive Coaching Alliance. See also Bigelow, Moroney, and Hall (2001), Coakley (2007), Engh (1999), Farrey (2007), Lancaster (2002), and Murphy (1999).

20 For a useful critique of many of the youth sport reform proposals, see Torres and Hager (2007). We share their view that a de-emphasis on winning is not the best path to reform. Still, in our view, Torres and Hager (2007) do not adequately consider developmental readiness for competition and dedicated athletic pursuits.

21 Young children are not psychologically ready to understand the social comparison process that is embedded within competition. For that reason, emphasizing winning with children before the middle elementary years is not helpful. For a discussion of children's cognitive readiness for competition, see Passer and Wilson (2002).

22 Elite travel teams, in addition to promoting a distorted view of excellence, are also inherently discriminatory. Children from poor or single-parent families, for example, are often unable to participate because of the costs and time involved. It is also important to recognize that there is very little evidence that such programs benefit the youth who participate in them, either athletically or otherwise. The child "star" is often simply the child who is maturing somewhat earlier than his or her peers. Being an "elite" nine-year-old does not mean that the child is likely to be a star by the time he or she reaches high school. Moreover, the expectations that many peers and adults place on the child star, not to mention the adulation, is often detrimental.

Postlude

Reclaiming Competition

Competition is powerful. It is also precarious. It is easy to set up a contest, but impossible to ensure that true competition will follow. So why establish contests in the first place? Why do we use them to structure our games, our economy, our politics, and some of our educational practices? We do so primarily because contesting is a way to elicit efficiency, effort, and enthusiasm. Ultimately, we hope that contests promote excellence and enjoyment.

In the real world, contests often bring about neither excellence nor enjoyment. Quite frequently, in fact, their actual impact is downright negative, occasionally even tragic. The idea that contests can serve excellence and enjoyment sometimes seems laughable. Where is the enjoyment in mob violence at soccer matches? Where is the excellence when a dad pays a 12-year-old pitcher to bean an opposing player? Or when a mom actually tries to have her daughter's cheerleading rival murdered? Where is the excellence in corporate raiding, political attack ads, and teachers teaching to the test? Virtually everywhere contests are found, there is overwhelming evidence of cheating, scandal, corruption, hostility, dishonesty, collusion, and crime. This has led many critics, based on a wealth of evidence, to reach the disturbing conclusion that contesting is inherently counterproductive and morally bankrupt.

Are the problems that attend contests simply a result of ethical weaknesses within some individuals? Certainly not everyone cheats. Not everyone acts aggressively toward opponents. Yet many quite normal people act in less than desirable ways when they are under the sway of a contest. Contests exert a structural tug toward poor ethics.

The core argument of this book is this: If we are to reclaim the real power and legitimacy of contests, it is vitally important to distinguish between two fundamentally different processes: competition and decompetition. The outward contest structure allows for both, and yet they are radically different.

Benefit 1: Competition optimizes performance.

Supporting Arguments:
- Competition orients the participant to the pursuit of excellence.
- It focuses attention on the task at hand.

Benefit 2: Competition has positive psychological consequences.

Supporting Arguments:
- Competition builds lasting enjoyment.
- It strengthens intrinsic motivation and a task goal orientation.

Benefit 3: Competition builds positive character.

Supporting Arguments:
- Competition fosters cooperative interpersonal relationships.
- It encourages a belief that we can all benefit together.
- It aids in developing commitment to ethical norms.

The Case for True Competition.

Competition involves contesting *with* opponents. Despite the contest's goal structure, real competition is fundamentally a cooperative process rooted in a metaphor of partnership. It has the characteristics and benefits summarized in the above figure. Decompetition, by contrast, is guided by a metaphor of war. It replicates at the psychological level the external structure of conflict. The deeper values of the process are drained, leaving only a shallow focus on coming out on top.

From a practical standpoint, how do we reclaim true competition? We have suggested that part of the answer is to employ the new vocabulary of competition and decompetition. This is important because the natural default setting in a contest is for decompetition. To benefit from the positive values of real competition, we need to distinguish its features and pursue it with knowledge and diligence. Not only is decompetition the natural default, but it is even more likely when certain internal and external factors are present. Thus, we have noted that true competition becomes more challenging to sustain when significant real-world benefits to winning are present, as they often are. When the outcome is important, it tends to draw attention away from the values inherent in the process. Competition is also threatened by wounded egos that need to be propped up by the superficial boost of winning, as well as by overly narrow gender roles. We have also discussed the threats posed by external pressures to win and the internal pressure created by overextended loyalties. Decompetition can also be triggered by perceived unfairness, lopsided contests, and emotions run wild.

In everyday life, most contestants are influenced by several of these factors. Given all the internal and external pushes and pulls toward decompetition, is it really worth trying to preserve a role for true competition? Should we, as Alfie Kohn suggests, simply seek to eliminate contesting from our lives as much as possible? We believe that such a solution throws the proverbial baby out with the bathwater. What we need to toss out is decompetition.

It is often said that the Chinese character for *crisis* is created by combining the words *danger* and *opportunity*.[1] A contest creates a kind of crisis in which we are thrust up against our own limits and challenged to transcend them. Within a contest lurks, indeed, both danger and opportunity. Culturally, however, we haven't adequately appreciated the perils. Failing to recognize the dangers, we are all the more easily ensnared by them. If we are to tap into the rich opportunities that contests provide, we must *name the dangers.* We must be able to name decompetition and recognize the various pathways that lead to it. We must be able to clearly separate it from true competition. *We can't move into true competition passively. We must choose it deliberately.*

We have focused much of our attention in this book on sports. We have done so, in part, because we believe sports can provide a vital setting for learning how to respond to the challenges posed by all types of contest. Transfer of learning does not occur automatically, of course. Nor are sports the only venue for learning about competition and decompetition. Nevertheless, if we can learn to maintain integrity within sports, there may be opportunity to extend the spirit of true competition elsewhere.

Sports are also advantageous to consider because young children, youth, and adults all participate in them. They provide a rare opportunity for a cross-generational discussion of the meaning and value of true competition. Also, the pressures toward decompetition in sports tend to increase with advancing age and competitive level. This fact lends itself to a learning progression. The gradual increase of temptations to deviate from true competition should, if combined with an educational approach to teaching the values of true competition, enable people to take on increasingly difficult challenges as they gain the competencies, skills, and dispositions needed for sustaining true competition.

We would like to close this book by responding to questions that we frequently hear when talking about true competition. Obviously, these are bare-bones responses. Each deserves to be fleshed out in considerably more detail. Nonetheless, we hope that these brief responses will indicate something of the direction we would take in elaborating more complete answers. We also hope to hear from you about your questions, experiences, and reflections.

You have relied extensively on illustrations from sports. How closely does your model of competition and decompetition fit other settings?

It is easy to think that sports are totally different from other forms of contest. After all, sports take place in a highly limited time frame, the rules and goals are rather artificial, and there is no intrinsic meaning to the activities involved (e.g., tossing a ball through a hoop). In some sense, sports operate within a separate world-within-a-world. So we understand why some might conclude that insights gained about competition within sports will not translate beyond the world of athletics. However, we believe that with appropriate adaptation, similar reflections apply to contests wherever they may be found.

Businesses, in most countries, operate within a capitalist economy, and competition is said to be the heart of capitalism. Competition in the economic sphere is said to reduce costs, increase innovation, discourage waste, and expand productivity. Yet these benefits can be undermined by decompetitive practices. Sometimes, for example, companies focus less on producing quality products than on selling inferior but cheap goods through deceptive advertising. Another way companies practice decompetition is through depersonalizing their own workforce in an effort to reduce costs and boost the bottom line. Interestingly, such decompetitive practices often fail to achieve their objectives. The cost-savings achieved through layoffs, downsizing, outsourcing, and reductions in benefits are often more than offset by the increased costs associated with demoralized workers who have little sense of loyalty to the company.[2] A disgruntled workforce, though leaner and meaner in theory, lacks the positive motivation of a workforce that has been treated with more respect and dignity.

Some assume that businesses and corporations must necessarily adopt a cutthroat orientation toward competitors and a bottom-line orientation toward their own productivity. When CEOs think they are in a war against opponents, decompetition may show up in the form of shoddy products, lack of attention to safety, price gouging, deceptive advertising, market manipulation, book cooking, outright fraud, and cover-ups. Businesses certainly need to make a profit, but they can do so in either a competitive or decompetitive way.

Competition within the economy, like that in sports, rests on a foundation of cooperation, enforced as much by ethics as law. On the grand scale, economic competition rests on the cooperative underpinnings of democracy. As former U.S. secretary of labor Robert Reich points out in his book, *Supercapitalism*, the relationship between the economy and democracy has become distorted in recent decades. His book, along with numerous other analyses of contemporary capitalism, reads like an essay on how to free true competition from the grip of decompetition. Once again, because we haven't had a vocabulary to distinguish competition from decompetition, we often accept the latter as if it were the former.

Democracy itself, of course, is based on contesting —for votes, of ideas, and of policies. The contests embedded within democracy, however, can evolve in two fundamentally different ways. Democracy, when it reflects true competition, is rooted in genuine dialogue and dispute about what serves the common good. Democracy that has devolved into a decompetitive form gives way personality cults, distorted political campaigns replete with dirty tricks and negative advertising, and shallow sloganeering designed more to trick than to educate.

Those who think the sport contest is fundamentally different from other contest forms often point to the important consequences of contesting in "real life." Although a focus on process over outcome may make sense in amateur sports, they argue, such a mental framework is less relevant when outcomes matter a great deal, such as on the job. Of course, outcomes also matter in sports. Even in sports, jobs can be on the line. So can scholarships. Even in youth sports, prestige and status are often on the line. As the outcomes become more important, it is true that genuine competition becomes more challenging to sustain. It is also vital, however, to recognize that as outcomes matter more, so does the importance of sustaining true competition. Rather than becoming irrelevant, the ability to distinguish true competition from decompetition becomes even more vital.

Is decompetition always inappropriate?

In sports, education, politics, and business, the answer is *yes*. In war, *no*. Obviously, in situations of armed conflict, war is no longer a metaphor. The opponent is not a partner, but a literal enemy. Relatively few values can be gained through the process, and the quicker the whole "contest" is ended, the better. Although some ethical norms must be followed even in battle, war is not a setting in which true competition is the goal. Aesthetics are hard to find in real combat. War is ugly. Apart from genuine war, however, contests are healthier when they are truly competitive.

Do you mean if I'm competing against someone for a job, I should think of them as a partner?

Yes. Although other job applicants (your opponents) may be reluctant and invisible partners, they are not enemies. The challenge that your rivals pose can stimulate you to thoroughly assess your suitability for the position and your areas of strength and vulnerability. It can help you bring out your best. Of course, you hope to win. You hope to get the job. But there is real value in going through the process of discernment regarding the job, carefully considering how it would and would not match your own goals and talents.

Consider the situation also from the perspective of the employer. She wants the best person for the position. If one applicant inflates his resume, the contest is undermined. Genuine competition, far better than decompetition, will provide the employer with the information she needs to make an informed choice. Ultimately, sustaining true competition is in everyone's best interest.

You have talked almost entirely about formal contests. What about informal contests?

There are many ways to contest. In this book we have, indeed, talked mostly about formal contests. Yet informal contests are probably even more common. Brothers and sisters contest for parental attention; we call it sibling rivalry. Young teen girls contest for the affection of guys, and many, despite the sexism, refer to these contests as catfights. Office workers seek recognition from the boss; we label it ambition. Scholars compete for professional accolades, and we bless it with the label drive. Informal contests are everywhere.

Whether the contest is formal, such as in sports, or informal, such as in a family, similar dynamics are at work. Informal contests have competitive and decompetitive forms. Even in an unspoken, undeclared contest, opponents can be viewed as partners who can bring out each other's best. They can also be viewed as enemies. In fact, it is usually more difficult to maintain the spirit of true competition within informal contests.

Often, when we view another negatively, that view triggers a sense of rivalry and we silently contest with them, often in decompetitive ways. Similarly, when we perceive that someone is contesting with us, feelings of rivalry, hostility, and resentment are likely to arise. Because informal contests lack formal rules and modes of regulation, it is even easier to think that "anything goes." Antagonistic feelings are likely to be amplified. Nevertheless, even in these informal settings, there is an opportunity for true competition; there is opportunity to grow and learn from the challenge posed by others. There is also the need to follow the ethical norms of civility. Having said that, the best response to many informal contests is neither true competition nor decompetition. It is to end the contest altogether.

An interesting question is whether attitudes learned in formal contests carry over into informal contests or whether it is the other way around. In reality, of course, it probably works both ways. No doubt, family dynamics provide the first context for learning about contesting. By the time a child signs up for T-ball, she may well have experienced a plethora of informal contests in the home. These early learnings may well provide a blueprint, a model, for thinking about formal contests. Yet children's early experiences in more formal settings no doubt provide powerful learning opportunities as well. These experiences may feed back into ways of thinking about informal contests.

From our standpoint, the most important point is this: We need to use whatever opportunities are available to us to teach children about the qualities and characteristics of true competition. Often, we also need to reduce the sense of contesting within our homes, schools, and workplaces. Where contests do exist, we need to overtly teach about the values and norms of genuine competition.

Is competition the only way to push for excellence and enjoyment?

Absolutely not. In fact, we believe that the contest structure is overused. If you want to enjoy the taste of salt, it is better not to turn everything into salt. The contest structure works best when it salts our experience, rather than dominates it. We shouldn't contest too much. The research literature is clear: *If you want to improve performance and enjoyment, build cooperation.* Of course, as we have emphasized, true competition is a form of cooperation, but it is not the only form. More straightforward cooperative arrangements are often preferable.

In schools, cooperative learning—done correctly—is a powerful way to deepen the educational process. Competition, if used at all, should be used quite sparingly. When contests are used with students, they should be voluntary, and winning should be inconsequential. Used in educational settings, contests often have the negative effect of undermining intrinsic motivation. The emphasis on grades and test scores, for example, pushes students away from valuing learning for itself. Learning simply becomes a means to an end.

Similar comments apply to most work settings. Cooperative teams—done correctly—are potent means of organizing for maximum productivity and job satisfaction. Although teams are not a panacea and have their own challenges, creating well-structured opportunities for increased cooperation is a surefire way to improve both the quality of work and workers' enjoyment of it. In contrast, contests often undermine performance. Such practices as employee-of-the-month rewards, bonus pay for higher performance ranking, honorary pins, and preferred parking space assignments are based on the mistaken assumption that internal competition is helpful to an organization. Such practices have a tendency to decrease intrinsic motivation, while fostering hidden resentments and antagonistic relationships. The predictable result is that they undercut performance.[3] A better incentive would be bonuses to all employees when customer satisfaction ratings increase; such an approach is likely to augment internal cooperation. On the macro level, one illuminating study found that national economic growth is correlated with higher levels of internal organizational cooperation, not competition.[4]

In many situations contesting is simply harmful, regardless of whether it is done in a truly competitive or decompetitive manner. The famous "tragedy of the commons" story, popularized by Garrett Hardin in 1968, illustrates this.[5] Hardin wrote of a hypothetical pasture that is shared by local herders. Each herder wants to add additional animals to his flock, but there is a limit to how many animals the common pasture can support. If the herders contest, if they seek to maximize individual gain, as Hardin assumed they would, then the common pasture would be destroyed to the detriment of everyone. They all would be better served if they cooperated and agreed to shared restraints. The moral of the story: Public goods—including rivers, forests, the atmosphere, and the earth itself—can be preserved only through cooperative strategies.[6]

We do not claim that contests are the only pathway to excellence. Far from it. Rather, we make the much more modest claim that contests *can be*, under the right circumstances, supportive of both excellence and enjoyment. We have suggested that contests need not, as many critics claim, replicate at the psychological and interpersonal levels the antagonism built into their goal structure. They can, contrary to the view of many, support positive character. For these benefits to occur, however, we need to teach the dispositions and skills of true competition from an early age.

In short, true competition is a powerful process, but there are other pathways to excellence and enjoyment. When available, these pathways are often preferable. In fact, only people with well-developed skills in less complicated forms of cooperation are likely to have the competencies necessary for sustaining true competition within contests.

Your approach to competition sounds fine in theory, but get real! Most people are decompetitive, and you aren't going to change that.

This isn't a question; it's a statement of belief. People who are firmly convinced that we live in a dog-eat-dog, cutthroat world are unlikely to change their viewpoint regardless of the evidence. A mountain of evidence contradicts this view, but like the neighborhood bully who thinks everyone is born to fight and proves it by backing people into confrontations, this view becomes a self-fulfilling prophecy.

Can we create the external and internal conditions needed for true competition? Admittedly, strong winds are blowing against us. However, we believe that change can happen. Sure, it won't happen all at once, but it can happen—person by person, team by team, league by league, school by school. Only a few people are required to help the concept catch fire. If a couple of people in a league, for example, want true competition to happen, they can teach it, practice it, and help it take hold. When it comes to promoting change, there is both good and bad news.

The Bad News: Even well-intentioned people can get caught up in victory fever. Because it is fun to win and be on the winning side, we tend to develop blind spots toward those who propel us toward victory. For example, when it came to light that Coach Bill Belichick had stolen signals from the opposition, how did the fans respond? With shock and dismay? Quite the contrary. Most rallied around their coach. I suspect the level of support that he received from both the fans and the organization would have been substantially lower if he had had a mediocre record on the field. Winning covers a multitude of sins, but this needs to change. Those of us who believe in true competition need to hold ourselves and others to a higher standard. Whether in sports, school, business, or politics, ethics should be first; winning, second.

The Good News: We believe that, when given the choice, most people, the vast majority in fact, prefer true competition. They may sometimes get discouraged because it is easier to knock competition off balance than to sustain the balance needed for true competition. Nevertheless, numbers are on our side. One problem has been that we haven't had a way to talk about the difference between true competition and decompetition. We've tried to talk about being good sports or being positive competitors, but such language is too vague and weak. We hope this book has made a small contribution to creating a vocabulary for change.

How can we make a difference? Where do we go from here?

Whenever an effort for change is needed, it has become almost cliché to refer to the popular book, *The Tipping Point: How Little Things Can Make a Big Difference* by Malcolm Gladwell. In the book, Gladwell, a writer for *The New Yorker*, suggests that major changes in culture, fashion, ideas, practices, and products come about much like the spread of a viral epidemic: They start small, gain momentum, reach a tipping point, and then rapidly spread. Ideas can catch fire. What is needed is for people to talk about them.

It is our hope that you—whatever your setting, whatever your role—will find a way to talk about competition and decompetition, about genuine competition and its polar opposite. Create a buzz. Include it in your staff training. Incorporate it into your coaching. Include it in your league training seminars. Teach it in your classrooms and physical education programs. Share the ideas. Make them sticky.

We are also interested in a follow-up book brimming with stories about how people are reclaiming competition in their settings. So e-mail us your stories at: authors@truecompetition.org. We'd love to hear from you.

Thanks for journeying with us.

For additional resources, please also visit us at: www.truecompetition.org. ■

---

1   Although the claim that the Chinese character for *crisis* is created by combining two separate elements that independently signify *danger* and *opportunity* is widespread, it is probably at best a misinterpretation. For a discussion of the issue, see the Web site: www.pinyin.info/chinese/crisis.html.

2   This issue is taken up at length in Rosenau (2003), especially chapter 4.

3   See Prusak and Cohen (2000) and Coens, Jenkins, and Block (2000).

4   Hicks and Kenworthy (1998).

5   Hardin (1968).

6   Related to this point is the tendency of contests to focus attention on short-term gain. The contest puts the focus on winning the game; considerably less attention is paid to the external costs of playing the game. For example, corporations, in an effort to boost immediate profits, often ignore longer-term environmental costs.

References

Alberts, C.L. (2003). *Coaching issues & dilemmas: Character building through sport participation.* Reston, VA: National Association for Sport and Physical Education.

Alzola, M. (2008). Character and environment: The status of virtues in organizations. *Journal of Business Ethics, 78,* 343-357.

Amabile, T.M. (1982). Children's artistic creativity: Detrimental effects of competition in a field setting. *Personality and Social Psychology Bulletin, 8,* 573-578.

Amdur, N. (1971). *The fifth down: Democracy and the football revolution.* New York: Coward, McCann & Geoghegan.

Ames, C. (1992). Achievement goals, motivational climate, and motivational processes. In G.C. Roberts (Ed.), *Motivation in sport and exercise* (pp. 161-176). Champaign, IL: Human Kinetics.

Azzi, A. (1998). From competitive interests, perceived injustice, and identity needs to collective action: Psychological mechanisms in ethnic nationalism. In C. Dendeker (Ed.), *Nationalism and violence* (pp. 73-138). New Brunswick, NJ: Transaction.

Barash, D.P. (2003). *The survival game: How game theory explains the biology of cooperation and competition.* New York: Holt.

Bateson, G. (1972). *Steps to an ecology of mind.* New York: Ballantine.

Ben-Shahar, T. (2007). *Happier: Learn the secrets to daily joy and lasting fulfillment.* New York: McGraw-Hill.

Berger, R. (2003). *An ethic of excellence: Building a culture of craftsmanship with students.* Portsmouth, NH : Heinemann.

Berkowitz, M. (2006). *Parenting for good: Real world advice for parents from the character columns of Dr. Marvin W. Berkowitz.* Chapel Hill, NC: Character Development Group.

Bigelow, B., Moroney, T., & Hall, L. (2001). *Just let the kids play: How to stop other adults from ruining your child's fun and success in youth sports.* Deerfield Beach, FL: Health Communications.

Blake, R.R., & Mouton, J.S. (1961). Reactions to intergroup competition under win-lose conditions. *Management Science, 7,* 420-435.

Blasi, A. (2005). Moral character: A psychological approach. In D. Lapsley & F.C. Power (Eds.), *Character psychology and character education* (pp. 67-100). Notre Dame, IN: University of Notre Dame Press.

Bobo, L. (1983). Whites' opposition to busing: Symbolic racism or realistic group conflict. *Journal of Personality and Social Psychology, 45,* 1196-1210.

Bradley, B. (1998). *Values of the game.* New York: Artisan.

Bredemeier, B., & Shields, D. (1985). Values and violence in sport. *Psychology Today, 19,* 22-32.

Case, J. (2007). *Competition: The birth of a new science.* New York: Hill and Wang.

Clark, D.C. (1969). Competition for grades and graduate-student performance. *Journal of Educational Research, 62,* 351-354.

Clifford, C., & Feezell, R.M. (1997). *Coaching for character.* Champaign, IL: Human Kinetics.

Coakley, J. (2007). *Sports in society: Issues and controversies* (9th ed.). Boston: McGraw-Hill.

Coens, T., Jenkins, M., & Block, P. (2000). *Abolishing performance appraisals: Why they backfire and what to do instead.* San Francisco: Berret-Koehler.

Csikszentmihalyi, M. (1990). *Flow: The psychology of optimal experience.* New York: Harper & Row.

Damon, W. (2004). *The moral advantage: How to succeed in business by doing the right thing.* San Francisco: Berrett-Koehler.

Deci, E.L. (1995). *Why we do what we do: The dynamics of personal autonomy.* New York: Putnam.

Deci, E.L., & Ryan, R.M. (Eds.). (2002). *Handbook of self-determination research.* Rochester, NY: University of Rochester Press.

Deutsch, M. (1949a). A theory of cooperation and competition. *Human Relations, 2,* 129-152.

Deutsch, M. (1949b). An experimental study of the effects of cooperation and competition upon group process. *Human Relations, 2,* 199-231.

Deutsch, M. (1973). *The resolution of conflict.* New Haven, CT: Yale University Press.

Deutsch, M. (1985). *Distributive justice: A social psychological perspective.* New Haven, CT: Yale University Press.

Deutsch, M. (2000). Cooperation and competition. In M. Deutsch & P. Coleman (Eds.), *Handbook of conflict resolution: Theory and practice* (pp. 21-40). San Francisco: Jossey-Bass.

Devereux, E. (1976). Backyard vs. Little League baseball: The impoverishment of children's games. In D. Landers (Ed.), *Social problems in athletics* (pp. 37-56). Champaign, IL: University of Illinois Press.

Dewey, J. (1916/1966). *Democracy and education.* New York: Free Press.

Dewey, J. (1934). *Art as experience.* New York: Minton, Balch & Company.

Diab, L. (1970). A study of intragroup and intergroup relations among experimentally produced small groups. *Genetic Psychology Monographs, 82,* 49-82.

Dreikurs, R. (1964). Children: The challenge. New York: Hawthorn/Dutton.

Duda, J.L. (1987). Toward a developmental theory of children's motivation in sport. *Journal of Sport Psychology, 9,* 130-145.

Duda, J.L. (2001). Achievement goal research in sport: Pushing the boundaries and clarifying some misunderstandings. In G.C. Roberts (Ed.), *Advances in motivation in sport and exercise* (pp. 129-182). Champaign, IL: Human Kinetics.

Dweck, C.S. (1999). *Self-theories: Their role in motivation, personality, and development.* Philadelphia: Psychology Press.

Elliot, A.J. (1999). Approach and avoidance motivation and achievement goals. *Educational Psychologist, 34,* 169-189.

Elliot, A.J. (2005). A conceptual history of the achievement goal construct. In A.J. Elliot & C.S. Dweck (Eds.), *A conceptual history of the achievement goal construct* (pp. 52-72). New York: Guilford Press.

Engh, F. (1999). *Why Johnny hates sports: Why organized youth sports are failing our children and what we can do about it.* Garden City Park, NY: Avery Publishing Group.

Farrey, T. (2007). *Game on: The all-American race to make champions of our children.* New York: ESPN Books.

Fine, G.A. (1987). *With the boys: Little League baseball and preadolescent culture.* Chicago: University of Chicago Press.

Flett, G.L., & Hewitt, P.L. (Eds.). (2002). *Perfectionism: Theory, research and treatment.* Washington, DC: American Psychological Association.

Ford, G. (1985). In defense of the competitive urge. In D.L. Vanderwerden and S.K. Wertz (Eds.), *Sport inside out: Readings in literature and philosophy.* Fort Worth, TX: Texas Christian University.

Fraleigh, W.P. (1984). *Right actions in sport: Ethics for contestants.* Champaign, IL: Human Kinetics.

Frankfurt, H.G. (1988). *The importance of what we care about.* New York: Cambridge University Press.

Gallwey, T. (1974). *The inner game of tennis.* New York: Random House.

Gallwey, T. (2000). *The inner game of work.* New York: Random House.

Gill, D.L., & Deeter, T.E. (1988). Development of the Sport Orientation Questionnaire. *Research Quarterly for Exercise and Sport, 59,* 191-202.

Gladwell, M. (2000). *The tipping point: How little things can make a big difference.* Boston: Little Brown.

Gumbrecht, H.U. (2006a). *In praise of athletic beauty.* Cambridge, MA: Harvard University Press.

Gumbrecht, H.U. (2006b). They have a powerful aesthetic appeal. *Chronicle of Higher Education, 52(42),* B10-B11.

Haan, N., Aerts, E., & Cooper, B. (1985). *On moral grounds: The search for practical morality.* New York: New York University Press.

Hardin, G. (1968). The tragedy of the commons. *Science, 13,* 1243-1248.

Hayes, N. (2003). *When the game stands tall: The story of the De La Salle Spartans and football's longest winning streak.* Berkeley, CA: Frog.

Hicks, A., & Kenworthy, L. (1998). Cooperation and political economic performance in affluent democratic capitalism. *American Journal of Sociology, 103,* 1631-1672.

Huizinga, J. (1955). *Homo ludens: A study of the play element in culture.* Boston: Beacon.

Hyland, D. (1978). Competition and friendship. *Journal of the Philosophy of Sport, 5,* 27-37.

Hyland, D. (1984). Opponents, contestants, and competitors: The dialectic of sport. *Journal of the Philosophy of Sport, 11,* 63-70.

Jackson, P., & Delehanty, H. (1995). *Sacred hoops: Spiritual lessons of a hardwood warrior.* New York: Hyperion.

Janssen, J. (1999). *Championship team building.* Tucson, AZ: Winning the Mental Game.

Janssen, J., & Dale, G. (2002). *The seven secrets of successful coaches.* Cary, NC: Winning the Mental Game.

Johnson, D.W., & Johnson, F. (2006). *Joining together: Group theory and group skills* (9th ed.). Boston: Allyn & Bacon.

Johnson, D.W., & Johnson, R. (1978). Cooperative, competitive, and individualistic learning. *Journal of Research and Development in Education, 12,* 3-15.

Johnson, D.W., & Johnson, R. (1989). *Cooperation and competition: Theory and research.* Edina, MN: Interaction Books.

Johnson, D.W., & Johnson, R. (1999). *Learning together and alone: Cooperative, competitive, and individualistic learning* (5th ed.). Boston: Allyn & Bacon.

Johnson, D.W., & Johnson, R. (2003). *Cooperative, competitive, and individualistic efforts: An update of the research.* Research Report, Cooperative Learning Center, University of Minnesota, Minneapolis, MN.

Johnson, D.W., & Johnson, R.T. (2005). New developments in social interdependence theory. *Genetic, Social, and General Psychology Monographs, 131*(4), 285-358.

Johnson, M. (1993). *Moral imagination: Implications of cognitive science for ethics*. Chicago: University of Chicago Press.

Jowett, S., & Lavallee, D. (Eds.). (2007). *Social psychology in sport*. Champaign, IL: Human Kinetics.

Kaelin, E.F. (1968). The well-played game: Notes toward an aesthetics of sport. *Quest, 10*, 16-28.

Kavussanu, M. (2007). Morality in sport. In S. Jowett & D. Lavallee (Eds.), *Social psychology in sport* (pp. 265-277). Champaign, IL: Human Kinetics.

Kohn, A. (1992). *No contest: The case against competition* (Rev. ed.). Boston: Houghton Mifflin.

Kohn, A. (1993). *Punished by rewards: The trouble with gold stars, incentive plans, A's, praise, and other bribes*. Boston: Houghton Mifflin.

Kretchmar, R.S. (1975). From test to contest: An analysis of two kinds of counterpoint in sport. *Journal of the Philosophy of Sport, 2*, 23-30.

Kretchmar, R.S. (1994). *Practical philosophy of sport*. Champaign, IL: Human Kinetics.

Lakoff, G., & Johnson, M. (1980). *Metaphors we live by*. Chicago: University of Chicago Press.

Lancaster, S. (2002). *Fair play: Making organized sports a great experience for your kids*. New York: Prentice Hall.

Langford, T., & Ponting, R. (1992). Canadians' responses to aboriginal issues: The roles of prejudice, perceived group conflict, and economic conservatism. *Canadian Review of Sociology and Anthropology, 29*, 110-166.

Liu, X., Oda, S., Peng, X., Asai, K. (1997). Life events and anxiety in Chinese medical students. *Social Psychiatry and Psychiatric Epidemiology, 32*(2), 63-67.

Luban, X. (2006), Making sense of moral meltdowns. In D.L. Rhode (Ed.), *Moral leadership: The theory and practice of power, judgment, and policy* (pp. 57-76). San Francisco: Jossey-Bass.

Lyubomirsky, S. (2007). *The how of happiness*. New York: Penguin.

Mastrich, J. (2002). *Really winning: Using sports to develop character and integrity in our boys*. New York: St. Martin's Press.

McArdle, S., & Duda, J.K. (2002). Implications of the motivational climate in youth sports. In F.L. Smoll & R.E. Smith (Eds.), *Children and youth in sport: A biopsychosocial perspective* (2nd ed., pp. 409-434). Dubuque, IA: Kendall/Hunt.

Messner, M. (2007). *Out of play: Critical essays on gender and sport*. Albany, NY: State University of New York.

Murphy, A. (2001). *The sweet season*. New York: HarperCollins.

Murphy, S.N. (1999). *The cheers and the tears: A healthy alternative to the dark side of youth sports today*. San Francisco: Jossey-Bass.

Nelson, M.B. (1998). *Embracing victory: Life lessons in competition and compassion*. New York: William Morrow and Company.

Nicholls, J.G. (1978). The development of the concepts of effort and ability, perception of attainment, and the understanding that difficult tasks require more ability. *Child Development, 49*, 800-814.

Nicholls, J.G. (1989). *The competitive ethos and democratic education*. Cambridge, MA: Harvard University Press.

Orlick, T. (2008). *In pursuit of excellence* (4th ed.). Champaign, IL: Human Kinetics.

Osborne, T. (1999). *Faith in the game: Lessons on football, work, and life*. New York: Broadway.

Passer, M.W., & Wilson, B.J. (2002). Motivational, emotional, and cognitive determinants of children's age-readiness for competition. In F.L. Smoll & R.E. Smith (Eds.), *Children and youth in sport: A biopsychosocial perspective* (2nd ed., pp. 83-103). Dubuque, IA: Kendall/Hunt.

Pensgaard, A.M., & Duda, J.L. (2002). 'If we work hard, we can do it,' A tale from an Olympic (gold) medalist. *Journal of Applied Sport Psychology, 14,* 219-236.

Pensgaard, A.M., & Duda, J.L. (2003). Sydney 2000: The interplay between emotions, coping, and the performance of Olympic-level athletes, *The Sport Psychologist, 17,* 253-267.

Pepitone, E.A. (1980). *Children in cooperation and competition: Toward a developmental social psychology.* Lexington, MA: Lexington Books.

Power, F.C., & Higgins-D'Alessandro, A. (2008). The Just Community approach to moral education and the moral atmosphere of the school. In L. Nucci & D. Narvaez (Eds.), *Handbook of moral and character education* (pp. 230-247). New York: Routledge.

Power, F.C., Higgins, A., & Kohlberg, L. (1989). *Lawrence Kohlberg's approach to moral education.* New York: Columbia University Press.

Price, T. (2006). *Understanding the ethical failures of leadership.* New York: Cambridge University Press.

Prusak, L., & Cohen, D. (2000). *In good company: How social capital makes organizations work.* Cambridge, MA: Harvard Business School Press.

Putnam, R. (2000). *Bowling alone: The collapse and revival of American community.* New York: Simon & Schuster.

Rabble, J., & Horwitz, M. (1969). Arousal of ingroup-outgroup bias by a chance win or loss. *Journal of Personality and Social Psychology, 13,* 269-277.

Ralbovsky, M. (1974). *Lords of the locker room: The American way of coaching and its effect on youth.* New York: P.H. Wyden.

Ramsey, H. (1997). *Beyond virtue: Integrity and morality.* New York: St. Martin's Press.

Reich, R. (2007). *Supercapitalism: The transformation of business, democracy, and everyday life.* New York: Alfred A. Knopf.

Rhoden, W.C. (2008, February 3). Two personalities: One for game day, one for every other day. *The New York Times,* SP, 6.

Roberts, G.C. (1989). When motivation matters: The need to expand the conceptual model. In J.S. Skinner, C.B. Corbin, D.M. Landers, P.E. Martin, & C.L. Wells (Eds.), *Future directions in exercise and sport sciences* (pp. 71-83). Champaign, IL: Human Kinetics.

Roberts, G.C., Treasure, D.C., & Conroy, D.E. (2007). Understanding the dynamics of motivation in sport and physical activity: An achievement goal interpretation. In G. Tenenbaum & R.C. Eklund (Eds.), *Handbook of sport psychology* (3rd ed., pp. 3-30). Hoboken, NJ: John Wiley & Sons.

Rosenau, P.V. (2003). *The competition paradigm: America's romance with conflict, contest, and commerce.* Lanham, MD: Rowman & Littlefield.

Ryan, R.M., & Deci, E.L. (2000a). The darker and brighter sides of human existence: Basic psychological needs as a unifying concept. *Psychological Inquiry, 11,* 319-338.

Ryan, R.M., & Deci, E.L. (2000b). When rewards compete with nature: The undermining of intrinsic motivation and self-regulation. In C. Sansone & J. M. Harackiewicz (Eds.), *Intrinsic and extrinsic motivation: The search for optimal motivation and performance* (pp. 13-54). New York: Academic Press.

Ryan, R. M., & Deci, E. L. (2002). An overview of self-determination theory. In E. L. Deci & R. M. Ryan (Eds.), *Handbook of self-determination research* (pp. 3-33). Rochester, NY: University of Rochester Press.

Ryan, S. (2007, July 14). Lions are ready to move on; Players hoping worst of dorm-fight fallout is over. *The Philadelphia Inquirer,* p. D01.

Sack, A.L. (2008). *Counterfeit amateurs: An athlete's journey through the sixties to the age of academic capitalism.* University Park, PA: Pennsylvania State University.

Sansone, C., & Harackiewicz, J.M. (Eds.). (2000), *Intrinsic and extrinsic motivation: The search for optimal motivation and performance.* New York: Academic Press.

Sarrazin, P., Roberts, G.C., Cury, F., Biddle, S.J.H., & Famose, J.P. (2002). Exerted effort and performance in climbing among boys: The influence of achievement goals, perceived ability, and task difficulty. *Research Quarterly for Exercise and Sport, 73,* 425-436.

Scanlan, T.K. (1978). Social evaluation: A key developmental element in the competitive process. In R. Magill, M. Ash, & F. Smoll (Eds.*), Children in sport: A contemporary anthology* (pp. 138-152). Champaign, IL: Human Kinetics.

Schmitz, K. (1976). Sport and play: Suspension of the ordinary. In M. Hart (Ed.), *Sport in the sociocultural process* (pp. 35-48). Dubuque, IA: Brown.

Scholtz, G.J., & Willemse, J.W. (1991). Antecedents of aggression in sport. *Journal for Research in Sport, Physical Education and Recreation, 14,* 51-62.

Searle, J.R. (1969). *Speech acts.* Cambridge, MA: Cambridge University Press.

Seligman, M. (1995). *The optimistic child.* Boston: Houghton Mifflin.

Seligman, M. (2002). *Authentic happiness: Using the new positive psychology to realize your potential for lasting fulfillment.* New York: Free Press.

Senge, P. (1990). *The fifth discipline.* New York: Doubleday.

Sheehy, H. (2002). *Raising a team player.* North Adams, MA: Storey Books.

Sherif, M., Harvey, O.J., White, B.J., Hood, W.R., & Sherif, C.W. (1988). *The Robbers Cave experiment.* Middletown, CT: Wesleyan University Press.

Shields, D. (1986). *Growing beyond prejudices: Overcoming hierarchical dualism.* Mystic, CT: Twenty-Third.

Shields, D., & Bredemeier, B. (1995). *Character development and physical activity.* Champaign, IL: Human Kinetics.

Shields, D., & Bredemeier, B. (2007). Advances in sport morality research. In G. Tenenbaum & R.C. Eklund (Eds.), *Handbook of sport psychology* (3rd ed., pp. 662-684). Hoboken, NJ: John Wiley & Sons.

Shields, D., & Bredemeier, B. (2008). Sport and the development of character. In L. Nucci & D. Narvaez (Eds.), *Handbook of moral and character education* (pp. 500-519). New York: Routledge.

Shields, D., Bredemeier, B., LaVoi, N., & Power, F.C. (2005). The sport behavior of youth, parents, and coaches: The good, the bad, and the ugly. *Journal of Research in Character Education, 3,* 43-59.

Shields, D., LaVoi, N., Bredemeier, B., & Power, F.C. (2007). Predictors of poor sportsperson-ship in youth sports: Personal attitudes and social influences. *Journal of Sport & Exercise Psychology, 29,* 747-762.

Shulman, J.L., & Bowen, W.G. (2001). *The game of life: College sports and educational values.* Princeton, NJ: Princeton University Press.

Simon, R.L. (2004). *Fair play: The ethics of sport* (2nd ed.). Boulder: CO: Westview Press.

Sperber, M. (1998). *Onward to victory: The crises that shaped college sports.* New York: Holt.

Stapel, D.A. (Ed.). (2007). *Social comparison theories: Key readings.* New York: Psychology Press.

Stendler, C., Damrin, D., & Haines, A. (1951). Studies in cooperation and competition: The effects of working for group and individual rewards on the social climate of children's groups. *Journal of Genetic Psychology, 79,* 173-197.

Still, B. (2002). *NASO special report: Officials under assault: Update 2002.* Racine, WA: National Association of Sport Officials.

Suits, B. (1967). What is a game? *Philosophy of Science, 34,* 148-156.

Theeboom, M., De Knop, P., & Weiss, M.W. (1995). Motivational climate, psychological responses, and motor skill development in children's sport: A field-based intervention study. *Journal of Sport and Exercise Psychology, 17,* 294-311.

Thompson, J. (2003). *The double-goal coach: Positive coaching tools for honoring the game and developing winners in sports and life.* New York: HarperCollins.

Torres, C.R., & Hager, P.F. (2007). De-emphasizing competition in organized youth sport: Misdirected reforms and misled children. *Journal of the Philosophy of Sport, 34,* 194-210.

Torres, C.R., & McLaughlin, D.W. (2003). Indigestion? An apology for ties. *Journal of the Philosophy of Sport, 30,* 144-158.

Triplett, N. (1897). The dynamogenic factors in pacemaking and competition. *American Journal of Psychology, 9,* 507-533.

Turiel, E. (1983). *The development of social knowledge: Morality and convention.* New York: Cambridge University Press.

Urry, H.L., Nitschke, J.B., Dolski, I., Jackson, D.C., Dalton, K.M., Mueller, C.J., Rosenkranz, M.A. Ryff, C.D., Singer, B.H., & Davison, R.J. (2004). Making a life worth living: Neural correlates of well-being. *Psychological Science, 15,* 367-372.

Vallerand, R.J. (1997). Toward a hierarchical model of intrinsic and extrinsic motivation. In M. P. Zanna (Ed.), *Advances in experimental social psychology* (vol. 29, pp. 271-360). San Diego: Academic Press.

Vallerand, R.J. (2001). A hierarchical model of intrinsic and extrinsic motivation in sport and exercise. In G.C. Roberts (Ed.), *Advances in motivation in sport and exercise* (pp. 263-319). Champaign, IL: Human Kinetics.

Van Yperen, N.W., & Duda, J.L. (1999). Goal orientations, beliefs about success, and performance improvement among young elite Dutch soccer players. *Scandinavian Journal of Medicine and Science in Sports, 9,* 358-364.

Vealey, R.S. (1986). Conceptualization of sport-confidence and competitive orientation: Preliminary investigation and instrument development. *Journal of Sport Psychology, 8,* 221-246.

Vealey, R.S., & Campbell, J.L. (1988). Achievement goals of adolescent figure skaters: Impact on self-confidence, anxiety, and performance. *Journal of Adolescent Research, 3,* 227-243.

Watzlawick, P. (1976). *How real is real? Confusion, disinformation, communication.* New York: Random House.

Watzlawick, P., Beavin, J.H., & Jackson, D.D. (1967). *Pragmatics of human communication: A study of interactional patterns, pathologies, and paradoxes.* New York: W.W. Norton.

Weinberg, R., & Butt, J. (2005). Goal setting in sport and exercise domains: The theory and practice of effective goal setting. In D. Hackfort, J.L. Duda, & R. Lidor (Eds.), *Handbook of research in applied sport and exercise psychology: International perspectives* (pp. 129-144). Morgantown, WV: Fitness Information Technology.

Weiss, M.R., & Stuntz, C.P. (2004). A little friendly competition: Peer relationships and psychosocial development in youth sport and physical activity contexts. In M.R. Weiss (Ed.),

Developmental sport and exercise psychology: A lifespan perspective (pp. 165-196). Morgantown, WV: Fitness Information Technology.

Weiss, M.R., & Williams, L. (2004). The why of youth sport involvement: A developmental perspective on motivational processes. In M.R. Weiss (Ed.), *Developmental sport and exercise psychology: A lifespan perspective* (pp. 223-268). Morgantown, WV: Fitness Information Technology.

Weston, D.R., & Turiel, E. (1980). Act-rule relations: Children's concepts of social rules. *Developmental Psychology, 16,* 417-424.

White, H. (2006). They have betrayed their educational purpose. *Chronicle of Higher Education, 52(42),* B10.

Zarate, M.A., Garcia, B., Garza, A.A., & Hitlan, R.T. (2004). Cultural threat and perceived realistic group conflict as dual predictors of prejudice. *Journal of Experimental Social Psychology, 40,* 99-105.

Index

Note: The italicized *f* and *t* following page numbers refer to figures and tables, respectively.

About the Authors

David Light Shields, PhD, is an affiliate associate professor at the University of Missouri-St. Louis. Previously, he was codirector of the Mendelson Center for Sport, Character, and Community at the University of Notre Dame. In that role, he conducted research, designed educational programs, engaged in community outreach, built coalitions, and sponsored conferences and symposia. He also worked as a consultant with coaches, athletes, school administrators, and league officials to foster a better understanding of the relationship between competition and character. He coauthored the book *Character Development and Physical Activity* in 1995. Shields is founder and executive director of TrueCompetition.org, a nonprofit

David Light Shields

research and education organization focused on understanding and promoting true competition.

Dr. Shields is a member of the Moral Education Association. In 2007, he was named Sport Ethics Fellow by the Institute for International Sport in conjunction with National Sportsmanship Day.

Brenda Light Bredemeier, PhD, is an associate professor at the University of Missouri at St. Louis and a certified sport psychology consultant. Along with her husband, David, she was codirector of the Mendelson Center for Sport, Character, and Community at the University of Notre Dame. She coauthored the book *Character Development and Physical Activity* in 1995. She was a founding board member of the Association for Applied Sport Psychology, a consultant for the NCAA, editorial board member of several professional journals, and an academy member of the American Academy of Kinesiology and Physical Education.

Dr. Bredemeier was the McCoy Lecturer for the American Alliance for Health, Physical Education, Recreation and Dance Research Consortium. With her husband, she has authored more than 50 books, articles, and book chapters.

Brenda Light Bredemeier

*You'll find
other outstanding
socio-cultural issues resources at*

www.HumanKinetics.com

In the U.S. call

1-800-747-4457

Australia.............................. 08 8372 0999
Canada 1-800-465-7301
Europe.....................+44 (0) 113 255 5665
New Zealand.................. 0064 9 448 1207

HUMAN KINETICS
The Information Leader in Physical Activity
P.O. Box 5076 • Champaign, IL 61825-5076 USA